W0036001

SAGE was founded in 1965 by Sara Miller McCune to support the dissemination of usable knowledge by publishing innovative and high-quality research and teaching content. Today, we publish over 900 journals, including those of more than 400 learned societies, more than 800 new books per year, and a growing range of library products including archives, data, case studies, reports, and video. SAGE remains majority-owned by our founder, and after Sara's lifetime will become owned by a charitable trust that secures our continued independence.

Los Angeles | London | New Delhi | Singapore | Washington DC | Melbourne

ADVANCE PRAISE

Sacred and Profane is a narration of social customs, unusual events and mythical stories, prevalent in our part of the universe, some of which are embedded in religion and others are not, but all are mostly accompanied by rituals and practices that have gained certain obligatory force and a power of compulsion to abide by a regimen of performance for their followers. Their succinct description and accompanied ethos, without any religious connotation, coming from a renowned scholar, makes it a compulsive reading, which succeeds in arousing the curiosity of an inquisitive mind.

Prof S. K. Verma, *Vice President,*
Indian Society of International Law,
New Delhi and Professor of Law (Retired),
Delhi University

An intriguing book for both academic and non-academic readers. G. S. Sachdeva's compilation and secular presentation of several rituals and customs that are treated as 'unusual' or 'strange' by outsiders, but normal by its practitioners, illustrate that they all have their own life and meaning that grow and adapt with time. The book provides plenty of food for thought for the scholars of society and culture to carry out in-depth research in order to better appreciate, with emic and etic perspectives, the many dazzling customs and rituals of both indigenous and non-indigenous peoples.

Krishna B. Bhattachan, *PhD, Indigenous Expert, Lawyers' Association for Human Rights of Nepalese Indigenous Peoples (LAHURNIP), Kathmandu, Nepal*

This is a fascinating book. It introduces us to a wide range of religious practices, many of which may appear 'strange' and 'unusual'. However, they continue to be popular with the common people and also play an important role in their lives. Professor Sachdeva does not simply condemn or decry them, as a rationalist would do. Nor does he celebrate them as a traditionalist would do. Instead, he invites us to acknowledge their presence and understand the value they have to their practitioners. He also provides his analyses of these realities, using theories and categories from social sciences, theology and philosophy.

Surinder S. Jodhka, *Professor of Sociology, Centre for the Study of Social Systems, Jawaharlal Nehru University, New Delhi*

Gripping narrative of the intricacies of religious order in the ultra-modern era with a blend of functional and pseudo-secular analysis. The work uncovers the observance of unbelievable ritualistic practices associated with myths and realities of the sacred in South Asia. No doubt, the compilation set forth the everyday religion in motion with rational and non-logical acts, expressing an instrumental bearing of men towards the mysterious religious cosmos.

Ashish Saxena, *Sociologist, University of Allahabad*

The book seeks to focus on some aspects of culture or religion or faith-based human practices. These are so interwoven with the lives of people that the dividing line between sacred and profane often gets blurred. Derived primarily from information in the public domain, the author has audaciously tried to make sense of customs and rituals around which lives of ordinary people revolve, ordained by scriptures, need of the hour, born out of beliefs, having scientific basis to bring about colour and discipline in life. Their sublime divinity is difficult to fathom by ordinary mortals as the compass of logic just does not work here. For an inquisitive mind, this work lucidly provides a good food-for-thought. The scholar-author has made a commendable effort, without being judgemental, to ignite the interest of other connoisseurs to pursue research in this field.

Prof (Dr) Bharat H. Desai, *Professor of International Law, Centre for International Legal Studies, School of International Studies, Jawaharlal Nehru University, New Delhi*

SACRED
AND
PROFANE

SACRED
AND
PROFANE

Unusual Customs and Strange Rituals

G. S. SACHDEVA

Los Angeles | London | New Delhi
Singapore | Washington DC | Melbourne

First published in 2020 by

SAGE Publications India Pvt Ltd
B1/I-1 Mohan Cooperative Industrial Area
Mathura Road, New Delhi 110 044, India
www.sagepub.in

SAGE Publications Inc
2455 Teller Road
Thousand Oaks, California 91320, USA

SAGE Publications Ltd
1 Oliver's Yard, 55 City Road
London EC1Y 1SP, United Kingdom

SAGE Publications Asia-Pacific Pte Ltd
18 Cross Street #10-10/11/12
China Square Central
Singapore 048423

Published by Vivek Mehra for SAGE Publications India Pvt. Ltd. Typeset in 11/14 pt Sabon by Fidus Design Pvt. Ltd, Chandigarh.

Library of Congress Control Number: 2020943285

ISBN: 978-93-5388-515-1 (PB)

SAGE Team: Namarita Kathait, Satvinder Kaur, Aanchal Jain and Rajinder Kaur
Photo Credit: Amit Kumar

To my Grandchildren
Who have given me
Love, affection and inspiration
Keerat—Sweta
Sehaj
Sayam

Thank you for choosing a SAGE product!
If you have any comment, observation or feedback,
I would like to personally hear from you.

Please write to me at **contactceo@sagepub.in**

Vivek Mehra, Managing Director and CEO, SAGE India.

Bulk Sales

SAGE India offers special discounts
for purchase of books in bulk.
We also make available special imprints
and excerpts from our books on demand.

For orders and enquiries, write to us at

Marketing Department
SAGE Publications India Pvt Ltd
B1/I-1, Mohan Cooperative Industrial Area
Mathura Road, Post Bag 7
New Delhi 110044, India

E-mail us at **marketing@sagepub.in**

Subscribe to our mailing list
Write to **marketing@sagepub.in**

This book is also available as an e-book.

CONTENTS

FOREWORD

To be able to sit in your favourite chair at home and read at leisure is the stuff dreams are made of, particularly in the fast-paced life that we are living today. It is, therefore, increasingly becoming *de rigueur* to surround oneself with ready-to-cook meals, fast foods, household appliances that save time—the aim being that one can then spend more time in pursuit of one's passions in life. For some, it is engaging in one's favourite hobby—gardening, painting, playing or watching a sport, listening to music, watching movies, gaming, etc.; for the more cerebrally inclined there is nothing better than to curl up and read a 'new' book. More so if the 'new' book promises to take you on a virtual journey down the ages into all corners of the world—some which you may not have travelled to—and exposes you to the beliefs and superstitions that have been responsible for the various customs and traditions of societies and people around the globe (despite the fact that most such customs and traditions have the stamp of religion writ large across them); you are assured of a better appreciation of your fellow homo sapiens from different lands.

Sacred and Profane is one such book that has been 'crafted' and created for the sole purpose of educating the reader and making him/her aware of the 'person next door'—what is the 'baggage' he/she is carrying, and why does he/she behave in a particular way in certain situations. It is NOT a book on human psychology, but a narration of rituals and customs practised by people across the world. Through a lifetime of painstaking collection of articles/snippets on customs and traditions from newspapers and magazines, the author, whose primary areas of interest are Space Law and drones, has attempted to take you through a journey back in time to explain how customs and rituals were 'created' by sages and men of intellect and how they ensured abidance in their execution. Of course, religious underpinnings were always (mostly) present. While some customs are sure to bring a smile to your lips, for example, the groom not being permitted to join his own marriage procession (yes, it happens!), and a flutter to the heart of those in love ('The World's Most Romantic Letterbox'), the reader would be well advised to also steel himself/herself for some weird customs such as ones that cause injury (sometimes loss of life or limb) to the goats tossed from the belfry, or customs that involve piercing one's cheeks with an iron rod, apparently without any blood or pain during the process.

The author has gone to great lengths to inform the reader about the institution of marriage and how it evolved, the various customs related to the selection of one's partner (sometimes by the woman and sometimes by the man, depending on which part of the world the custom is practised in), live-in relationships (that persist till today in some tribal communities), polygamy and polyandry and how the caste system evolved in India (as outlined in the Manu Smriti). While outlining some of the social ills that existed in India in the past, he is quick to add a subtle message on how things could be improved.

That society is ever evolving has never been challenged by the author and he has quoted the Hindu and Chinese philosophies in support of this observation. He quotes from the Bhagavad Gita that explains the concept of continuous change: 'Of what is not there is not becoming; of what is there is no ceasing to be.'

This promises to be an easy-to-read book that would tickle your imagination and amaze you, 'Was this how it actually happened in those days?' Like the author has clarified, this work is a collection of snippets that he has pieced together and stitched up with his craftsmanship to present a one-stop shop for those keen to know about some of the customs and rituals of days gone by. Deeper research into individual cases would be necessary to fully understand the 'Why' and 'How' of things mentioned in the book.

Happy reading!

Life is a Journey…Complete it
Life is a Mystery…Unfold it
Life is a Goal…Achieve it
—Bhagavad Gita

K. K. Nohwar, AVSM VM
Director General, Centre for
Air Power Studies, New Delhi

PREFACE

This book is the reflection of my interest in social customs, unusual events and mythical stories and understanding their 'parable-like' guidance towards human virtues for living a natural life. With this background and desire to learn, I started collecting cuttings and clippings from reports appearing in widely circulated magazines and newspapers relating to such events, places, fables, festivals and rituals. Persistent collection of this informative material, for almost three decades, has prompted me to narrate all this in the form of a book. I honestly concede that this information is already in the public domain through circulation in print media, and has been acquired, compiled and systematized. Nevertheless, its collation, classification, styling, presentation and language are mine.

Customs and rituals have different menaings and a purpose in human life and are effective in inducing a certain regularity and solemnity in the performance and/or observance of ordained acts, the obscured origin of which may be difficult to explain to convince devotees and posterity into believing in them, without raising inconvenient and inquisitive questions. Thus, for engaging all generations into abidance, the sages of yore introduced rituals, mostly religious, which, over the years, gathered a certain obligatory force and a power of compulsion to act or behave in the prescribed manner or abide by a regimen of performance. Therefore, customs and rituals are generally habit-forming and tend to get observed almost reflexively without overt questioning or unusual demur. Some interesting and lesser known rituals and some apparently unusual customs have been described or narrated with conjecturable explanation, adduced logic and obvious vindication in favour of them.

This book, encompassing various shades of faith, is not a religious exposition, but a singularly objective and secular treatment of the same. Some of the rituals narrated may appear irreligious or even blasphemous, but their purposeful psycho-cathartic import cannot be denied or discounted. In the process of evolution, over a period of time, some of the festivals have shed their original religious hook, import of observance or the accompanying fervour, and tend to become 'areligious' or inter-community or secular. For example, Diwali is visibly celebrated by all communities in India, irrespective of their religion or affiliation to a particular deity and certainly with renewed societal impact, new social moorings and pan-cultural importance. Some such customs and rituals, sacred and profane, depicting different shades of faith and hues of cultural expression find place in this volume. Thus, this is a book of common interest, with a repertoire of social information and anthropological knowledge. It is aimed at scholars of sociology, theology and anthropology providing them research hypotheses for future investigation and exposition. The book will also be of great interest to the literate layman as light reading or short repartees.

I appreciate the sensitivity of the narrated events, customs and rituals; there may possibly be gaps or inaccuracies in my portrayal due to lack of original sourced material, imperfect appreciation of published facts or fallacy in logic of appraisal. Moreover, there could be a lack of comprehension of the sublimity of divine implications of sacrificial rituals or a lack of grasp on the native significance of customs or understanding of adherents' ingrained belief in rituals. I am conscious that my effort is humble, and the task is huge and deserving of sensitivity. It is, therefore, assured that any error is entirely inadvertent and there is no intention, whatsoever, to hurt anyone's sentiments. This small volume is, thus, an honest, open-minded presentation of the material that is already in public domain.

It will become apparent to any reader that the gamut of narration is global and so large and diverse that better appreciation of the text would be difficult without deeper insights into the information, which can be achieved through thorough research, reading dedicated interviews and personally surfing the web for investigation and verification of veracity of the stories narrated in this book. The handicap is obvious, but this has not been possible for the narrator due to old age. The author, therefore, acknowledges that the descriptions are in bald facts of bare events and observance of rituals as adapted and cited from published media.

The book is a bold experiment, eliciting greater engagement on new format cross-cutting, multi-disciplinary topics. The task of verification and elaboration is, perforce, relegated to future initiatives and study endeavours by devoted scholars pondering over this elementary information providing skeletal leads and simple clues. They may undertake research to put the same in revised perspective or portray haloed values and the espoused virtues in them. Even the 'unusuals' and 'strange' to modern prudery may have certain significance in understanding the old mindset or unravelling the social compulsions or cultural goading of the olden times.

At a few places in the book, it will be seen that the citations are incomplete in certain aspects. These narrations relate to periods over two decades old and requisite details have been either missed out at that time or news-reporting practice did not exist or vernacular papers did not bear that information. Anyway, this deficiency is sincerely regretted. Nevertheless, relevant cuttings and clippings are available and well preserved with the author. In case, any scholar or reader so desires to reach the source material, he/she would be welcome to approach the author through the publishers.

This book is not a work of fiction, even though it is interspersed with stories of mythical fantasy or interesting behaviour embedded in age-old beliefs and legends behind cultural ethos and pseudo-religious rituals. Hence, it may, thus, be treated as a non-fiction collation of seminal raw material for future research. For its avowed intention, it is sure to serve as a collection of short narrations imparting exciting knowledge and reasonably factual information for an inquisitive, yet receptive and open-minded academic or as leisure reading of a miscellany full of fun-factoids, unusual legends, strange rituals and interesting snippets.

ACKNOWLEDGEMENTS

It is rather otiose to fully and faithfully acknowledge the academic and inspirational debt in the accomplishment of such a project because as one progresses towards completion, one tends to be less conscious and more oblivious to the educed support and voluntary contribution of others. I also suffer from same impairment, yet I make an honest and sincere attempt to recollect my intellectual owings and advisory help to record due acknowledgment here. Inadvertent omissions are, therefore, human and unavoidable.

Some times are really fortuitous when ideas bloom and find fruition much faster than one had envisaged. This is one such undertaking with a lucky start after having been bundled and cast aside for decades. In fact, basic material for this book was studiously collected and held in raw shape for nearly three decades. Once inspiration dawned, the work of translation, adaptation, narration, stylisation and presentation in book form was accomplished in just one year.

I must list my debts by first acknowledging an intellectual contribution of my son-in-law, Rear Admiral (Retired) A. S. Sethi, recipient of the Vishisht Seva Medal (VSM), for his studious reading of an early iteration of the text and his suggestions for improvement. He has also greatly helped me in rearrangement of the narrations under different chapters and collation of homogeneous content. He has, thus, considerably improved presentation and readability of the book. My heartiest thanks are also due to my daughter, Dr Manpreet Sethi, for going through and correcting certain portions of the book despite her own academic commitments and publication deadlines. Her inspiration has been highly valuable to me.

Last but not the least, I sincerely recognize and affectionately acknowledge the sacrifice of time and companionship of my wife, Chan, during different stages of processing and iterations of the book. Truly, without her willing cooperation, unflinching support and sustained goodwill this project may not have been accomplished at all. My loving thanks to her.

Sage Publications, New Delhi, amply deserves my whole-hearted thanks and boundless gratitude for having accepted to publish this volume and, thus, having made my dream come true. This book is my sincere pay-back to the academia and society at large for everything I got from them, without even asking. In this connection, I record my special thanks and deep appreciation due to Manisha Mathews, Namarita Kathait and Satvinder Kaur Sandhu for their pain-staking editorial effort and professional contribution to improve the quality and marketability of the book in good measure.

INTRODUCTION

'Sacred and Profane' have no religious connotations in this book. Narrations are descriptive of social expressions that have neutral, 'areligious', altruistic, temporal or secular credentials. Any oblique relevance to religion is purely denominational or 'sect-al' (which means belonging to different sects of any religion or denomination) or totemic or a sheer coincidence. In pedagogic discourses, sacred has been taken to imply a broader social aspect or refers to collective representations like ceremonies, celebrations and festivals that transcend mundane life of 'ordinariness' or familiarity and which are for the welfare of community as a whole. These are for cohesive bonding or cumulative betterment of the societal group.

Similarly, profane does not denote evil or mystical or 'irrev-erential' but encompasses self-observances and utilitarian practices and rituals at a personal level. These are intended for wish-fulfilment, individual good or familial prosperity in accordance with group usages and personal values but still within the social instincts and community justice. In fact, profane bears connotation of an attitude of common-ness, familiarity and utility; and has little pertinence with religion. As Sumner postulates, folkways, mores and institutions shape individual behaviour in the group and lead to conformance. In fact, he asserts more vehemently, 'The mores can make anything right and prevent condemnation of anything.'[1] This vindicates societal approval and social justice.

Emile Durkheim, a well-known French sociologist, treats 'sacred and profane' as a concept of religion, whether old or

---

[1] William Graham Sumner, 'Folkways', in *Social Control*, ed. Joseph S. Roucek, (Toronto: D Van Nostrand Company Inc., 1965), 5.

new, established or totemic. He maintains, 'Religion is a unified system of beliefs and practices relative to sacred things.'[2] At the same time, he posits the idea of a dichotomy that divides sacred and profane as distinct and distinguishable, if not entirely antithetical domains. To him, this separation is vivid and clear. Sacred represents interests of the group in a wider perspective and its affinity and unity through group symbols or clan totems. On the other hand, profane relates to individual concerns and personalized observances within the societal architecture. But this simplistic dichotomy does not appear tenable on several criteria. In fact, this pedagogic construct has greater salience to the worshipped divinities and the awe-inspiring extraordinariness of the religion and is not primarily related to the social manifestations and ethno-denominational expressions.

Some other scholars on sociology preach differently and do not promote this hypothesis. Jack Goody laments that some societies do not even have appropriate native words that may approximate to a translation of 'sacred and profane'. Evans-Pritchard also differs with this simplistic classification and its strict separation.[3] Again, Tomoko Masuzawa points out that this dichotomy cannot be found to be accepted and practised in all societies and, therefore, the universality of this concept comes under shadow and deserves a re-statement.[4] The division, in empirical context, is nebulous and without clear boundaries. Thus, the doubts raised appear compelling and bear validity and merit.

The author, too, does not wholly subscribe to the views of Durkheim. He believes that the situation is not sheer binary

---

[2] Emile Durkheim, *The Elementary Forms of Religious Life*, ed. Karen E. Fields (New York: The Free Press, 1995), 35.
[3] E. E. Evans-Pritchard, *Theories of Primitive Religion*, (Oxford, London: Oxford University Press, 1965).
[4] Tomoko Masuzawa, *The Invention of World Religions: Or, How European Universalism Was Preserved in the Language of Pluralism*, (University of Chicago Press, 2005).

with discernible separation and concentration at the figurative ends. Rather, the gamut is a variegated dispersion and full of plurality of practices, intensity of faith and subjective devotion of the believer. Sacred and profane, at best, can be treated as two extant bounds of social expression where all solemnities, customs, traditions, practices, observances, modalities, rituals, formalities and the like fall within this range and spectrum to assume different shades of faith determined by the vigour of emotional attitude, language of reverence, posture of obeisance, depth of religiosity or even denial of subordination to the holy. To put it succinctly, reformations often 'stress the inner dimension of faith with its clarity of purpose and sincerity of worship as opposed to institutionalised and formal religiosity devoid of personal devotion.'[5]

Ergo, sacred and profane do not portray a dichotomy of faith or beliefs. The society, in totality, reflects variety in hues of faith and dispersion in beliefs that gradually extend on a bandwidth from the sacred to the profane; or even co-exist, imbued in divergent shades of grey. Despite this, there are certain customs and rituals that are cocooned within relative opacity and are performed in exclusive privacy and secrecy. In social context, sacred need not only be holy or pious or revered, and profane need not be merely evil or bad or sacrilegious. There could be an overlay of either or a blended mix of both.

Based on the above premise as also on the liminality of human consciousness or the resilience in societal acceptance, sacred and profane do not appear to be contradictory or mutually exclusive and could, *vice versa*, possibly abide as mutually inclusive or co-habit in graded medleys. This brings out in sharp relief the magnanimity of social phenomena,

---

[5] Douglas Davies, 'Introduction: Raising the Issues', in *Worship*, eds. Jean Holm and John Bowker (London: Pinter Publishers, 1994), 4.

flexibility of the societal architecture and humane play of altruism which exert profound and fundamental influences on the structured system of social life and its patterns of belief and behaviour. No wonder, 'Society is a synthesis of human consciousness.'[6]

It also seems pertinent to allude to a verity that society as a living organism is always under transition, whether slow or fast. It is processual rather than substantial. Bhagavad Gita illuminates the concept of continuous change and provides, 'Of what is not there is not becoming; of what is there is no ceasing to be.'[7] Buddhism echoes the same idea that phenomenal reality is an uninterrupted process, where 'One state ceases to exist and another comes to exist'.[8] The Chinese conception is also similar:[9] thus change is ever-continuous.

Therefore, transformation of society could be internal due to evolving values and changing perceptions or it could be extraneous due to the migration of ethnicities and exposure to new contacts, thus, creating collective or metamorphosed identities that manifest themselves in due course. As a result, every society has a different way of doing things, or doing the same thing differently and there should be no imposed urge to detoxify these. Traditions and customs may not yield an apparent rational explanation, yet these have an inherent purpose and intrinsic meaning, possibly lost in the journey of the community or in obscurity of time.

It is equally essential that there is no necessity to permanently label social customs or cultural traditions into moulds or subsets because societal expressions in the form of traditions, customs, ritual and even beliefs remain in flux leading to a

---

[6] K. S. Bose, *A Theory of Religious Thought,* (New Delhi: Sterling Publishers, 1991), 1.

[7] Bhagavad Gita. Translated by R. C. Zaehner, (Oxford: Clarendon Press, 1969), 127.

[8] Lucien Stryk, ed., *World of Buddha*, (New York: Doubleday & Co., 1969), 95.

[9] Bose, *Theory of Religion*

change in meaning, understanding, importance and tolerance of the basic context of sacred and profane. The constant flux is a result of several reasons, influences and initiatives like literacy, prosperity, education, personality domination, trauma, legislations and administrative actions. Consequently, views and attitudes of society, or certain sections of society, towards these concepts and their manifestations, can and do, continuously undergo a transformation.

Therefore, sacred and profane are not determinable constants or static concepts with invariable meaning or unchanging importance. These are dynamic and evolutional and 'mutatory', and as a result, may undergo a shift in their position or status with the passage of time or may be influenced by other pressures, either internal or external, positive or negative. In conclusion, 'sacred and profane' are not universal or eternal concepts nor are they a perpetual or enduring dichotomy. They are variable in essence with passage of time and significance to different practitioners and cannot be proclaimed either way for everyone and once for all times. Change is undoubtedly, a constant factor and immutable inherence when it comes to the sacred and profane.

Religion, as Vivekananda said, does not consist of doctrines or dogmas. It is not what you read, nor what belief you deem important, but what you realize is important. Therefore, in the right sense, this book is not a religious exposition nor is it specific to India. It also describes some secular traditions, 'areligious' customs, community rituals, mixed legacies and less-known legends. These are presented as a worldwide panorama to highlight similarities in thought, congruence of concepts and evolution on a socio-anthropological plane. At places, plausible explanations and selective vindication has been attempted while at the same time, judgemental commentary has been deliberately eschewed. This volume thus has no doctrinal agenda or affiliation.

Some of the traditions, customs or rituals discussed in this book may not fascinate the millennial mind. They may also not be agreeable to the professed modern prudery; nevertheless they may be read and understood as ideas relating to an era gone by, which are held dear and have been ardently perpetuated by the believers in rustic faith and regular observance. They bear and nurture social virtues and a moral connection thus promoting affinity and trust within the group of believers. Further, the social values of implicit acceptance, group conformance and totemic cohesion so transmitted within the community appear enabling, meaningful and essential.

To some, the traditions may appear overstrung, customs may seem 'culturized' and rituals may give the idea of being steeped in religiosity, yet one may be able to discern the mundane reality of individual proclivities, personal self-interest, social identity and cohesive bonding in their behaviour revealing a rustic elegance in their collective observance and a certain dignity in the personalized performance. These tend to be totemic symbols of tribal unity and societal coherence that accord them a unique identity and distinctive recognition. These social groups inherit ingrained discipline, learn of social integration and abide by their community mores and norms almost instinctively and without inconvenient inquisitiveness. In this manner, posterity is educated in lessons of conformity, solidarity and continuity[10] by the processes of social sympathy, conceptual learning, abstracting[11] and vicarious acquisition of concepts[12], thereby, making social control complete and

---

[10] Kimball Young, *Sociology*, (Cincinnati: American Book Co., 1942), 898.
[11] Norman L. Munn, *Psychological Development*, (Boston: Houghton Mifflin co., 1938), 349. Also see C. L. Hull, 'Quantitative Aspects of the Evolution of Concepts', in *Psychological Monographs*, XXVIII, 1920, 349–350.
[12] Joseph S. Roucek, *Social Control,* (Toronto, D Van Nostrand Company Inc., 1947), 24.

unchallenged in society.[13] Thus, a deep-rooted psychological reality and sociological manifestations crave to be unravelled and vindicated.

The contents of this book have been documented, structured and arranged in seven chapters. Each chapter bears a title from one of its narratives though it covers a wider gamut of coherent and cognate topics. At times, the contents of a chapter may appear diverse or heterogeneous, however, there is an underlying nexus and a thread of tautology or a shared theme that strings them together. This also brings to consciousness a co-evolution of similar thought processes in societies geographically scattered all over the world with little contact or communication. At the end of each chapter are a few snippets along the same lines.

Chapter one titled 'A Living Deity', celebrates goddesses and womanhood. Human belief in gods has existed since pre-historic times. Gods were benefactors and protectors of the social groups inhabiting the jungles. At that time any adversary animal, bird or reptile was an enemy, so were the obstructive, destructive and insurmountable objects of terrain like rivers or mountains and disasters of nature like droughts or floods. Any object, animate or inanimate, beyond the human prowess to tame or control became a god and came to be propitiated for mercy and protection. Pre-historic gods were male, virile and powerful.

With time, the pantheon of gods became systematized and each clan picked up its own god or a set of gods relevant to its terrain and environmental inclemencies, thereby, leading to the evolution of some form of totemic religion. Worship of gods became an integral part of their religion, howsoever, rudimentary or primitive. 'So, theologically speaking, worship

---

[13] Ibid.

is a response. People worship because they are aware of something.'[14] In other words, people's awareness could relate to their fear for survival or the potency of god as a viable protector and saviour.

However, coincidences do not always happen and the gods, generally male, did not rise up to their expectations in certain trying times of dire need. Disappointment was natural and obvious. So, the next option was to create female gods who were wildly ferocious and extremely dreadful yet equally protective brimming with motherly instincts. This confidence in Durga, the deity who killed the demon Mahishasur and is worshipped during Durga Puja, particularly in West Bengal, worked wonders. 'Taleju' in the form of Kumari Devi in Nepal is another such example. Later, the pantheon of gods became a wholesome mix of male and female deities offering choices as per individual belief and necessity.

The history of the celebration of womanhood has been chequered and not so smooth or consistent. Women, who were respected so much a few millennia ago like in times of Ramayana, were later relegated and repressed. A similar cycle occurred in Western societies also. So different societies have treated women differently. The Indian social system, for instance, has given women a status inferior to men since the last few centuries whence the treatment of women as captives of male guardians such as father, brother or husband has been considered not only acceptable but also preferable. The custom of segregation of women during menstruation is yet another instance of such denigration. Revival has started in the last century, but progress is slow and appears to be generational in its traction. On the contrary, reference may be made to the case of Juchitán de Zaragoza, a town in Mexico,

---

[14] Douglas Davies, 'Christianity', in *Worship*, eds. Jean Holm and John Bowker (London: Pinter Publishers, 1994), 59.

which is ruled by women and where men play second fiddle to women.

In the Indian social system as well, an example of gender equality may be seen in the tenets of the Sikh theology according to which women are considered equal in status and treatment. The Sikh gurus have rejected any ill-will towards women and have extolled them in many ways. The preaching in their Holy Book reads, '*so kiyon manda akhiye, jit jammey raajaan.*'[15] This means that 'why call them (women) wretched or bad of whom kings are born'. Thus, women are held in high esteem. In many other psalms (shabads) in the Holy Book, references to women are complimentary and salutary. Womanhood has been celebrated in Sikh egalitarian concepts.

Worship of gods embodies customs and rituals. Howsoever unusual, they give a lot of meaning and purpose to human life and have the effect of inducing certain regularity and religiosity in performance or observance of self-promised or ordained acts. At times, it may be difficult to fully explain or elicit devotion to traditions and beliefs or make posterity adhere to them. Thus, for engaging all generations into implicit acceptance or submissive abidance, rituals over the years have garnered a certain obligatory force and a binding normative power of compulsion to prompt prescribed action or behaviour and adherence to a prescribed regimen of celebration of such rituals from people.

There are many such interesting and lesser known rituals and some apparently unusual customs described in chapter one. Howsoever naive to our hegemonic urban civic sense or prudish millennial mindset or 'educational' arrogance, they should not be deprecated, stigmatized, condemned or

---

[15] Raag Asa, 'Asa di Var', Sri Guru Granth Sahib (SGGS), ang (page) 473. The original text has been put in Romanized Punjabi phonetics. Translation is in gist. SGGS has standardized pagination in all editions.

demonised in any manner, as they provide a lot of purpose and significance to the lives and mindset of their followers. Those who think, believe or practice differently also deserve equal space and due freedom to do so. Hence, they need to be respected for their 'otherness', individuality and uniqueness. Some such practices have been described with conjecturable explanation, though at times, groping for good vindication.

Chapter two titled 'Marry a Dead Person' (Unusual Marriages and Strange Customs), is a documentation of mate selection and marriage systems of the past and present. The institution of marriage is a 'civilizational' baggage because in primitive societies no such formality or formalization either existed or was considered necessary. Even Adam and Eve were not married by any custom or ordainment. Procreation was dictated by mating instincts expressed in a natural carnal urge and willing partnership of the two sexes. Fidelity was not always a cherished virtue in many societies.

As birth of children led to evolution or innovation of the family system, clusters of families started living in close proximity to each other for safety and reciprocal support to collectively fight for survival against natural dangers lurking around. 'Village' became a close-knit unit of habitation and village elders began to regulate the affairs. Mate selection then got formalized and took on many different forms of fanciful likeability or testing criteria, for both people in the partnership, to make a free and perhaps a deliberated choice. At that time, giving birth to children prior to wedlock or out of wedlock was not uncommon and was socially acceptable because marriage was not a pre-requisite to bearing children.

As society became more evolved, civilized, prosperous and regulated, the incidence of marriage became pertinent in itself and relevant to paternity of children and succession of property. It became a social norm to celebrate marriage with pomp and show by hosting a meal with drinks for the community as form of a public announcement of the event. Thus, while the marriage was blessed by the elders, it also became an occasion for fun, mirth and rejoicement for the young members of the family. As a result, marriage became institutionalised.

Mate selection, too, has evolved through generations, giving rise to many methods of selection such as *swayamvar*, which involves choosing a partner based on merit or the *ghotul* system of experimental mating or eloping, where the couple marries in secret in ostensible defiance. Similarly, pre-marital selection systems have evolved over time and resulted in many options and alternatives. Dating culture, live-in relationships and same–gender companionships are not new developments in our modern society. These have been in existence since long ago in Egypt as well as in many communities in India and abroad. Some facets of such systems, and their latest innovations, have been presented in this chapter.

Chapter three titled 'Human Sacrifice with Safety Measures' (Sacrifices and Penances), deals with the concept and practice of sacrifice among primitive as well as present-day societies in the world over and across religions. For most societies, these are rituals that are formal ceremonial activities. These generally have religious importance and involve sacrifices, whether human or animal, offered at religious shrines. Blood-letting on the ground to be absorbed by the Earth is an important aspect of the offering and a pre-requisite for performing the sacrifice. It is believed that Mother Earth has been over-exploited by humans through agricultural cultivation and mineral extraction and thus virtually tortured and famished from times immemorial. Therefore, Mother Earth needed rejuvenation of fertility and rehabilitation of its reproductive powers which, it is believed, could be achieved by offering it sacrificial blood.

In Hindu theology, blood is considered as a powerful vitalizing force which may be used to refurbish the productive strength and restore fertility of the Mother Earth. Human blood was considered as the most potent agent for the purpose. This concept was imbibed by the followers of the *Shakti* cult and devotees of the *Devi* among the *Shaivites*. Initially, the cult ordained in *narbali* or compensatory human sacrifice and consequent spilling of blood on the ground. This practice of human sacrifice has continued for centuries but lately, in some cases, is performed using safety measures. The titled narration relates to such sacrificial rituals performed with reasonable safety.

With the passage of time, compassion dawned and the chilling experience of *narbali* was replaced by *pashubali* or animal sacrifice. The ardent clergy reluctantly yielded the vigour of age-old traditions to accept animals as sacrificial offerings. But animal sacrifice was no less cruel either as it was equally gory and gruesome. Excruciating pain was the common factor whether suffered by the condigned man or dumb animal. Therefore, even animal sacrifice was protested against and resisted worldwide to prevent cruelty to the animals.

Paying due regard to protests against animal sacrifice, some temple organizations and shrine trusts, for example, *Gadhimai* temple in Nepal, have relented and put restrictions on the number of animals to be sacrificed. There are also some shrines that have started to accept offerings of coconuts, *kaddu* (gourd), earthen pots filled with milk, etc., which are broken on the ground in symbolic sacrifice. Yet there are some shrines, like Kamakhya temple where the die-hard devouts still persist in performing the traditional sacrifice, stealthily at night. Faith can seldom be tested on the template of logic or rationality and there is a classical rigidity about beliefs that tends to facilitate their perpetuation.

At some places, local resentment has prodded the administration for intervention to check and control inhuman practices against animals and humans, deemed repugnant to society in general and resisted by rationalists and humanists, in particular. Some state governments in India have even passed suitable legislations to prohibit such *bali* rituals but enforcement of such laws is weak and half-hearted. The temple at Kharchi in Tripura is one such example of weak execution of anti-sacrificial laws for animals.

Incidentally the concept of sacrifice exists in Muslim and Christian theologies also. Among Muslims, the concept of *qurbani* (sacrifice) of animals exists though in a different context, having different meaning and motive. Shariah law approves of animal sacrifice and such sacrifice is ritually offered on the Muslim festival of Bakr-Id. In Islam, belief is exalted above deeds (18:105)[16] and 'the main object of human endeavour ... is to secure heavenly bliss',[17] and belief demands sacrifice. The Christian custom of Holy Communion in churches also represents the spirit of sacrifice by the Lord. Bread represents the body of Jesus and red wine symbolizes His blood and it is shared after benediction. Apart from this, there is a Spanish custom of throwing down a goat from the church belfry that has been narrated in this chapter.

Chapter four is titled, 'A Feast to the Monkeys' (Of Stratified Societies and Prasads). First part of this chapter provides a narrative of the *Varna* (caste) system in Hindu society that was formally and systematically introduced by sage Manu. His architecture of the caste system arranged the society in four tiers of hierarchy and prescribed main avocations for each of them through a litany of rules. Over time, these

---

[16] Diwan Chand, *Fundamentals of Religion,* (Kanpur: Nanakchand Wazirdevi Trust, 1953), 80.
[17] Ibid, 148.

developed into hereditary professions and stratification became rigid and almost unbreachable.[18] This stratification and impermissibility in crossing over from one caste to another, engendered social inequality and caused human injustice. This prevailed for many centuries and is being neutralized by legislation and social engineering.

A similar self-imposed caste system also crept into Islamic society that vehemently preached equality and fraternity. With the passage of time and contact with other stratified societies in India, Muslims also developed a nominal hierarchy that duly hardened later. Here Sayyids and Qureshis and Ashrafs ruled the roost and Ajlafs were considered lower riff-raff of the society. Besides this clannish superiority, Muslims also arranged themselves in *zats* or professional *biradaris* like Khans, Ansaris, Momins, Khojas and so on and so forth.[19] Other societies with similar classification for their population, for example, classification in the Egyptian society, have also been briefly discussed, for providing a global perspective.[20]

Some festivals have their origin in spontaneous and accidental celebrations that turned out to be memorable and were, thereafter, celebrated periodically for rejoicing. Some festivals originated circumstantially for fun and frolic, for example, to celebrate a seasonal glut in the tomato crop in Spain when its uneconomical sales in the market led to protests and dumping of the tomatoes as waste on the roads. Perhaps, some children started playing with the dumped tomatoes, dirtying their clothes in impulsive spontaneity, gaily throwing tomatoes at each other, enjoying themselves. Possibly, la Tomatino festival

---

[18] Refer Dubois, J. A., and Henry K. Beauchamp (trans.), *Hindu Manners, Customs and Ceremonies*, 3rd ed. (Delhi: Oxford University Press, 1978).

[19] Refer Hakeem Abdul Hameed, ed., *Islam at a Glance*, (New Delhi: Vikas Publishing House, 1981).

[20] For more details refer Emile Durkheim, *Division of Labour in Society*, trans. George Simpson (New York: MacMillan, 1933).

in Spain was born out of this unrestrained spirit of children and came to be enjoyed by all with 'carnivalesque' abandon.

The festivals may also have historical moorings to certain past events, good or bad. For example, the legend of 'devil gets the boot' is reminiscent of an evil person; it is an event that evokes painful memories even though the legend has a happy ending. People take cathartic revenge against a depraved ruler of the past and pray that the bad events do not happen again. Whereas, Chittirai Thiruvizha, celebrated in Madurai, is a festival of dance and music and felicitously calls for yearly celebrations. A festival may also have oblique religious affiliation. Although, not a pleasant celebration, yet such festivals are commemorated for a known purpose, for example, the Thookam festival of Kerala.

Festivals may even be earmarked specifically, by an authority for a specific community, to be celebrated in a particular manner. This happened when Rishi Manu propagated his social reorganization and stratification of the Hindu society. While allocating different castes or *varnas* their avocations, he also allotted them festivals according to their status and living styles. He, however, kept in mind the fundamental idea that festivities are generally accompanied by dancing and music, merrymaking, prolific eating, over-drinking and, occasionally, licentious revelry.

Another aspect of festivals, particularly those celebrated at shrines or temples, relates to the type of offering to the deity and its subsequent distribution as *prasad*. Most of us are familiar with the usual sweets or sugary *batashas* consumed as *prasad*. But some festivals and shrines have peculiar rituals associated with the offerings which include meat or fish; *bhang sharbat* or another alcoholic drink; butter for seeking benediction; or even a piece of sanctified thread. This chapter narrates the legends behind some such kinds of *prasad* and the associated socio-psychological importance of the celebration with a particular kind of *prasad*.

Chapter five is titled 'Hurling Obscenities in front of a Deity—Celebrating with Abandon'. It describes some taboos with legends of their origin. The rites discussed in this chapter involve irreverent behaviour or irreligious conduct or sacrilegious language in front of deities and within the campus of the shrine. Normally, religion and religious practices are viewed with piety and held sacrosanct to evoke spontaneous veneration and spiritual devotion. So, delinquencies like impious body posture, disrespectful language or sacrilegious conduct in religious places is a total taboo, invoking social disapproval and community condemnation. Hence, utmost respect, reverent obeisance and unflinching obedience to religiosity are normal and normative.

However, despite such societal and religious injunctions, there are certain rituals and practices associated with some shrines that may appear socially offensive and outright blasphemous like singing vulgarity or hurling obscenities in front of the deity or worship by women in nude in Renukemba temple. Even a secular custom of women abusing an opponent with expletives or dirty language would seem highly indecent and patently unacceptable even though a plausible explanation may be culled out from the cathartic import of spewing out cuss words against repressed emotions and pent up resentment in the extant social milieu of domination of women.

Another not so pleasant aspect of religious or 'demi-religious' practices discussed in this chapter pertains to attainment of salvation from human bondage or acts of self-mortification. Examples adduced include the religious practice of *santhara* in the Jain community, the practice of *suttee* primarily and most popularly by Rajput women to showcase *Rajputi maryada* and the ritual of penance in Malaysia. Indian practices have been held contrary to law but enforcement is lacking because these practices happen to be rooted in theistic faith, cultural tradition, societal exaltation and sentimental value. Ergo, these exist and are sporadically practiced in some regions and need not be validated on the template of rationality, law or modernity.

Chapter six is titled 'A Tale of Platonic Love that Bestows Boons—Miracles, Myths and Boons'. It narrates tales of miracles, myths and wish-fulfilling boons. In real life, certain events and occurrences cannot be explained by rules of science or by principles of rationality or their visual physicality. These events are variously known as miracles, myths or mysteries. Miracles are caused by saints and sages with occult powers in places of faith. Miraculous facts appear so real and genuine that people unsuspectingly accept and believe in the surrealism with devotion and fervour, without scientific inquisitiveness, optical analysis or rational affirmation. Some events narrated are truly miraculous and submit to no logical explanation.

Again, mysteries are surely cryptic and generally remain unexplained on logic. But not all mysteries can be deemed illusory or non-existent. There must be an iota of explanation for some of these happenings so as to be believed by such a large audience. Similarly, myth is not falsehood; it is only a different kind of truth. The wise people accept that there are many types of truth; some objective, some subjective; some logical, some intuitive; some deductive, some inductive; some cultural, some universal; some are based on evidence, others depend on faith. Hence, a myth is a truth that is subjective, intuitive, inductive, cultural or grounded in faith.

Therefore, a general condemnation of miracles, myths and mysteries by the rationalists as optical illusion or blind faith would be in denial of God's supremacy and His unbounded powers of action and variations in creation. However, in the age of scientific temper and uber rationality such manifestations are viewed with skepticism or disbelief and deemed devoid of logic or rationality. Nevertheless, their occurrence and the patent end result can neither be denied nor wished away. Some such legends are narrated in this chapter.

Chapter seven is titled '*Sadasuhags*: The Cross-dressers— Veneration of the Oddities and Peculiar Practices. It discusses a miscellany of unusual customs and social practices—meta-religious, non-religious and secular. In fact, during the evolution of human society and community living, religion, howsoever primitive or elementary, has always been accepted and observed in some form or manner. Even aboriginal tribes had pseudo-religious totemic faiths, which are still carried forward with unwavering belief and staunch fervour, though religion then had a different meaning and purpose in community life or belief ecosystem.

In a way, religion was more relevant for sheer survival, mun-danity of life and actual living and only later, came to be sought for higher values, cherished virtues and sublime aim of salva-tion from rebirth. A few select adherents, in different faiths, got blessed with elevated divinity and spiritual experiences that impelled them to branch off with distinct beliefs and tenets, and grow a separate sect with independent identity. *Sadasuhags*, the cross-dressers, came to exist as a separate sect in the same way. They considered themselves as eternal brides of the eternal God and groomed themselves with feminine grace.

Again, religions are generally wish-fulfilling and known for bestowal of boons on the believers. In this regard, Hindus, Muslims, Christians, Sikhs and other religious denominations are all alike. However, each religion has subaltern deities or *gram devtas* (locally worshipped gods) or revered sages who benevolently grant wishes of bigoted beseechers. Islam also believes in insubordinate divinities.[21] Delhi alone has a host

---

[21] Chand, *Fundamentals of Religion*, 61.

of them and each one gets a heavy footfall. Christianity, too, has ordained saints. But how many wish-makers are actually granted their wishes and are satisfied in the end can be anybody's guess!

Further, there are other secular traditions that tend to get verily transformed with changing needs and expectations of the believers. For example, 'deity turns banker for loans' is a unique concept of seeking returnable funds with goodwill and blessings of the deity for a profitable business venture. Thus, this chapter is a miscellany, a broad-spectrum collection of lesser known legends and unusual rituals that are nonetheless interesting and informative and also promote social trust and nurture moral virtues.

In a nutshell, this book illustrates how a religious doctrine or a social custom or a community ritual is like an organism that grows with time and in the process undergoes a change. New elements get absorbed in its evolution and some of the old and archaic practices are discarded due to social discomfiture or varied pressures, internal or external. Nevertheless, their haloed aetiology, historical legacy or sociological significance cannot be summarily discounted; and it surely deserves to be investigated and resurrected. This task has been left for posterity.

This book is an ode to unusual customs and strange rituals and thus presents a repertoire of variegated material that would inspire and prompt students and scholars of sociology and anthropology, and even theology, for undertaking further dedicated research and provide a more informed articulation of these customs and rituals and other related topics. Besides, this book would also appeal to a wide array of literate audience for sheer informative pleasure or for leisure reading.

1

A LIVING DEITY
Goddesses and Womanhood

From pre-historic times, even when man roamed and inhabited the jungles, he would often encounter fearful enemies in animals, birds and reptiles as also in elements of nature that obstructed him, appeared insurmountable and caused disasters. Whenever he found them to be over-powering or invincible, he exalted them to the level of gods to propitiate them for their mercy, friendship and protection. At this stage, no formal or even totemic religion existed, and beliefs were the mainstay of human survival and gods were the visible protectors. Favourable coincidences reinforced the efficacy of beliefs and confirmed them for posterity. Thus, gods were invented for invocation and supplication, with self-interest and circumstantial necessity in mind.

Sometimes, male gods failed and could not ward off a disaster or defeat the demons or kill a powerful *asur* for deliverance from evil. So female gods were ingeniously created and figured to be unexceptionally powerful, highly ferocious with motherly protection unlike the male gods; Goddess *Durga* of Hindu pantheon is an example of this belief. So is Goddess Taleju, manifesting in Kumari Devi, as a living deity of Nepal. Here, the traditions may be different yet the instinct is the same. Thus, goddesses have personified indomitable strength, dignified valour and a killer instinct. Moreover, goddesses were kind and motherly and, thus, easier to supplicate and please for favourable blessings and benign protection.

Goddesses have been venerated and worshipped in almost all ancient communities as also modern social groupings across the globe. Further, there is another aspect of goddesses that deserves a respectable mention. Man created female gods for his psychological completeness. Hence, the goddesses in female form were the embodiment of stunning beauty, graceful charm, sprightly gait and other ethereal qualities. Vak Ambrini is an apt example of this godly feminine personality.

Goddesses have been celebrated in all societies spreading over time including in the Greek and Roman and other societies. Similarly, womanhood has also been celebrated for similar qualities and above all, for being blessed with the unique ability to procreate. Best example of acknowledgement of this unique ability can be seen at Kamakhya temple where female genital parts are worshipped and female menstruation is held in high esteem during the Ambubachi festival when the doors of the temple are closed for four days. Another illustration could be Juchitán de Zaragoza town that has been ruled by women and continues to be so. Thus, this chapter collates narrations that eulogize goddesses and womanhood.

THE ORIGINAL AND OLDEST DEVI

Vak Ambrini is the original *Devi* and possibly the oldest feminine deity in the Hindu pantheon. The legend has it that the *Devi* first took shape as *Aapstambha*[1], that is, the column of water that came forth from the breath of *Prajapati*, also known as *Brahma*, the Primal Being or the Original Creator. The *Devi* is an embodiment of ethereal qualities; she is free in spirit like air, sprightly in gait like water and dances maidenly with abandon on poppy-swathed steppe. This daughter of Brahma, attractive, active and strong, thus, freely roams the meadows, uplands and rivers and wherever else she desires, enjoying her life. She also wields a lot of super-powers bestowed upon her by Brahma, her Father.

There is a resplendent hymn in the *Rig Veda* (in Sanskrit) in which Vak boasts of her powers. The Veda states, '*Ahem rudrebhir-vasubhischaraami*' which roughly translate to, 'I roam where I please with the *Rudras* and *Vasus*.' She also asserts, '*Ahem rudrayadhanuratanomi, Brahmadvishesharaanehantavavu*',

---

[1] *Aapstambha* is also the name of a Sutra.

which means, 'It is I who bend the bow of Rudra to slay the Creator's enemies.' She further announces her powers *'Tvambrahmaam, tvamhrushiam, tvamsumedha'* which means, 'Whom I love, I make a priest, a sage, a person of good mind.' It is important to note the ascending order: from being a mere 'ritualist', to a 'seer', to a realized *'jnani'*, the knowledgeable.

While on one of her frolics, one day, Vak is caught by *Prajapati* and is made to be his wife. Even though he is the Original Creator, he did not restrain his baser impulses and enslaved his own daughter, his own creation, into being his spouse. *Prajapati*, thereafter, shrouds the wildness in her nature and seats Vak Devi, clad in purist white robes, on a white lotus flower. He also chooses the name Saraswati, meaning the one who gently flows, for her as his wife, a name which signifies something is sweet but watery and weak. A heavy lute (a stringed musical instrument) is thrust into her unwilling arms. A *hamsa* bird is appointed as her *vahan* (designated transport) to chaperone her wherever she fancies. The *vahan* is believably also supposed to spy on her movements and report the same to the suspicious *Brahma*.

Due to her enslavement at the hands of Brahma, Saraswati transforms into a different deity altogether, uncharacteristic of her true free spirit. She embodies womanly beauty and wifely submissiveness as a dulcet toned creature. She is revered as *Devi* and is, therefore, dressed in silk with a crown on her head and thick bejewelled anklets on her stilled feet. This signifies, Vak's evolution into a different role, a role more refined, cultured and matured. On the other hand, Brahma's indiscretion is not condoned by *Rtam*, the eternal laws of God and his misdeed catches up with him so much so that he is hardly worshipped anywhere except at Pushkar and Uttamarkoil in Tamil Nadu while Vak lives on as *Devi* bestowed with the utmost reverence and devoted worship. It is believed that several castes in Tamil Nadu still flick three drops of liquor on the goddess every time they lift a glass.[2] It is a custom with some communities of South India.

KUMARI DEVI: A LIVING DEITY IN NEPAL

In most Asian temples, based on the beliefs of the proximate communities, there is, generally, an installed idol of a god or a goddess or a combination of both made of mud, stone, wood, metal or any other composition. But Nepal has a unique temple at Bhaktapur with sees a continued tradition of installing a living deity, Kumari Devi. The Kumari is revered, deified and worshipped as a living incarnation of Goddess Taleju, the powerful and fierce demon-slaying goddess worshipped in Nepal. Taleju, in one of her numerous forms, is ferocious, menacing, powerful and a fearful deity; she is an embodiment of all horrors of the mortal mind and at the same time is accepted as the protector capable of shielding the kingdom from all adversities, natural or man-made. This patron goddess is the deity protecting the king of Nepal, his kingdom and its people.

According to a legend, many centuries ago, Taleju befriended a king of Nepal and would often come to him in the form of a stunningly attractive woman to play a game of dice with him. One day, a royal princess inadvertently interrupted them. Infuriated at being seen by another mortal, Taleju vanished in anger. But after much persuasion and beseeching by the king, she relented and said she would continue to guide him on the condition that he will no longer be able to see her in her physical form. From then on Taleju's spirit has been brought to life in the form and body of a virgin girl called Kumari Devi.

The living Kumari perches on her throne 'dressed in brilliant red cloth bordered with brocade, hair pulled back tight, eyes

---

[2] Renuka Narayanan, 'Devi Loves a Drink', *Indian Express*.

lined with kohl, forehead painted in emphatic black and white paint, vermillion around a third eye situated at the centre of the forehead and a bejeweled crown on her head'.[3] Always on display to bestow blessings, she lives a life cocooned and cosseted, inside the red brick, grandly built medieval palace with intricate wood carvings of almost every god in the Hindu pantheon. The highly venerated living goddess sits calm and composed, immaculate and unperturbed—as the royal Kumari Devi of Nepal, highly pampered yet most feared.[4]

Once a year, the King of Nepal bows down before the tiny, imposing girl-goddess to seek her permission for another year of continuing his reign; and the Kumari Devi, believably imbued with supernatural powers of the erstwhile dreaded goddess, Taleju, benignly assures the King of her protection and blesses the royalty with peace and prosperity in the country and otherwise. The Kings of Nepal have followed this annual practice rather religiously and with abiding belief in its efficacy. For most Nepalese, this customary tradition is an amalgamation of myth and reality and remains a continued living practice and an intrinsic part of their *sanatan* culture and popular belief system.

The necessity of a virgin girl has an anthropological twist in the story. The conjectured explanation is that the king developed a strong fascination for Goddess Taleju and desired to sexually possess the beautiful goddess.[5] That, possibly, is the reason for the *kumaris* being virgins who have not yet started menstruating. The onset of puberty and first sign of menstruation is the signal that the spirit of Taleju is leaving

---

[3] 'Tryst with the Gods', a photo feature on 'Nepal: Former Kumaris', with text by Vijay Jung Thapa and photographs by Sibal Das, published in *India Today*, 11 January 1997. Words in parentheses have been added for clarity.

[4] Ibid.

[5] This explanation has been offered by Michael Allen, an anthropologist who has studied and investigated the *Kumari* tradition.

or has abandoned this body, so the reigning *Kumari* is settled back to an ordinary pedestrian life and a new *Kumari* is duly selected in her place and reverentially enthroned. Thereafter, the new *Kumari* is highly protected and surprisingly, as the *karmacharya* (priest of the Kumari temple) asserts, even the King is not allowed entry into the Kumari temple during all hours of the day.

The selection of a *Kumari* is also an elaborate and arduous process and ends with a final trial of grit for the chosen candidate. The criteria for the selection of a *kumari* include her caste, beauty, poise, confidence and grit. All *kumaris* are chosen from the Buddhist Sakya community of goldsmiths and can be as young as three years of age. A special council, so constituted, starts the search guided by a list of 32 attributes of the *kumari* that include physical attributes like a neck like a conch shell, a voice like a running stream, cheeks like a lion, skin, the colour of gold and soft as a duck. Once the prospective *kumaris* are shortlisted, the royal astrologer determines the competence and compatibility of the prospective *Kumaris* with the King, from their *kundlis* (horoscope).

Finally, the chosen one has to go through several arduous processes and ordeals. Yet the ultimate nightmarish initiation rite is to sit in a dark room full of 108 slaughtered heads of buffaloes and goats, the floor shining with blood and each head illuminated by a lamp light. Thus the final, toughest and truest test of the *Kumari's* intrepidity and temper is her courage, fearlessness and will to not get scared and run away from the gory room. Overcoming this horrifying ordeal successfully, she is deemed fit to be crowned as the living deity *Kumari Devi* and it is believed that the spirit of Goddess Taleju has enshrined herself in her. It is a tryst with divinity, and her reign of bliss in *Kumari Ghar* with dancing camphor flames, which release when camphor tablets are burnt for spiritual aura of fragrance, begins till puberty when she menstruates for the first time and the spirit of Taleju forsakes her. She is then treated as notionally married to an inanimate object like a fruit[6] and is obliged to retire as the *Kumari Devi* following such symbolic wedding.

Kumaris are known to have supernatural and ominous powers and can, by their spontaneous actions, body language and/or physical disposition foretell upcoming events. The *Kumari* temple priest loftily proclaims that the *Kumari* has latent occult powers of clairvoyance that may manifest at any time for an ominous prediction.

An angry squeal would convince startled devotees that she was predicting imminent doom, whereas, a good-natured laugh would presage peace and prosperity for the entire kingdom. Thus, every natural calamity or mishappening would be attributed to her wrath; a bout of illness or other expressions would foretell a lot more.

The *karmacharya* recalled an incident when King Tribhuvan went to the *Kumari Devi* for receiving yearly blessings from her. The goddess, as wonted and normal, was supposed to anoint the monarch's forehead with vermillion; instead she tried to place it on the head of the young crown-prince. The priest had to literally force the girl's hand onto the King's forehead. It was deemed a bad omen that foretold an ill-happening. Six months later, King Tribhuvan died and his son ascended the throne. It is believed that the *Kumari* divinely senses and innately experiences what the kingdom is going through. Superstition cuts both ways. More so, if at times coincidences occur to reinforce the belief.

The *Kumari* cult comes wrapped in numerous such tales. One of the former *Kumaris*, by name of Anita, shared her life

---

6 Sajani Shakya who reigned as Kumari Devi for nine years was notionally married to a fruit after retirement as the Devi at the age of eleven years in 2008. 'Search for a deity: Nepal's Fruity Wedding', *Hindustan Times*, 4 March 2008.

story and narrated that she once chipped her tooth and three days later a huge earthquake shook Kathmandu. This *Kumari* again fell seriously ill in the year 1979, during a time when the *Shah* monarchy was in crisis. The royal palace sent the king's personal physician for the *Kumari's* treatment, but he could do little to cure the goddess. Thereafter, a tantric was summoned but he died the night before he could complete his incantations for the *Kumari's* recovery. Miraculously she came around from the illness and it was then that the threat to the king started virtually diminishing.[7] The prophetic powers and physical life cycles of fitness and ill-health endured by the Kumari means a lot to the king and his Nepali subjects.

In an ironic twist of fate, the life of a dethroned *Kumari* is rather difficult. It is a free fall from the pedestal of a revered goddess to the harsh ordinariness of the materialistic world. This demotion from grand medieval pomp to the fast modernizing society is psychologically and emotionally devastating and it becomes difficult to grapple with contradictions of mundane reality in the normal society. The everyday plight of these cast-off deities is pitiable, and their trauma is unbearable. Many former *Kumaris* rue their fate and wonder if it was indeed lucky to be chosen as a *Kumari*. For example, there is a myth about *Kumari* cult which provides that an incarnation of Goddess Taleju, even a former *Kumari*, is not likely to take on a life partner because of a saying, 'marry one and you will die'. Sure, coincidences do occur, but myths are difficult to counter with reason or logic and may take eons to die out.

Lately, however, there is talk about rehabilitation of the former *Kumaris* and the need for them to forge a life ahead, to accept reality at a time when shadows of the past do not hover, memories do not haunt them and they can discover a purpose

---

[7] Monarchy in Nepal has been replaced by an elected government.

in life again. Serenity and acceptance that comes with age, prepares for the inevitability of fate and acknowledgement of neo-reality. Not much thought has been devoted to the plight of the erstwhile goddesses who were once considered reincarnations of Goddess Taleju, but everyone rightly stresses on the need for the *Kumaris* to forge ahead. *Kumaris* hold no money because all offerings, in whatever form, went to the *Kumari Ghar* or the temple Trust. Equally damningly, *Kumaris* are not formally educated due to the conviction that mortals cannot teach a goddess. At any rate, the government has of late started doling out a monthly stipend of ₹1,000 per month to the unmarried *Kumaris*. However, the amount is hardly beneficent and not worth a mention.

AMBUBACHI FESTIVAL AT KAMAKHYA TEMPLE

India is a big country with incredible diversity and conflicting customs, where in most parts of the country menstruating women are looked down upon and are forced into seclusion and solitude for the duration of their monthly periods, *Ambubachi* festival celebrated at *Kamakhya* temple in Guwahati (the capital of Assam), commemorates the goddess who bleeds. This ritualistic fair celebrating the annual menstruation of the Mother goddess, symbolic of Mother Earth, is generally held in the month of June and lasts for four days.

The concept of *Shakti* or primordial energy symbolized in a woman is an amalgam of many elements drawn from various sources, pre-Aryan, Aryan and aboriginal. The processes of fertility and motherhood are energizing forces that have apparently led to the emergence of a concept of a supreme goddess who is considered to be the repository of all energy governing the universe. Thus, the deity is said to preside over creation, preservation and destruction.

During the Ambubachi fair, Devi Kamakhya goes through her annual cycle of menstruation and what is worshipped at this time is not the image of the goddess but rather the process of fertility which is considered profoundly sacred. Primitive people identified the earth with women. Devi Durga symbolizes universal motherhood. Similarly, the earth and soil have always been associated with the concept of mother. The traditional belief is that our sacred Mother Earth is like a fertile woman and Ambubachi festival represents this phenomenon of ancient agrarian culture.

In a similar vein, it is believed that Mother Earth also becomes unclean during these days and separates from the environmental forces. It is believed that if humans plough and dig the earth during this period, they violate her and make her unhappy and reduce her fertility or productive powers. It is in conformance to this belief that farmers across Assam do not indulge in any kind of agricultural activity during these days and worship daily or perform other religious ceremonies.

During these days the doors of the temple are shut for visitors to let the goddess go through her period peacefully and undisturbed. Further, during these four days all Hindu temples across the region also remain closed. Doors of all temples in the region open to the devotees only on the fifth day and that too after the deity has been bathed and rituals are executed ensuring that the goddess has retrieved her pristine cleanliness and re-incarnated her usual purity.

As the doors of Kamakhya temple open on the fifth day, thousands of devotees gather at the door to receive *prasad*. The *prasad* distributed is of two types: One is *Angadhak,* which is the fluid part of the body which is symbolically the menstrual fluid but actually water from the spring within the sanctum. The second is *Angabastra,* which is a cloth for covering the body. The *prasad* is distributed in the form of small bits of red cloth that have been used to cover the stone *yoni* during the days of menstruation. This piece of cloth, supposedly moist with the menstrual fluids of the goddess, is considered highly auspicious and potent blessing for fertility.

Ambubachi fair is the biggest annual congregation of *Shakti-worshippers* in the subcontinent and nearly one lakh devotees visit Guwahati during the four days of the festival. Apart from locals who flock in large numbers, the devotees include godly saints and traditional singers belonging to the *Shiva* sect and *tantrics* who display their tantras and penance and practice of body contortions. In conclusion, Ambubachi festival is a grand show of devotion, worship and merriment, celebrating the concept of fertility of the earth and women too. It is believed by the temple priests that celebration of Ambubachi is one of the reasons why the taboo associated with menstruation is less stringent in Assam compared to other parts of India. Moreover, Ambubachi Mela can be an appropriate occasion to promote awareness on menstrual hygiene. In fact, the attainment of womanhood for girls in Assam is no secret occasion or a hush-hush affair but is welcomed and celebrated with a ritual called '*Tuloni Biya*', which means small wedding.

THE CUSTOM OF SEPARATION OF MENSTRUATING WOMEN

The discourse on menstruation is not complete with celebration of the *Ambubachi* festival. Of course, menstruation is a hush-hush affair generally, with varying intensity of taboos almost all over the world. In several parts of India, menstruation is not considered a natural and biological function of the human body but a dirty process that renders a woman unclean and as a result she is not considered fit to live with the rest of the people in the house during this period.

The superstitions and unfounded beliefs connected with menstruation are so strong that women are made to suffer in solitude, in a secluded hut or thatched shelter often detached from the family residence. Such customs with minor variations prevail in several tribes, communities and areas in India. In many of these places, there is not much progress in countering the beliefs associated with menstruation even with the spread of education and general advancement. The regressive practice continues.

In Thanjavur district of Tamil Nadu, it is a belief that girls who attain puberty are considered impure during their period and are isolated from the rest of the family and are forced to stay in a hut away from the main house. It can cause physical and psychological injury to these girls. An example of such injury has been relayed here. A 14-year old girl, Vijaya, from Annaikkadu was a student of eighth standard. Her father was a labourer and they lived in a coconut grove. The girl, during onset of menstruation, was banished to a hut a little away from their main family dwelling. During these nights, her mother joined her. However, one fateful night the cyclone Gaja struck the district and the heavy winds uprooted a coconut tree in the grove which fell on the hut occupied by the girl and her mother and injured both of them. The mother shouted for help but no one could hear over the strong winds. By morning, Vijaya was dead and the mother seriously injured and bleeding was taken to the hospital.

Apart from Thanjavur, there is a village in Karur where menstruating girls are sent to an isolated location during their menstruating period. In Agram village in Perambalur, there is a building in the outskirts of the village where menstruating women are supposed to stay.

This discriminatory and denigrating practice of treating women undergoing menstruation as impure is also prevalent in certain parts and tribes of Maharashtra, Chhattisgarh and Andhra Pradesh. The Madia and Gond tribes of Gadchiroli and Chandrapur in Maharashtra, Bastar in Chhattisgarh and the people in parts of erstwhile Andhra Pradesh treat menstruation as a social taboo. Nowhere in South India is it accepted as a normal, biological process women are subjected to periodically, on a monthly basis.

The women of Gadchiroli district, undergoing menstruation, are banished to a 'periods hut' known as *kurmaghar* or *gaokar* in the local dialect. These huts are located on the outskirts of the village, usually in a dilapidated condition with no toilet and bathing facilities and electricity and lighting. For this duration, the women are prohibited from doing household chores, kept away from the common dwellings and forced to live in seclusion in unsanitary conditions which cause infections, illness and sometimes, may lead to even death. Local NGOs (non-governmental organization) such as *Sparsh* have collected statistics of deaths but they haven't appealed to the community or the relevant authorities to curb these discriminatory and unhealthy practices. There is little realization that the women need additional physical help, mental care and emotional support during their menstrual periods.

Some brave tribal women have tried to resist this age-old practice and rebelled against compulsory seclusion but such women are brought before the Panchayat which then imposes exorbitant penalties on these women like forcing them to cook an entire meal of expensive meat and provide liquor for the entire village. The poor and hapless women cannot afford such expenses and cater to such luxurious and sumptuous meals and, hence, are forced to resign to their fate of social exile and remain within the shackles of the customary beliefs of the society.

NGOs are involved in amelioration of the conditions of women through mental change and spreading awareness about the biological realities of menstruation and healthy handling but these NGOs often faces resistance from men and older women who are set in their beliefs. Further, support of the government is non-existent because the government is wary of intervening in matters of age-old social beliefs. Therefore, the change has to come from within the community through active participation from the younger and educated members of the community. On the issue of Kurmaghar, it can be improved, a *pucca* structure with proper sanitary facilities can be built but an ugly practice sanctified by society or an unsympathetic custom seeped in history which treats women in such an unsympathetic manner cannot be eradicated easily.

The prejudice against women undergoing menstruation also prevails in the Hindu society of Nepal as an ancient tradition. This practice is called '*Chhaupadi*' that banishes menstruating girls and women as they are thought to be impure. This banishment forces them to live in animal sheds or even windowless huts for the duration of their period. Apart from poor sanitation, lack of hygiene and proper utilities for maintaining health, such living conditions may prove fatal even otherwise. An incident that occurred in Bajura district of western Nepal is recounted here. Amba Bohara, aged 35, was segregated in a hut as a result of the customary practice of *Chhaupadi*. She brought her two sons with her. In the freezing winter night, in good faith, she lit a small fire in the windowless hut to keep herself and her children comfortably warm. But to the family's horror they were discovered dead the next morning, having been suffocated to death. This age-old Hindu practice lead to these deaths even after having been banned by the Supreme Court of Nepal in 2005. This practice is still widespread in Nepal due to the stranglehold of customary practices and community's backward mindset.

THE LEGEND OF THE BIRTH OF GODDESS DURGA

A war between the *asuras* (demon warriors) and *devtas* (gods) had been going on for hundreds of years. Finally, the king of *asuras*, Mahishasura, defeated God Indra and became the Lord of the *swaraglok* (comparable to heaven). Victorious and full of pride, Mahishasura not only assumed the powers of the defeated God Indra, but also of other *devtas* including Surya, Agni, Chandra, Yama and Varuna. The vanquished gods had no choice and wandered around in the universe for a while like helpless mortals. Weary and tired, they finally reached Vaikunth[8] to take a safe shelter with Lord Vishnu.

The *devtas* pleaded of their pitiable plight to Lord Vishnu and told him that the mighty Indra has been deposed, Surya has no light, Agni has turned cold as ice while Vayu and Varun are still and more or less lifeless; Chandra has faded in its beauty and Yama stands as helpless as a mortal man. They collectively sought Vishnu's help to destroy the evil Mahishasura who had reduced them to this state of penury.

On seeing the *devtas* plight and hearing their tales of sorrow, Lord Vishnu was filled with compassion as also anger. His face trembled and a fierce light shone like a streak from his eyes and darted straight as a lance. This awakened Lord Shiva who too appeared enraged and emitted a blinding light. They were joined by Lord Brahma, his face seemingly on fire and seething with intense rage. Encouraged by the trinity's favourable reaction, the divine powers of other *devtas* also shot forth from their ethereal bodies, bursting arrows of powerful light and rays of strong energy.

The combined concentration of light and energy rose like a blazing mountain, its flames lighting up all three worlds (earth, atmosphere and netherworld) with a unique golden light. To the *devtas'* surprise, the light slowly gathered and composed itself into a lustrous female form. By that which was Shiva's light, her face came into being, by Yama's light, her hair was born, by Vishnu's light, her arms were formed, by Chandra's light, her breasts were created, by Indra's powers, her waist was formed, by Varuna's light, her thighs grew and earth's light formed her hips. Further, from Brahma's light, her feet came into being, from Surya's light,

---

[8] Vaikunth in mythology is believed to be the abode of Lord Vishnu and a place of bliss.

her toes were created, Vayu formed her ears and from Agni's powers, her three eyes were formed. The light and energy within the control of other *devtas*, too, surged forward for bestowal of collective embellishments and sundry powers upon the female form. No wonder the *devtas* were filled with joy and hope as they beheld the auspicious and beautiful *devi* who had, thus, been formed. This is how Goddess Durga was born, with a collective contribution of supernatural powers and divine will to defeat and destroy the demon king, Mahishasura and restore the original order of peace and worship in the *Brahman* (the universe).

THE CUSTOM OF SUTTEE

The ancient custom of *suttee* put an obligation, particularly, on the widows of *Kshatriya* kings and nobility, to compel them to be burnt alive on the funeral pyre of their deceased husbands. The custom was established many centuries ago and it began as a voluntary practice where the widow, out of expression of her intense love, affection and fidelity for her husband, or as a mark of honour or act of devotion, of her own volition, immolated herself on the funeral pyre of the dead husband. As Abbe Dubois commented nearly two centuries back, '...women are only too frequently offering themselves as victims of this horrid superstition, and, either through motives of vanity or through a spirit of blind enthusiasm, giving themselves up to a death which is as cruel as it is foolish.'[9]

Over a period of time, however, this voluntary sacrifice of the highest order became an ingrained social practice and came to be imposed on the women as a duty even if the widow herself was reluctant and unwilling to commit *suttee*. Thus, it became an obligation and was stringently enforced in areas

---

[9] Dubois, *Hindu Manners, Customs and Ceremonies*, 355.

forming parts of the then Rajasthan, Gujarat, Maharashtra, Madhya Pradesh, the Bengal Presidency, parts of North India and provinces bordering on the Ganges.[10] The rituals of *suttee* have slightly varied in different regions but the core practice has always required a voluntary desire to commit *suttee* and the willingness of the widow was deemed to be expressed by placing of the head of the husband in her lap while sitting in the funeral pyre.

Once acceptance was indicated, the widow would be adorned like a bride. Customarily, she would commit *suttee* as a bride and not as widow. After that, she would be given a large platter filled with coins, jewellery and *sandhoor* (or *sindoor*, a mark of a bride) and prompted to go around the village symbolizing her willingness and desire for committing *suttee*. On her return to the palace, she was offered a coconut and thereafter, wrapped and embellished with *sandhoor*, called *sadhaura*. Till this stage of the ritual, she was allowed to change her mind but once she willingly accepted *Sadhaura,* she could not recant her decision and had to compulsorily climb onto her husband's funeral pyre.

The Mohammedan rulers utterly disapproved of this practice of suicidal sacrifice and never tolerated it. But notwithstanding their orders prohibiting *suttee*, 'the fanatics more than once succeeded in bribing the subordinate representatives of the ruling authority to give them permission to commit the deed in violation of the laws of humanity and common sense.'[11] The British rulers of India also tried, by all possible means of persuasion, to put an end to this callous custom, but their efforts were only partially successful. Admittedly, the administration was obliged to shut its eyes to this dreadful practice because any attempt to remedy it by force of authority

---

[10] Ibid.
[11] Ibid., 356.

would have exposed it to dangerous opposition from ardent believers of the custom. Gradually, native social reformers and activists like Rajah Ram Mohun Roy, raised their collective voice against this practice. This encouraged the British Indian government to abolish the practice of suttee by law in the year 1829. This happened during the governance of Governor-General Lord William Bentick (1825–1835).

This law, passed in the year 1829 prohibited this practice till a few decades back, but isolated incidents still happened on the sly and sometimes, even openly, in defiance of the government machinery and the statutory law. One such recent case is of Roop Kanwar who committed *suttee* on her husband's funeral pyre in Deorala on 4 September 1987. The incident became highly publicized and was collectively criticized ny the entire nation and jolted the country to re-enact the old and forgotten law as the new Sati Prevention Act, 1987. Criminal proceedings in this case are still going on in a court at Jaipur.[12] Nevertheless, the *suttee* women are glorified and venerated as a symbol of 'caste culture'. The *suttees* are even worshipped for their devotion to their spouse and are hailed for bringing honour to their family. A few such women have even been elevated spiritually as benign deities who can fulfil wishes and bless seekers with boons. Despite the ongoing legal proceedings, the shrine of Roop Kanwar, even now, exists in Deorala, though visited on a low-key, i.e., few people visit the shrine and no fair is held.

As mentioned above, the custom of *suttee* principally originated and prevailed within the noble castes of *kshatriyas* and 'was looked upon (*sic*) as a highly honourable proof of wifely attachment and conjugal love which ostensibly enhanced the glory of the family'. In most cases the sites, where unburnt

---

[12] Final arguments in this case are going on in a Special Court at Jaipur constituted for trying cases under Sati Prevention Act, 1987. Refer Yeshika Budhwar and Shoeb Khan, 'Sati a crime, bult cult of Roop Kanwar thrives', *The Times of India*, 5 September 2019, p. 7.

bones of the *suttee* woman are buried, have been decorated within tomb-like structures or pyramid memorials to celebrate their heroic feat and to perpetuate the memory of an ideal wife as an example for posterity. Over time, these monuments have grown into shrines as places of worship. Many such *suttee* temples are spread all over Rajasthan and northern parts of Gujarat and the enshrined *suttees* are venerated as local deities. Rani Sati Mandir of Jhunjhunu with its famous *Chunri* ceremony is one of these. There is also a belief that *suttee devis* are blessed with divine powers and can bestow boons on devotees.

In case a widow, by reason of a natural fondness for life or lack of courage or rightly frightened by the barbarity of the act, tried to avoid being burnt alive on the funeral pyre of her deceased husband, she was considered to be offering a gross insult to her husband's memory and causing ineffaceable dishonour to the distinguished lineage of the family as also bringing ever-lasting shame and life-long humiliation to widowhood. The *purohit Brahmin* and the relatives would still try to entreat the widow and convince her with inducements of fame and carriage in a palanquin. They would highlight the distinctiveness of the act and promise her immortal glory as well as posthumous exaltation to the dignity of a godly stature. An affirmative decision, even by mistake or under coercion, could be retracted or revoked and 'the sorry widow' could even be dragged and put on the pyre, forcibly, despite her wailing and remonstrations. The invoking of superstitions or promising intangible inducements like fame and glory may have worked on some widows but did not succeed in the case of the widow of the *poligar* prince of Cangoondy in Karnataka who stubbornly refused to commit *suttee*. Ultimately, the deceased prince was obliged to depart alone to the other world.[13]

---

[13] Dubois, *Hindu Manners, Customs and Ceremonies*, 358.

'Some authors have maintained that this... age-old practice originated primarily due to the jealousy of husbands, or rather, perhaps, from their fear that their discontented and young wives might seek to get rid of them by poison.'[14] But 'this writer-researcher[15] has been unable to find written accounts of such suppositions or any such suggestion in his interaction with Hindu elders during his long stay in India'. At the same time the writer-researcher is not 'inclined to attribute these voluntary sacrifices to an excess of conjugal affection'[16] or abiding mutual attachment of the heart. Suffice it to say, the end of life of widows on a funeral pyre has almost always been tragic for the victim and heart-wrenching for the mourners.

There is another variant of the custom of submitting oneself to death on the funeral pyre of the husband. This variation exists because most *Sudras* communities as well as the Hindus of the Shiva sect, do not cremate, instead they bury their dead. Therefore, in their observance of *suttee* custom, the wife is buried alive with the dead husband. 'There are several instances of wives having been buried alive with their deceased husbands. But the *suttee* ceremonies in either case are nearly the same.'[17]

This practice of *suttee* also prevails among the upper classes of Marathas, records chronicler, John-Henry Grose; and whispers confide that this custom was invented by the brahmins, i.e., this reason is not openly discussed but secretly shared, as Grose writes, 'to put a stop to the frequency of the women poisoning their husbands, on every slightest quarrel.' He further comments, 'If true, it would appear to have been a very drastic remedy for an equally drastic response to a

---

[14] Ibid., 359.
[15] Ibid.
[16] Ibid.
[17] Ibid., 361.

domestic tiff.'[18] Whatever be the origin of this custom, the needle of suspicion points towards complicity of *brahmins* who presided over the *suttee* ceremony and were the ultimate beneficiaries of sumptuous *dakshina* and other charities for overseeing the performance of such rituals of death.

Another area in the grip of this mindset is Bundelkhand where, in the last decade, over five widows have committed *suttee* despite the existence of an enforceable Sati Prevention Act, 1987. The region literally seems to be caught in a time warp between medieval feudalism and liberal ethos of the twenty-first century. People still appear to be steeped in stigmas, superstition and parochial beliefs. Scores of temples dot the rugged countryside and thrive on generous donations by the believers.

Suttee worship by married women is common practice; and hordes of them can be seen visiting the *suttee* temples on Basant Panchami (a spring festival generally celebrated in the month of February in India) and offering prayers with the belief that '*sati maiya*' fulfils every wish of the devotee. Brides usually visit the *suttee* temples before entering the house of the groom and her in-laws, wishing and praying for a long life for the husband.[19] Customs do have a strong grip on society and it indeed becomes difficult to breach the stranglehold of these norms. Enough strength to break off from these customs and societal awareness to accept the contemporary reality, both are vitally essential to cut the shackles of these age-old practices.

Let us now explore the *Vedas* for a discourse on the practice of *suttee*. To put it cryptically yet succinctly, the scriptures do not sanction *suttee*. However, 'some assert that the Rigveda,

---

[18] John-Henry Grose, *The Statesman*, 20 January 1992.

[19] Sunita Aron, 'Stigma smoulders: Bundelkhand out of sync with time', *Hindustan Times*, 23 May 2006.

through *richa* X.18.7 (7th richa of 18 *Sukta*, Chapter X) commands a Hindu widow to mount the pyre of her deceased husband.'[20] One website quotes Kane's translation of this *richa*: 'Let these women, whose husbands are worthy enter the house with ghee applied as collyrium (to their eyelids). Let these wives first step into the pyre, tearless without any affliction and well adorned.'[21]

This interpretation has been contested and the richa is differently translated by scholars like Wilson and O 'Flaherty. Firstly, because the translation itself mentions a wife and not widow, the latter status befalls only after the death of the husband. Secondly, the referred *richa* itself does not contain the word *vidhwa* (widow), hence the context appears unrelated. On the contrary, *richa* eight of the same *Sukta* and chapter, demands of a Hindu widow, to return alive to her home, to the world of living beings.[22] So the custom of *suttee* seems to carry no Vedic approbation.

FEMALE BONDING: AN INTERESTING COMMUNITY CUSTOM

A closely knit community called Bhatia community comprising of 250 is settled in Jaisalmer. The Bhatia's originated as a trader community in the 9th century and are an off-shoot of Bhatti Rajputs. Over time, 84 sub-castes evolved from them but they have always lived within a short distance from each other and have been concentrated within a single locality of the town. *Bhatia* women are considered liberal though very few of them have studied beyond graduation or taken up jobs. They do not have the dowry system and believe in endogamy.

---

[20] O. P. Gupta, 'From the Rigveda, a thing or two about sati', *Indian Express*, 4 October 2002.
[21] Ibid.
[22] Ibid.

Thus, the maternal house of the women is never too far from the husband and in-law's residence. As per popular Indian traditions and prevalent customs, the parent's household normally becomes secondary to that of the in-laws for a woman after marriage.

However, married Bhatia women believe differently and have an unusual but accepted practice, where they visit their parent's home every evening to spend time with them. Most of them dine at their parent's house and then return to their husband's house. This practice is encouraged by the women's husbands. Bhatias believe that unhindered communication between a woman and her maternal family harmonizes the relationship between the two households and therefore, this system of interaction is encouraged by the families. Despite this freedom, the mothers motivate their daughters with advice to adjust with their parents-in-law and ignore minor dissensions. As such, daily, or at least, frequent meetings release a lot of tension and remove perceived misunderstandings.

The daily dinners at the maternal house become less frequent as mothers age and cooking for a large number of people becomes difficult to manage; or daughters get busy with their own growing families and expanding household duties. The evening visits, nevertheless, continue though less frequently. In fact, a long break in such visits duly elicits worried queries from the parents or is indicative of a family discord that needs urgent amicable resolution. This system, therefore, rightfully serves as a social coolant or as a release valve for mundane tensions.

It is difficult to establish and pin-point as to when or ascertain as to why exactly the custom of married women visiting their parent's house every evening started. But its rationale and basis appear to be a basic concern among the Bhatia community that women should remain equally in touch and involved with the life and affairs of their parents, even after marriage. A possibility can be surmised that this custom originated at a time in the past when child-marriages were prevalent and a common occurrence in society.

SNIPPETS

SUN GODDESS THAT MOVES TO NEW RESIDENCE EVERY TWENTY YEARS

Goddess Amaterasu is revered as the ancestral goddess of Japan's imperial family and treated as the guardian deity of the nation. According to ancient chronicles, she first took up residence at Ise's inner shrine in the year 4 BC. This Sun goddess is believed to shift her abode every twenty years. In the year 1993, she moved through towering Hinoki Cypress trees to her grand new shrine of Ise, the heart of Japan's indigenous Shinto religion. White robed priests, following ancient rites, ceremonially transport the goddess to its new abode every time the new building is ready. In the year 1993, this ceremony was held in October to mark the rice harvest. This was believed to be 61st recorded divine house-transfer. After the shift to the new site, which is generally identical in appearance and just a short distance away from the old abode, the old temple is razed down to the ground as part of a purification cycle. This tradition is said to travel back to the dawn of Japanese history.[23] The shrine of Amaterasu is highly revered and deemed holiest by the Japanese.

---

[23] 'New abode for Sun goddess', *The Statesman*, 13 March 1993.

A MEXICAN TOWN RULED BY WOMEN

The Mexican town of Juchitán de Zaragoza is ruled by women where men play second fiddle to women in all aspects of life. The town is inhabited by people from the Baputak racial stock of aboriginal Indians where, for centuries, women are highly respected, rated superior to men and enjoy total freedom. Of course, Mexico has a traditional *Manual of Conduct* to regulate the behaviour of menfolk, but its implementation is relaxed. However, in the Joshitian way of governance, it is rather strictly followed to keep the men on their toes. In this town, women dominate and rule almost every walk of life. Joshitian women consider that men are incapable of handling money; therefore, they preside over money matters and maintain all financial accounts while men as earning members, work as artisans and labourers and hand over their entire wages to their respective wives who are virtual rulers.[24]

They have to request their wives for pocket money and even legitimate, regular and normal personal expenses, though granted, are doled with a tight fist. In case of any mal-transaction or concealment of finances, the wife can divorce her husband. He loses all his relations and privileges in the society as well as his job because men have no right to do any trade in the market under their own identity, which is the sole monopoly and prerogative of the women.

In fact, almost all, important decisions, whether relating to town governance or family matters or personal issues

---

[24] A report by Chris Fuller, translated and published in *Hind Samachar* (Urdu), 8 September 1993. Retranslated and amplified.

of men, are taken by women, individually or in concert. Even in matters of sexual indulgence, women decide the time, mood and place.

The women on the other hand freely enjoy among themselves with wine, beer and good food; while men remain segregated and are treated with inferior status and permitted to lesser enjoyments in life. This mindset is groomed and instilled by mothers in their sons right from childhood; and it gets imbibed and docilely accepted without demur or resistance.[25] The tradition has continued since ages and no one knows till when it will remain. Amen!

---

[25] Ibid.

2
MARRY A DEAD PERSON
Unusual Marriages and Strange Customs

Marriage is a civilizational baggage because in primitive societies, no such formality or formalization either existed or was necessary. Adam and Eve were not married by any custom or ordainment. Procreation was dictated by a natural urge and willing partnership. When the civilization evolved as a society, it birthed the incident of marriage, to maintain accounts of paternity of children and succession of property. Marriage became a social norm to be publicly announced and celebrated with pomp and show, hosted with grand meals and drinks for the community. Thus, marriage became a ritual to be blessed by the elders and to be enjoyed by the young.

In olden days, particularly during the periods of Ramayana and Mahabharat, young girls selected their own spouse prescribing some sort of a test or criterion to be satisfied by the young suitor. This system of choosing a partner was called *swayamvar*. This word when conjugated is a combination of two words: *swayam*, meaning oneself or of own volition, and *var*, meaning partner or husband. In other words, it means self-selection of a husband. This system has worked well, more so, among the royal and noble families where equality in status, leverages of nobility and social pressures were conducive to longevity of marriages.

With the passage of time, the norm became an obligation and society became compulsive about its observance. If these obligations are not adhered to, marriage wouldn't be socially recognized or accepted by the fraternity or blessed by the elders. The economically weaker sections suffered the brunt of these norms of celebration, and in certain communities, they were forced to live-in and beget children before formal marriage with a prescribed ceremony. In some cases, marriages were delayed till children started contributing to the family fund. However, this simple social norm of marriage gradually found its way into legislated statutes as its registration or official solemnization became a legal necessity. This requirement now exists in almost all civilized societies of the world. However, even in large countries with plurality of religions and multiple communities, aborigines still living in their original habitat, follow their own, old customs. Diversity in their marital systems, methods of mate selection and customs of marriage celebration is observed. What is fascinating to note is how diverse marital systems are adopted by societies, communities or tribes, due to various factors such as compulsive economic reasons, ethnic duress, force of domineering norms and sometimes sheer voluntary societal acceptance.

Time flies and people evolve resulting in mutations of traditions that have erupted over time and metamorphosized. New and modern marital arrangements include acceptance of multiple partners, live-in relationship or same-gender marriages, formal and informal. Many other permutations and combinations are coming in vogue and becoming visible. Reversal to old traditions and values seems impossible. Therefore, we must come to terms with the changing grammar of marital systems. It is conceded that the material presented here is neither comprehensive in content nor researched enough for assured veracity. It is intended for providing common information and as a base for further socio-anthropological research.

IN FRANCE ONE CAN MARRY A DEAD PERSON

In France, where a law permits 'post-mort' marriages, the 'dearly departed' can still be 'dearly beloved'. It so happened that in December 1959, floods devastated parts of France and inundated the town of Frejus and claimed hundreds of lives. When, President Charles DeGaulle visited the town later to inspect the extent of damage, a young woman named Irene Joddard pleaded with him to allow her to follow through on her wedding even though her fiancé, Andre Capra, had drowned. Later that month, the National Assembly drafted a law to permit marriage with the deceased. The law passed in December 1959 turned the wedding vow 'till death do us part' on its head and Joddard legally married her dead fiancé.[1]

Thousands of 'would-be' widows and widowers have since applied for 'post-mortem matrimonial' permission and many have successfully received official clearance for solemnization of such marriages and were joined in love and matrimony. However, for obvious tragic reasons surrounding the events, most of such posthumous weddings are kept quiet and low-key affairs and rarely publicly announced or propagated in society.

One brave lady, named Christelle Demichel, however, decided to marry and celebrate her wedding with her dead lover complete with rituals and the usual customs. Her fiancé, Eric Demichel was riding his motorcycle when he was killed by a drunk driver in a road accident. She applied for postmortem matrimony and got approval on 22 December 2003 but decided to wait until 10 February 2004 to get married as that would have been her fiancé's thirtieth birthday. The wedding ceremony was held at Riviera in Nice.

As if in a traditional wedding, Christelle showed up at Nice's town hall wearing a black pantsuit, carrying a bouquet of yellow roses. An empty armchair represented the groom, and as a substitute for his vows the Mayor read the decree, 'I declare you man and wife'. The pomp and celebration were reminiscent of a customary wedding and the bride gleefully ducked rice after the ceremony. Later, about forty people attended her reception at a local restaurant, merrymaking, and drank champagne from bottles which bore customary labels with the names of the newlyweds printed on them. It bore complete resemblance to the usual wedding celebrations

---

[1] Craig S. Smith, 'In France, dearly departed can still be dearly beloved', *New York Times*, 19 February 2004. Published in *Indian Express* (Delhi Edition), 20 February 2004.

and the only thing conspicuously missing, besides a wedding cake, was the groom. However, the spirit of celebration made up for the loss.

WORLD'S MOST ROMANTIC POSTBOX

From times immemorial, people have been able to send messages and letters to different recipients in different destinations via sundry modes and means even though public post departments operated by the governments have been in existence only for a couple of centuries. We are all familiar with a red letterbox situated on street corners that has nothing romantic about its looks, colour or shape; in fact, its presence evokes sentiments as well as comments to the contrary. Yet, there is one letterbox in Germany that is not really a conventional letterbox but a tree functioning as a letterbox. It is used to exchange love and romantic notes by people in Germany and is an unsung matchmaker.[2]

The legend of the tree goes like this: There was a girl called Minna living in Wilhelm in Germany. She was in love with a boy, but her father forbade her from meeting her lover. This was unbearable for both the girl and the boy, and their despair led them to discover an expedient alternative mode of communication. For one year they kept in touch by leaving letters to each other inside a knothole in a tree. They finally married each other under the same oak tree on 2 June 1891. This successful love story soon spread far and wide and the tree came to be considered as lucky and auspicious for lovers and culmination of the bond of their love.

As a result, 1891 onward, singles, with utmost belief, started writing letters and leaving them in the knothole of the tree hoping to find a desirable and loving match. It was customary

---

[2] Amplified from a pictory (picture story) published in *The Times of India* (Chandigarh Edition), 5 April 2018, p. 7.

for anyone to open a letter left in the round knothole, write a reply and leave it in the same place. The popularity of the tree has since risen and it gets around 1000 letters deposited in its knothole every year. Showing official courtesy and deference to public opinion, the German Postal Department, in the year 1927, allotted the tree a postcode number (number 23701) and a name, *Der Brautigamseiche,* the Bridegroom's Oak.

This lucky Oak Tree is located outside the town of Eutin in Germany. It is the only tree in the world with its own postal code as its unique identity. It may be of interest to know that this tree and its matchmaking are believed to have arranged over 100 marriages so far and the count is expected to increase since the sentimental and amorous practice continues.

KENYAN CUSTOM OF WIFE'S WIFE

Kenya has a custom of a wife marrying a wife though not for lesbian partnership. The wife's wife may also serve as a kind of second wife to the husband but it is not considered a polygamous relationship because the second wife enters the house through a contract between the two women only with no involvement or partnership of the husband. This tradition is called '*Iweto*' in which another woman is literally adopted to procreate or provide her own existing children to the family. Who fathers or fathered the children is irrelevant in this relationship.[3]

In many African societies being barren is a bane and infertility a virtual taboo. Even blessed with a home and a husband, a childless woman is considered worthless because the couple is unable to leave an heir resulting in the end of the family line. In such situations, while the Western world looks to

---

[3] Fiona O'Brien, 'Wake up, wife's wife', *Reuters* (also published in *Indian Express,* 12 May 2002).

specialist doctors and reproduction technology, the African communities prefer a more humanistic approach. In such circumstances, a woman who cannot beget children can simply marry another woman who is single and able to have children or already has children. She is a wife's wife, an 'Iweto', a woman married to a woman.

Anthropologists consider this practice as a practical way of solving a social problem of old-age neglect of the original family where a wife is acquired in adoption either along with children or in a hope that children will follow. In nutshell, the main purpose of wife's wife is to provide children for furtherance of the lineage and perpetuation of the family name as well as for looking after the adoptive parents in their old age. This solution may be practical as also socially accepted but it is not always a happy one.

Mutiso Ndwale married her husband many years ago but did not bear any children. The need for children was acute on a personal as well as social level. So, she negotiated with Syombua, a young woman in the same village, a member of Kenya's Akambe tribe. This woman was unmarried with four illegitimate sons and few prospects of finding a husband. After five years of negotiations, the two families came to an agreement for marriage and dowry and Syombua moved in with the Ndwale's becoming an 'iweto'. Mutiso, now 80 years old, is happy, for when she dies, she will leave a pillar standing instead of her, who will carry forward her name and remember her. She is glad that the sons call her *inya*, that is, mother, and call Syombua, who is the true mother, 'mwaito', that is, mum; and they officially carry her surname, Ndwale. The joy of leaving a lineage is unique and can only be appreciated as a social compulsion or as a peculiar satisfaction of personal advancement.

Syombua, the wife's wife seems to have had the rough end of the deal. This young woman does all the household chores, takes care of the old couple and has yet to get a cent against the dowry of fifty goats and two cows promised to her parents at the time of marriage. She may get some portion out of this for herself, but the pertinent question is, when? The couple is really old and poor. Nonetheless, she is resigned to a fate she has not voluntarily chosen for herself. Social compulsions led to her predicament. Of course, she meets other 'iwetos' when they occasionally gather to sing and dance and share their experiences and personal woes. She laments that she is yet to meet an 'iweto' who has ever benefitted from such a contract. Anthropologist David Maillu comments that there is no need to rationalize or find logic in such an unequal arrangement because it is part of a customary tradition of a community.[4]

MARRIAGE OF WOMEN TO THE HOLY QURAN

BBC has revealed in a programme that in the Sind province of Pakistan there was a custom where parents would marry their daughters to the Holy Quran so that they remained unmarried and childless till death. The purpose of this custom was to avoid division or fragmentation of landed property through succession rights. This practice is not only discriminatory and prejudicial to the affected women, but also detrimental to their health and happiness because some of them become mentally disturbed or insane.[5]

A reporter informed that this custom came into practice after the invasion of India by Mughals, when Hindus converted to Islam. As per the existing Hindu custom, widows had to accept the fate of committing *sati* on their husband's funeral pyre. To avoid this, converted Hindus adopted the practice of marrying the Quran, with an additional advantage that the women married to the Quran would be included

---

[4] Ibid.
[5] Suvera Features, 'Marriage with Quoran', *Hind Samachar*, 15 October 1992.

in the category of a 'peer' and be revered as a pious person, notwithstanding the other consequences of undertaking this step.[6]

MARRIAGES AMONG ANNIARAIKOTTAIS

There is an unusual system of marriage practised in South India. Melakalangal, better known as Pathinettu Patti (eighteen villages), now a cluster of 16 villages, ever since two villages disappeared due to death of their residents and migration of families. These villages fall in the district of Tirunelveli-Kattabomman of Tamil Nadu. This cluster was formerly part of erstwhile Oothamalai Zamin. Long time ago, the ruling family ruthlessly chopped down all the trees in the area, in a one last grab of wealth. So, this once green and verdant area became environmentally unsustainable and turned dry, dusty and semi-arid. Consequently, the inhabitants became poor.

The population of Pathinettu Patti villages averages about 300–400 families each and here women outnumber the male population. The villagers belong to Aniaraikottai sect of Thevar community who are highly traditional and zealously follow the traditions handed down by their forefathers. One such custom relates to marriage. For Aniaraikottai community, marriages are not made in heaven and marriage is considered far too serious a matter to be left entirely to the families of the young man and woman. As such, these sixteen villages are endogamous and do not marry outside their cluster. As a result, such marriages may happen within the legally prohibited degrees or in anomalous relationships where girls may again come back to their paternal family.[7]

---

[6] Ibid.
[7] E. G. Rajendran, 'Children precede weddings', *The Statesman (Sunday Magazine)*, January, 1992.

Therefore, marriages are arranged during covert discussions by a group of elderly men relaxing under the scanty shade of a scrawny shrub or at the dingy village teashop. At these sessions, the matchmakers draw up a list of nubile girls and eligible bachelors in all the 16 villages and then consider how best to pair them off while the actual participants in the marriage, that is, the girls and boys and their families, are in blissful ignorance. While matchmaking, the elders are not bothered in the least about mundane matters such as adhering to the minimum legal age for marriage or the biological risks due to endogamous inbreeding or the eugenic considerations for better progeny. On the contrary, they abide by self-proclaimed age-old customs that mandate a girl should be married by 15 years of age and a boy by 17 years of age. No wonder, by the time an Aniaraikottai couple reach the lawful age for marriage, they are usually the parents of a child or two.

The marriage ceremonies of this community are also different and strange. Once the matchmakers decide on a particular match, they awaken the boy and girl quietly and escort them to the house of a relative or friend in the neighbouring village, where the boy ties a *thali* (mangal sutra) around the girl's neck, under their supervision. All this happens so unexpectedly, when the boy and the girl, in all probability, are still in their night clothes and in that attire, are made man and wife. This ceremony and resultant transformation are accomplished without any fuss or bother and without payment of anything remotely resembling a dowry or a promise of *mehr*.[8]

After a few days of marriage, the couple moves in with the bride's parents and lives there until her parents decide that it is time for the couple to live with husband's parents. The

---

[8] Ibid.

decision to move to the husband's house is normally taken after a few years of marriage when in all likelihood, the couple have become parents to at least one or two children. The move to the groom's parents' house, accompanied by their off-springs, is considered a joyous occasion, marked by a feast for friends and relatives. At this celebration, the bride's parents are required to give presents of household articles and ornamental jewellery to their daughter, son-in-law and grandchildren. With this celebration, the formalization of marriage is accomplished.

INTERESTING CUSTOM AMONG SINGPHO CLAN

Singpho clan of North-East India makes for an interesting study of marriage customs. This community now resides in Tirap district of Arunachal Pradesh. However, originally, this clan, known to have consisted of Buddhists of the Hinanayana sect, migrated from the Humang valley of Burma at the end of the 14th century. They are akin to the *Ka Khiyens* of Burma whose chief habitat has been in the Irrawad valley in Burma. They have an interesting marital ecosystem.

Singpho clan treats its women as precious beings and their marriage system demands for a 'bride price' which is rather heavy. In fact, the possibility of a marriage is considered virtually on capacity to pay a traditional bride price of about ₹280, four buffaloes and two guns or an additional ₹280 in lieu of the guns. With the rise of inflation over the years, these figures may have escalated. Whatever be the present rates, this price is considered rather high in the area and acts as a deterrent to marriage among Singpho youth.

Generally, monogamy is practiced as the norm in this society. However, the rich who can afford the bride price are permitted to have several wives. The community also permits sororate polygamy. Under this system a man may either of his own volition, or under certain circumstances, be pressurized to marry his wife's sister. This could be a subsequent or concurrent marriage. Broadly speaking, this marital arrangement, apart from being polygamous, involves marriage of one man marrying two sisters. Thus, in this system of sororate polygamy, sisters may have one husband which is the inverse of polyandry, where brothers may have one wife.

Singphos as a society are exogamous and liberal yet impose certain riders on eligibility for marriage. For example, 'the daughter of a woman's brother is considered a potential wife for a man of the clan.'[9] However, 'a man's maternal first cousin cannot marry the daughter of his paternal aunt.' Indeed, tough rules of marriage relating to prohibited degrees of relationships in sanguanity.

Singphos' girls, once married, do not return to her parents' house under normal circumstances and it seems that there is no divorce system. In case a woman becomes a widow, she can remarry a younger brother but the widow's consent is necessary before such a marriage is settled. The second husband will consider the widow's issues from the previous marriage as his own children. If the widow rejects the marriage proposal, the bride price taken by the widow's parents will have to be returned to the brother of the deceased husband. Only after this repayment, the widow is considered free to return to her parents.[10]

Another unusual but not uncommon marriage custom among this community is a man's marriage with his daughter-in-law. But this liaison is permitted only if no children are borne from the first marriage. The purpose of this marriage is to ensure

---

[9] 'Singpho society permits polygamy', *The Statesman*, 30 June 1992.
[10] Ibid.

continuity of future generations and prevent the name of the family from becoming extinct.

PREVALENCE OF POLYANDRY WORLD-WIDE

Such systems of marriage are not confined to any specific communities, regional boundaries or national frontiers. They operate everywhere, perhaps exist sporadically and lately, have been vanishing gradually with spread of education and awareness. For example, an influx of wives from South India is happening in Haryana villages. A similar trend is noticed among the Chinese who are picking up Muslim brides from Pakistan.[11] Thus only the contours of necessity may vary yet the solution found may be the same.

Similarly, the practice of polyandry has existed in Himachal Pradesh, some areas in Sikkim and among the Nair community of Kerala till fairly recent times. The Todas of Nilgiri Hills have also followed this custom for generations because they believe that they are the descendants of the Pandavas. But lately, however, the threat of extinction has turned them towards monogamous relationships. But this switch to monogamy is yet to stabilize itself and prove its wisdom.

Polyandry is also known to have existed among other Asian people such as the folk of Tibet. In some areas of Tibet, it is still common and practised. Similarly, in Sri Lanka, the *Sinhalese* custom of fraternal polyandry, colloquially referred to as 'ekagekema' meaning eating in one house, still exits even though it is no longer legal. This tradition is also encountered in certain regions of China. Beyond Asia, it still exists in sub-Saharan Africa and among certain native communities

---

[11] This migration has since assumed scandalous proportion and is being investigated jointly by both countries. In the meanwhile, China has withheld visas of 90 Pakistani brides. Omar Farooq Khan, 'Trafficking scandal: China withholds visas of 90 Pak brides', *The Times of India* (Chandigarh Edition), 15 May 2019, p. 14.

of Latin America, notably the *Surui* community of north-western Brazil.

EARLIEST FRATERNAL POLYANDROUS SYSTEM

To have a holistic understanding of polyandry, it is relevant to discuss its etymology. The term polyandry is derived from the Greek language and is formed from the combination of two words—*'polys'* meaning *'many'* and *'aner or andros'* meaning man. The earliest reference to polyandry can be traced back to the age of Mahabharata when Draupadi is unwittingly married to five husbands. The circumstances that led to this situation, were purely co-incidental and unintentional. One can trace several variations of the legend that forced the royal family to accept this predicament which was neither the outcome of any royal tradition nor in pursuance of any native practice of the community. It so happened that the five *Pandava* brothers attended a *swayamvar* (a ceremony for selection of a bridegroom) where Arjun, one of the five brothers, won Draupadi's hand in marriage. After the wedding ceremony, they returned to their palace along with Draupadi.

The brothers were excited to break the news of their adventure and eagerly wished to inform their mother, Kunti, of Arjun's marriage to Draupadi. Kunti was busy in her chamber and could not come out to receive them. They implored her to come and see, rather than just hear their news. However, Kunti, in an unlikely turn of events, unwittingly and without knowing the fact of the situation, casually directed her sons to share whatever they had brought home. The embarrassment of sharing Draupadi as their wife was obvious, but the sons, completely devoted to their mother, took her wish as their command. Without remonstration and in due reverence, the five pandava brothers obediently abided by it and took Draupadi as their collective bride.

This relationship was not one of pure polyandry; it was a medley of polygamy too. Bhim was already married to Hidimbaa and had a son with her. Arjun married several princesses but only Subhadhra, Krishna's sister, came to Indraprastha to live with him. Nakul and Sehdev married the daughters of Shishupal and Jarasandh after their respective fathers' deaths, as a token of revival of friendship after the war. Thus, Draupadi's predicament confused, embarrassed and discomforted her. It is also evident that polygamy was, presumably, widely prevalent at that time as soldiers would die in wars and widows had to be rehabilitated in marriage for social harmony in the society.

Polyandry, in the case of the Pandavas, was a sheer accidental as is evident from the fact that this marital system was frowned upon in the patrilineal society existing during that time. It was essential for the society to know the paternity of the child, particularly a son's paternity, for establishing the succession rights and acceptance of the continuation of the family. Karna had faced this embarrassing predicament of unknown parentage. Interestingly, in order to ensure the correct knowledge of paternity of Draupadi's children from the five Pandava brothers, Rishi Veda Vyasa[12] had stated of a compulsory one-year period of cohabitation on a rotational basis for each of the five husbands of Draupadi.

In due course, Draupadi had five sons, one from each husband. Prativindhya was Draupadi's son with Yudhishtra, Srutasoma with Bhim, Srutakirti with Arjuna, Satanika with Nakul and Srutakarma with Sahdev. Vyasa had stipulated another condition for harmonious polyandrous relations between Draupadi and her husbands — during the tenure of any one husband, the other husbands were forbidden to enter Draupadi's chamber when the husband-of-the-year was alone and intimate with

---

[12] Veda Vyasa was an ancestor of Kauravas and Pandavas. It is believed that he, with clairvoyance, had foreseen these events of Mahabharta and had orally passed on to his disciples as a story.

Draupadi. It was, of course, for an urgent reason that Arjun violated this vow while Yudhishtra was with Draupadi and had to suffer exile, as prescribed.

Perhaps, many of us tend to believe that polyandry peacefully died with the age of Mahabharata, however, we are wrong in our belief. This system still perpetuates itself in many parts of India though in different forms, for different reasons and with different social, demographic or economic rationale. Many reasons can be surmised with logic and empirical evidence for the prevelance of polyandry. These may include inability to find a local wife due to physical disability or lack of respectable agricultural land ownership or similar reasons. A couple of reasons for polyandry are mentioned at the outset to introduce the tone and content of this chapter. Also a few case histories will illustrate and authenticate the narrative.

First, the blame goes to the infamous skewed sex-ratio due to foetus abortion or female infanticide. This unfortunate choice makes the number of women in the community, scarce, with the result that wife-buying, wife-importing or wife-sharing is not frowned upon by the some societies. Despite the upward trend, most such polyandrous relationships are contained in-house and are well-guarded from unwanted publicity. The other plausible reason could be economic because the agricultural land holdings have divided and sub-divided themselves in succession with the result these have become really small and uneconomical to cultivate or even successfully lease the same for rental or usufructs. The dilemma due to low female sex ratio or poverty due to uneconomic land holdings either way is obvious and compelling for societal adjustment, howsoever, unwanted.

CUSTOMARY POLYANDRY IN HIMACHAL PRADESH

Kinnaur is a district situated in the north-eastern part of Himachal Pradesh, bordering Tibet. The tribal women of Kinnaur are, in mythology, described as *'apasaras'* or celestially beautiful women. Apart from their beauty, they are also praised for their tactful and crafty household management. Further, these women are considered the most important economic asset of Kinnaur as they form the backbone of agricultural labour. Women of adjoining areas like Jubbal, Sirmour and Kullu are also equally praised for their beauty, tact and strength. In other activities of the household also their productive contribution is deemed to exceed that of men. They also play a very central and significant role in social bonding in the Himalayan polyandrous families.[13]

According to an anthropological study, the tribals of Kinnaur and other adjoining areas have a common custom of fraternal polyandry and this customary practice has continued for many generations. According to this age-old practice, a Kinnaur woman is married to a set of brothers of same parentage as a common wife; and it is by her tact, politeness and amiable behaviour that she maintains conviviality and domestic peace. Her advantage is that most of the time in a particular year, she cohabits with one husband owing to the customary division of labour among the male members of the family that makes them stay away on the fields to protect the crops or on outstation errands. Moreover, socially, the position of the eldest brother is supreme in the household and younger ones generally remain away from home for long periods on other tasks and errands.

Same anthropological study also reveals that the common wife has considerable influence and clout in the family and is invariably consulted on vital issues of the household even though true decision-making authority vests in the men. However, in political affairs of the village, the women have little say and no contribution. In religious matters, their position is still more insignificant because they do not have the right to directly worship the local *devta* (deity) or participate

---

[13] 'Unique role of women in Kinnaur', *The Statesman*, 25 August 1992.

in local festivities. A woman cannot become a temple func-
tionary either.[14]

THE CUSTOM OF 'REET' IN HIMACHAL PRADESH

Today, the socially acceptable way of entering into marital
relations the world over, barring isolated aberrations, is
monogamy; and divorce is the usual method of separation
between spouses. But Himachal Pradesh still remains in a
time warp despite better socio-economic living conditions and
transformation through improved literacy. In the Himalayan
region of Himachal Pradesh, polyandry and the practice of
reet still prevail. The stranglehold of tradition is difficult to
break and customs, as they say, die hard.

The *reet* system of matrimony involvs money exchanging
hands between the boy's family and the girl's family. The
boy's family pais a standard amount of money to the girl's
family in return for their daughter's hand in marriage to their
son. The system works like a sale and purchase of a woman.
Reet also works in favour of remarriage of a woman in case
of death of her husband or if she decides to leave her current
husband for another man. Even in the case of marriage to
another man, *reet* money is to be paid by the new husband's
family to the present husband's family. Thus, the custom of
reet involved marriage, divorce as well as remarriage. In a
way, it permits the possibility of remarriage for widows and
divorcees unlike in other Hindu societies.

The Himalayan population in the north-western hills
of Himachal Pradesh have been predominantly Hindu.
However, these Hindus are different from those living in the
plains of Punjab. In the hills, castes are graded hierarchically
into two levels. Between the castes of upper level there is

---

14 Ibid.

considerable social interaction and barriers of endogamy are thin. Polyandry is practiced by both upper and lower castes almost universally in Kinnaur, Sirmour, Jubbal and Kullu. Similarly, *reet* system has been in vogue, particularly in Solan and Shimla districts of Himachal Pradesh, and Chakrata in Uttarakhand.[15]

The importance of women is well recognized in the hills for their household management and economic contribution to the family. The *reet* system coupled with polyandry is the solution for multiple problems including adverse sex-ratio, unviable land holdings, avoidance of future fragmentation and the transfer of exacting household chores to the women folk.

The customs of *reet* allows remarriage and in the communities based in the hilly regions such remarriage carries no social stigma. There are instances galore of remarriage: A woman of Naini Dhar had 16 husbands in her lifetime; another woman in Bhatgar village is known for having performed *reet* marriage eight times; still another instance is of a woman having married each and every one of a set of brothers in Thanga village. On the contrary, the women always commanded higher compensation for their next marriage depending on their reputation for efficiency in household work, proficiency in familial cohesion and wisdom in social interactions.

The origin of *reet* has been traced back to the custom of forcible capture in the olden times. Possibly, mutual love or one-sided infatuation, further backed by the bride's economic importance, might have prevailed in society in giving her an option of release from previous unpleasant marriage or unwanted husband if she recompensed him for his loss.

---

[15] Sudesh Bedi, 'Himachalis victims of reet'. Excerpt from the doctoral thesis of Y. S. Parmar, submitted to Lucknow University, Lucknow, 1945.

It seems society may have evolved and accepted this system as a solution in lieu of modern divorce. This custom of *reet* is not known to the Hindus in the plains of Punjab.[16]

The society in the hill stations dealt with women in an ambivalent manner. Women were, in theory, not considered equal to men and could be sold to the highest bidder or could be inherited by her husband's kin. But the ground reality was different to the extent that men could not afford to mistreat their wives or behave callously with them. Women were, thus, the mistresses of their own existence and lived their lives without feeling handicapped nor did they have any restrictions placed on them. Women often used their position to their full advantage. To that effect, they had the option to stay married to their husbands only as long as they found things to their liking such as reasonable household work where men were not too fastidious or demanding and the family members lived cordially.

Reet rates of payment for marriage are different for different categories of women. *Reet* money to be paid for a widow is less than that for a woman prepared to abandon her present husband. If a woman does not wish to live with her current husband or live with her husband's next of kin on his death, nothing and no one can force her to continue the marital arrangements. In case a husband chooses not to accept the *reet* offer for his wife, she can go back to her parents denying the husband, both money as well as her services such as household chores and conjugal relations. But normally, husbands can reinvest the *reet* money received from the new husband's family to get another wife for themselves.[17]

Whatever may be the logic or rationale for keeping with the practice, the hard empirical fact is that the much misunderstood

---

[16] Ibid.
[17] Ibid.

and maligned *reet* custom has been the savior of hardworking and oft suffering women living in the hills. The system works to the advantage of both parties, keeps their relations amiable and accords due freedom to the usually oppressed class of women in Hindu society. Though the elderly population is still rigid about traditional customs, the younger generations are developing a dislike for the practices of *reet* and polyandry. Therefore, nowadays, these practices are in decline though still existent.

Given the population diversity in India, certain areas and old tribes have retained and perpetuated certain marriage customs that seem unusual to the literate urbanites. The so called unusual customs, have evolved in societies due to certain local necessities of demography or as expedient norms to tide over exigencies or even due to interpretation of scriptures. Whatever be the circumstances, these customs have grown and stuck with communities, some of which follow these practices religiously as peremptory norms. They believe in their efficacy and benignity for the concerned persons as well as for the society at large.

WIVES IMPORTED INTO MALWA REGION OF PUNJAB

'I cook for all three, clean for all three and share a physical relationship with all three brothers', says Gurneet.[18] Attired in a *kurti* and loose *salwar* and speaking fluent Punjabi, she almost perfectly blends in with the gaggle of women filling water at the village tube well. Only her dusky complexion and small-boned structure raise minor doubts about her antecedents. After considerable hesitation and on persuasive cajoling, she admits that an 'agent' brought her to Mansa, a town in Punjab, from Midnapore district of West Bengal 15 years ago after paying her family ₹4,000. My eldest husband

---

[18] Neelam Raaj, 'Modern Draupadis', *Sunday Times,* 7 August 2005, 6.

gave me a new name, Gurneet which was more aptly suited to the location, and no one has called me Sharmila in years. With a new home, three square meals a day and the comfort of having someone attend to her, she has forgotten her past altogether.

'My eldest husband could not find a wife here in Punjab as he was crippled and had no large land-holdings, signifying high status, so he bought me for ₹20,000', rues Gurneet. She continued, 'After a son was born, my husband persuaded me to enter into a physical relationship with his other brothers, the youngest being only 14 years of age. Initially, this arrangement was not acceptable to me, although, I was fully aware of their economic condition. He again tried to convince me that they could not afford to buy any more brides. He further pointed out that there would be nothing left of the meagre landholding of three acres which will drastically shrink, if his brothers got themselves wives, anyhow'.[19] Of course, the decision maker is the eldest brother but relations do get convoluted and disputes occur to the detriment of all parties.

'The situation was dichotomous: It was either to agree or starve', Gurneet added with a slight trace of bitterness in her tone betraying her pent-up emotions. The pathos was palpable. It is wisely said, tears don't cry; they just flow. Then she resignedly said, 'Possibly, there was not another decent option to depend upon. I had no other choice, so I gave in. Anyway, ultimate use of force, as happened in some other cases, would have subdued me. More so because I cannot return to my parents' house at my birth place as they see nothing wrong in this polyandrous practice which is a predicament of economic convenience combined with socially acceptable morality. Genuine familial bonding that I had developed here was another supporting reason. It is the same dilemma for

---

[19] Ibid.

such other wives, brought from Bengal and Bihar, across the Malwa region. No wonder, it is sheer economics that is behind the fate of these 'modern Draupadis'.[20]

This case history is not an isolated occurrence but indicative of a mutated system that is still prevalent, if not rampant, in the Malwa region. It is, therefore, no wonder that a *mandi* (market) to auction such destitute women is held in Mangharia village.[21] Surprisingly, the newly acquired brides adjust pretty well and fast enough with the strange families, the uncertain behavioural treatment, the unexpected relationships and unfamiliar culture, unknown life styles and different food habits.

Such systems are not confined to any specific community or national boundaries. These operate elsewhere also, perhaps sporadically and may be vanishing gradually with education and awareness. For example, similar influx of wives from South India is happening in villages in Haryana. A similar trend is noticed among the Chinese who are picking up Muslim brides from Pakistan. Thus, only the contours of necessity may vary yet the solution found appears the same.

DIFFERENT CUSTOMS FOR SELECTION OF MATE

As per Indian *shastras* and customs, a person is deemed to have an incomplete life if he is not married. It is a belief that human partnership provides complementarity for a complete living experience. With this necessity in mind, society has developed several expedients to solemnize marriage; some are simple and symbolic while others are elaborate and exhibitionist with the common intent to unite two people and bless them to consummate, procreate and live a happy married life.

---

[20] Ibid.
[21] Ibid.

For example, a *gandharva* marriage needed only a ritualistic putting of a ring on the bride's finger or placing of a *varmala* around groom's neck by the bride; marriages with these rituals were accepted as valid and proper. In modern times, wedding ceremonies have undergone great transformation to become drawn out celebrations with elaborate rituals and imitated customs performed in front of hundreds of guests with expensive grandeur and ostentatious aplomb accompanied by a cacophony of noise and boisterous merrymaking.

There are, however, some rare customs pertaining to the institution of marriage that are simple and specific. For example, a simple form of selection of husband prevailed among the hill tribe of Bonda Porjas. As per their custom, pits were dug in the ground in which children were kept at night during the winter season to keep them warm. Come spring, marriageable girls of the village were huddled together in one of these pits. Then a young man would come and propose to one of them. If she refused, he made the same proposal to the others, until he was accepted by any one of them. This acceptance of the proposal deemed the couple married.

According to another similar but harsher custom of mate selection, a young man and a maiden retire to the jungle and lit a fire. Then the maiden, pick up a burning firewood and brand his back with the burning wood. In case he was not able to bear the suffering and cried out loud in pain, he was rejected outright. The one who suffered it without a grimace or expression of anguish was the winner and the marriage was, at once, consummated, right then and there. Bravery and bravado, with capacity to silently withstand suffering, sometimes bear lifetime rewards.

In olden days, particularly during the periods of Ramayana and Mahabharata, young girls selected their own spouse based on some sort of a test or criterion to be satisfied by the young prospector. This system of choosing a partner was called *swayamvar*. This word is a combination of two words: *swayam*, meaning oneself or of own volition and *var*, meaning partner or husband. In other words, it means self-selection of one's husband. This system had worked well, more so, among the royal and noble families since in these families social pressures forced stability and longevity of marriages.

For some reasons, with time, this practice degenerated and eventually vanished. With Manu's codes of social living, women lost their independence and also this right of mate-selection as per their desire and liking. Marriages came to be arranged by the parents or the village elders based on societal parameters and family compulsions. Despite this strong hold of society and the wave-like change in its mindset, some communities still retain and honour the original custom of the bride-to-be picking a life partner of her choice. With passage of time and re-emancipation of women, there is a visible but gradual reversal of this trend and more affluent and educated families now easily consent to love marriages based on the preference and option of the children.

ELOPEMENT AS A CUSTOM OF MARRIAGE IN MANIPUR

One often comes across incidents of marriage by elopement in the epics. But this system, though considered lowly, is not yet dead. It is still preserved in India as a common practice for bride-choice in Manipur, a state cosily tucked in the north-eastern part of India. The starry-eyed lovers swear by it as the most romantic path leading to the altar. Truly, it is an integral part of the protracted marriage deliberations and ceremonies. Fortunately, this method of mate-selection is neither communally shunned nor legally banned and is socially accepted as a tradition.[22]

---

[22] *The Statesman*, New Delhi, 31 March 1992.

Research studies by anthropologists maintain that nearly 95 per cent of the marriages in Manipur are the culmination of a romantic association. When a boy and a girl decide to unite in wedlock, they announce their intention by eloping and spending a night with a friend of the boy's family. The next day, the girl's parents are informed of her whereabouts and taken to the 'hide-out' for a meeting with the daughter. After her concurrence, mutual negotiations between parents of both lovers lead to the finalization of the date for the marriage to be solemnized.

Often, the girls' parents, in sheer abundant caution, lodge a first information report (FIR) at the police station for their missing daughter not having returned home till late in the night. But this is more of a formality to cover the remote possibility of any untoward incident. Families, generally, have a hint of such vanishing acts and the anticipated absence from home actually heralds the good news of mate-selection by the daughter and highlights a possibility of an ensuing marriage. Once the meeting at the hide-out of the girl matures successfully, the FIR is withdrawn by the family and no further investigation is necessary.[23]

Interestingly, though geographically separated, Gond tribe of Chhattisgarh also follows a similar system of marriage by abduction. In their system, the girls are kidnapped and married, provided they consent to the marriage after a few days of stay with the abductor. Else, she returns to her parents' home and waits for another, possibly consensual, kidnapping and eventual marriage.

PICKING PARTNERS ON HOLI

On the day of the festival of Holi, the *adivasis* of Madhya Pradesh hold a *'haat'* at a place called 'Mangoh'. It is an

---

[23] Ibid.

occasion and an annual opportunity where boys and girls meet freely, without inhibition, to pick their future life partners. Here, the boy proposes and the girl must express proper willing consent by accepting the boy's 'offering of paan' (betel nuts in a green leaf that is edible and chewable) and then play Holi with colours. With this display of agreement, the couple elopes for a week for consummation and, presumably, also for understanding each other for compatibility.

They return after this trial period and go to the girl's parents who ask for bride price from the boy's parents. This dower price is negotiable and is ultimately decided by the village Panchayat. The dower money is used for organizing the wedding celebrations and during the celebrations, the couple is declared married 'and they live happily everafter'.

'GHOTUL SYSTEM' FOR PICKING A MATE

There is another small-numbered community of Abhujmarias settled in Bastar district of erstwhile Madhya Pradesh, also called *Bastars*. They have a similar system of mate-selection by a popular tradition of *Ghotul*. In this tribal denomination, young girls and boys, eligible for marriage, are sent to or voluntarily go to the *Ghotul*, a hostel for the young population of the village. They live here, select their choicest mate and cohabit with consent of the partner. In case of incompatibility or undesirability, they keep selecting the next person till they come across a suitable and acceptable mate.[24] Once the couple decides on their preferred and final choice, they return to their parents for respective matchmaking and negotiations. This practice of finding a mutually compatible spouse has worked successfully in this community for centuries. Disputes are hardly ever heard on such issues.

---

[24] Ashwani Sharma, 'For old tribe, kids can't wait, wedding can', *Indian Express*, 31 August.

MARRIAGE AFTER DEATH OF BOTH PARTNERS

Natt tribal community that performs acrobatics in cultural fairs and at other public exhibitions to earn their livelihood is mostly settled in the erstwhile state of Uttar Pradesh. Two Natt families from Haridwar and Saharanpur were blessed with a child each. Jogendra from the former place begot a son, who was named Tejpal and to Rameshwar from Saharanpur, a daughter was born who was named Puja. Both the families, as per their tribal customs, decided to marry their children once they attained marriageable age. Thus, a solemn pact was made, albeit orally, and the families patiently waited for the auspicious time to come.

Destiny, however, had other plans and both children fell victim to fatal diseases as toddlers and died. Eighteen years ago, Tejpal died at four years of age and Puja died at two years of age. Nevertheless, the promise of marriage was kept alive by the families to be performed at the mutually agreed time. Accordingly, the marriage party (baraat) of the bride-groom comprising of about 50 friends and relatives arrived from Haridwar and a marriage ceremony was held at the bride's house in Meerpur-Mohanpur village of Saharanpur district. Complete wedding rites were performed replacing the deceased bride and groom with dolls which were immersed in the river after the ceremony.[25]

Elders of the Natt tribe maintain that they have been following this tradition for generations. According to their custom, if their children die before marriage, they arrange their weddings even after their death else those who passed away as 'bachelors' will not get salvation. They also follow this practice in the belief to save their remaining children from an untimely death.

---

[25] Pankul Sharma, 'UP couple get married...18 years after death', *The Times of India*, 11 November 2015.

GIRL MARRIES A DOG TO WARD OFF ILL-LUCK

Santhal customs are tribal traditions and appear strange to us. One such custom is to ward-off ill-luck. It so happened that a little girl named Karnamoni, born in Khayan, grew her first tooth in the upper gum. This is considered a bad omen in Santhal culture and belief system. To escape this ill luck or to break this spell of inauspicious teeth, she had to be married off immediately. But her father, Baburam Handsa, was a share-cropper and too poor to afford expenses of a wedding ceremony, at least immediately. Even to find a suitable boy within the tribe was not easy and that arrangement would be expensive, too. The dilemma was, indeed, real.

A solution had to be found and it transpired that she could be married off to a dog instead and this would effectively break the spell. So the choice was between a boy and a dog. Baburam found a stray dog; and with his meagre means arranged his daughter's wedding on 11 June 2003 with a dog as the groom.[26] More than a hundred guests reportedly attended this ceremony.

It is believed that such ill-omen marriages with dogs are a common practice among Santhals. In fact its prevalence is so accepted that this ritualistic marriage does not interfere with the girls' lives later nor does she suffer any social stigma or societal discrimination. She is considered free to marry eventually under normal customs. Nevertheless, authorities have ordered an enquiry into this incident but no official action may follow against this accepted social practice.

MAN MARRIES A BITCH TO ATONE FOR HIS SIN

Selvakumar, aged 33 years, was struck with paralysis of hands and legs and he lost hearing in one ear. After 15 years

---

[26] Jaideep Mazumdar, 'Dog has his day, marries girl', *Hindustan Times*, 19 June 2003.

of treatment, he has managed to become mobile but that too with a crutch. It was a long spell of trouble and suffering. One day, he suddenly recalled that nearly 15 years ago, he had killed two dogs when they were mating and had strung their bodies from a tree.[27] The remembrance of this long-forgotten prank haunted him and he somehow linked this to the beginning of his ailment.

He shared this occurrence with his close friends and one of them duly took him to a local astrologer. The astrologer, after consulting his sacred books of knowledge, announced his sagacious advice that Selvakumar can be cured of his physical impairment provided he atoned for his sin of killing the mating dogs. For repentance, he had to marry a female dog. The astrologer's advice was accepted with due faith and search for a female dog began and soon a stray dog was found. The would-be bride was given a bath and was draped in a saree. The she-dog was named Selvi.

Selvakumar and Selvi then marched in a procession to the local Ganesh temple in Vilathikulam village, near Manamadurai in Shivganga district for a wedding ceremony. At the temple, Selvakumar duly tied the customary *thaali (mangalsutra)* around the neck of Selvi, the 'bitch'. Thereafter, the bride-groom and his relatives and friends shared a sumptuous feast while the bride was treated to an unbuttered bun.

It is not known if this marriage was consummated or that Selvakumar was cured of his remaining disability as assured by the astrologer. Nevertheless, faith prevailed and prescription was executed.

A VILLAGE THAT TRAINS PROSTITUTES

There is a small village called Dabar Pura in Ponki Tehsil near Shivpuri. This village has only 38 houses belonging to

---

[27] G. C. Shekhar, 'Man marries bitch to atone for his sin', *Hindustan Times*, 13 November 2007.

families of an erstwhile nomadic tribe. People from no other community live in this village. It was during the days of Gwalior state, before partition of India that some nomad families came and settled down here. The men among them had no vocation and would indulge in small thefts at night and minor crimes to gain some money which was never enough to run the household. Out of necessity, their women took to singing and dancing and would even live-in with rich and respectable people as 'the other woman'. As a result, prosperity bloomed and this village turned into a training place for prostitutes.

Over time, a custom developed here; the headman of the village would decide the fate of girls: Whether a girl would be a housewife in a local family in the village or be trained as a prostitute and sent outside the village to distant places for business.[28] This looks like an age-old practice and carries no stigma or prejudice or ostracism. On the contrary, families with daughters who have become prostitutes are generally rich with remittances from daughters and are considered influential in the village.

The village Dabar Pura enjoys festivities and celebrate when daughters of the village return to meet their parents and friends. This invariably happens on the occasions of Diwali, Holi and Rakhi. These important Indian festivals are cele-brated with pomp and abandon and the village atmosphere becomes festive and cordial and people indulge in exchanging gifts and revive familial bonds.[29] Irrespective of the views and opinions of the outsiders, the villagers are now prosperous and happy with the prevailing custom as also the operating systems.

---

[28] Anupam Shukla, 'The village headman decides whether a girl is to become a housewife or a prostitute', *Hind Samachar*, [in Urdu] 1 April 1992.
[29] Ibid.

'DULHAN'S BARAAT': A CUSTOM WITH A DIFFERENCE

In Dawoodnagar, a village on the outskirts of Lucknow, lives a poor, rustic, scheduled caste Pasi community. They have a uniquely different custom of marriage in contradistinction to the urban concepts of a wedding procession. Among the Pasis, marriage procession goes from the bride's house to the groom's residence for the wedding ceremonies. The people are poor and cannot celebrate with pomp and ostentation; the bride's party may move in procession using any old method of transportation, including pedal cycles. Despite the lack of pomp and show, the wedding is celebrated with joviality and excitement.

On reaching close to the groom's house, the *baraatis* (wedding party/procession) burst crackers to signal their arrival to the groom's family so as to give them time to prepare for a ceremonial reception. The groom's family not only arranges a feast for the *baraat* (wedding party/procession), but also provides the bride's attire and jewellery. In fact, the bride comes to the groom's house in ordinary clothes and dresses up at groom's house for the ceremonies. Thus, the entire expense for the wedding is borne by the groom's father, howsoever poor he may be, and he does not, under any circumstances, share the expenses with the bride's father.[30]

Explaining the perpetuation of this age-old practice, the village elders take pride in this tradition and insist on not changing this unique custom of their community.[31] The elders rued that at times their youngsters, having become familiar with traditions of other communities or urban wedding customs, demand a change in this old tradition. But for the elders, the parents, it is a matter of honour within the *biradari*

---

[30] Sunita Aron, 'A different custom', Off Track column.
[31] Ibid.

(community). Thus, the tradition is upheld steadfastly and this unique custom continues.

KNOT OF LUCK BETWEEN GIRLS

Marriage is an important event in one's life and young boys and girls expectantly keep waiting for this occasion. Sometimes, marriages get delayed due to non-availability of a suitable, compatible or auspicious partner. Among girls of marriageable age, such delay becomes a matter of serious concern for the parents who start looking for good omens and propitious prayers for benign intervention from the gods for early solemnization of marriage and wish for a good groom.

One such custom to hasten marriage or to seek a husband of choice or the most suitable bridegroom when they actually get married for real, is the notional marriage of 'Kumari Vivah'. This practice is popular and prevalent in different parts of Odisha (erstwhile Orissa). On the occasion of Kumar Purnima every year, little girls posing as the bride and the groom are 'married' to each other for good luck in front of an all-women *baraat*; even the priest is female.[32] The venue is fully decked and decorated just like for a normal wedding but no money exchanges hands as dowry between the families of the girls. The night of full moon is considered auspicious for the purpose. The girls garland each other in a traditional ceremony of *jaimala* and are notionally married. The knot of luck is tied.

Kumari Vivah is a celebration as big as a real wedding. Invitation cards are distributed among villagers and relatives days ahead of the occasion. The women *baraatis* dance their way to the venue even as fireworks light up the sky. After

---

[32] It happened in Navapada. 'Knot of Luck', *Hindustan Times*, New Delhi, 20 October 2005.

the marriage ceremony, even though notional, the guests are treated to a sumptuous dinner and, thereafter, all of them bless the little 'so called' couple.

Apparently, to a novice, it may appear as child marriage, but it is actually called *Kumari Vivah* and is an intrinsic part of Odisha's cultural landscape. Such events are annually organized by dedicated local associations and one such association is the Kumar Purnima Girls Association of Shyampur. The *'oriyas'* believe that the symbolic marriage educates the young girls and their parents about the fight against dowry and also helps them rise above class and caste considerations while looking for real-life partners for their daughters when the time comes.[33]

MANGAL SUTRAS OF SOUTH INDIA

In North India, there is a custom where the husband ties a *mangal sutra*, a sort of necklace, around the neck of the bride which she wears as a symbol of marriage during the lifetime of the husband. It is traditionally made of black beads but may also contain small ornaments of gold. Widows do not wear this necklace as it is considered a sign of survival of marriage.

In Tamil Nadu, the *mangal sutra* is known as *thaali*. It is also tied by the husband around the neck of the bride and the marriage ceremonies are deemed complete with this ritual. The *thaali* is also held sacred and treated as a symbol of survival of marriage.

In Telegu, it is called *manjil kiyaru* and carries the same significance and ritualistic fervour. It is made of cotton thread, dyed in turmeric and appears yellow in colour. Its contact with the skin is considered beneficial in many ways.

---

[33] Soumyajit Pattnaik, 'Valuable lessons for young brides', *Hindustan Times*.

EARTHEN POT AS PROXY FOR GROOM

Priests have interpreted scriptures to provide for a provision for unforeseen contingency of absence of the bridegroom at his own marriage ceremony. They explain that in such exigencies an earthen pot can be used to fill in for the groom. This custom was actually seen to be practiced at Hayoo village near Chakrata where the date of marriage was fixed with the consent of the groom who worked in the rank of *havaldar* in the Indo-Tibetan Border Police (ITBP), a para-military force. He was then posted on the India-China border of Manna.

His leave was duly sanctioned in time and he proceeded homeward but due to heavy snowfall enroute, the road links for the journey got blocked and he was stranded. As a consequence, the groom, Devender Singh could not reach home in time for the wedding ceremonies. The obvious option was to postpone the wedding till his arrival, but this was beset with uncertainty and monetary costs. All the arrangements were already in place and the *baraat* could not be hosted indefinitely. Therefore, instead of postponing the marriage, the families, in consultation with the priest, opted for the unique scriptural permission to replace the groom with a proxy earthen pot. In fact, the holy books provide for '*Kumbh Vivah*' to cater to such dire contingencies.[34]

MARRIAGE WITHOUT SAPTAPADI

Laddakhi (of Ladakh) customs of marriage are at variance with the rest of India and bear their own uniqueness. For instance, in Ladakh, the marriage party of the bridegroom goes to the residence of bride's father without the groom who stays in his own home waiting for the return of the party with the bride. The marriage procession is accompanied by a

---

[34] Utpal Prashar, 'Groom replaced by pot for arriving late', *Hindustan Times*, 10 March 2005.

band and with great rejoice reaches the bride's house where it is treated to a sumptuous feast. This is tantamount to an announcement of the marriage to the society. Thereafter, the party returns to the groom's house with the bride.

Thus, the actual marriage ceremony takes place at the groom's as per proper *Laddakhi* religious traditions. The rituals are accompanied by chanting of the appropriate *mantras*; the couple sits and listens to them. The groom and the bride do not perform *saptapadi* or take *pheras* (circumambulation or seven steps) to solemnize a marriage—a custom prevalent in North India.

SOME KERALA CUSTOMS OF MARRIAGE

Within the Nairs (or Naimars) of Travancore, there is a distinct caste of Nambudiris. It is a well-knit community having strong societal norms and customs which call for strict abidance. One such practice is to marry their girls before they attain puberty. However, in case a girl, who has attained puberty, dies before her marriage, she cannot be cremated till the religious rites usually associated with a Hindu marriage are performed on the dead body.

For this purpose, a suitable and eligible groom has to be found within the community, a competent relative who could have married her if she were alive. This man must formally marry her and tie a *thaali* (the equivalent of mangal sutra) around the neck of the corpse lying on the funeral pyre. Having performed the rituals for solemnization of the marriage, the dead body can then be cremated. If at all for some reason this customary practice is not performed, the family considers itself dishonoured.

There exists, in the same part of the country-side, another caste known as the Totiyars. A custom among Totiyars allows brothers, uncles, nephews and other near relations to possess their wives in a sort of common pool. In fact, it is an 'entitlement' permitted to this group of relatives. One wonders how paternity issues would have been solved and decided in such complicated situations when in the past there were no DNA tests.

In South India, the custom of endogamous marriages prevails. The castes and communities maintain close family alliances cemented by inter-marriage within the families. In an effort to maintain this familial purity, one such custom allows for 'a widower to remarry his deceased wife's sister, an uncle to marry his niece and a cousin to marry his first cousin. Persons so related possess an exclusive privilege of inter-marrying upon the ground of such relationship; and if they choose, they can prevent any other union and enforce their own preferential right', howsoever unsuited a match they may be for reason of age, education, economic status or any other consideration.

In connection with the generalities stated above, certain restrictions are socially prescribed to define prohibited degrees of this relationship. For example, 'an uncle may marry the daughter of his sister, but in no case may he marry the daughter of his brother or a brother's children may marry a sisters children, but the children of two brothers or of two sisters may not inter-marry.' The reason is that children of the male line belong to same *gotram* and are brothers and sisters. 'This rule is universally and invariably observed by all castes, right from the Brahmins to the Pariahs.'

Again, in the western countries also, as per *Laws of Moses*, marriages within the clan have been the norm. This practice was quite general among Chaldeans. Also, the *Holy Writ* mentions that Abraham espoused his niece while he sent his kinsmen to far off places to find a suitable wife from within the family for his son, Isaac. Rebecca was found, thus.

No wonder, she and Isaac could not pardon their son Esau for marrying amongst strangers, that is, Canaanites.

The details narrated as above have been extracted from the cited book which is old by nearly two centuries and has possibly presented existing customs or the then contemporary conditions. Many of these customs and practices may have mutated themselves or diluted in stringency of observance with passage of time and increase in literacy. Therefore, the present-day observances, if still continuing, may be at variance with the above presentation, which is more by way of anthropological anthology.

LIVE-IN RELATIONSHIP AS AN ALTERNATIVE TO MARRIAGE

Arguably, Adam and Eve have shared the first live-in relationship on this earth but then they were the only two human beings on the face of earth and the ritual of marriage had not existed. In fact, the custom of monogamous marriages grew with the evolution of civilization and is the hallmark of modern living. Many sociologists believe that it is a dying institution and under threat as never before. Possibly, it is due to diminishing virtues of mutual trust, abiding fidelity, hearty communication and dissolved egos. No wonder, youngsters are feeling scared of the bondage of marriage despite amicable exit routes. Probably, they are afraid of commitment in marriage and scared of a lurking disapproval of divorce in most societies in the event of failure of their marriage. Nevertheless, marriage remains the most popular form of companionship and a stable social institution.

Live-in relationship is by no means a taboo in modern living environment. This experimental system has existed in western societies for decades and in many cases is treated as a period of mutual adjustment or as pre-marital trial living. Therefore, 'young millennial generation' finds nothing wrong with this brand of 'marital plasm'; and this system of close-living in partnered residence is gradually gaining societal approval, if not total approbation. Thus, the brief discourse shows similarities in two extremities: A section of upper-middle-class urban population as well as poor tribal families have adopted live-in relationships. But the fascinating aspect of this social phenomenon is the disparity in their motives: The former lack will for commitment and the latter, the economic capacity for customary obligation of celebrations.

Historically, such loose relationships have existed from olden times even in traditional societies. Some tribal communities in India have followed this practice for many centuries with pseudo-social approval and family's acceptance. A few such prevalent customs with their intrinsic motives and nuanced attitude towards such couples with 'marriages-on-hold' will be discussed in the succeeding paragraphs.

FOR PAHARI KORBAS, WEDDING CAN WAIT, CHILDREN CAN'T

Pahari Korbas is one of the six primitive tribes of Chhattisgarh, within which, as a custom, the wedding of a couple can wait yet the birth of children cannot. The young population of this tribe enjoy full freedom to select their partner as per their choice but the partner has to be from within the community. Thereafter, they live together and beget children as a normal married couple. That is their way of living and such live-in couples are neither ostracized nor shunned out of the village. In this community, most marriages are performed after years of living together. Their off-springs are accorded proper legitimacy and equal status just like children of married couples. At times, children also attend their parents' wedding with equal celebratory fervour and joy.

The live-in arrangements with independent living can begin as early as the age of twelve years and the couple may beget children, out of wedlock, as and when they choose to. Even though solemnization of marriage is necessary sooner or later, it is not time-bound and there is no urgency for a formal marriage. One of the reasons for delayed marriages is rampant poverty and a wedding function requires the boy's family to spend a lot of money since custom makes it binding on him to organize a feast with country liquor and food for relatives and the entire community of the village in order to get the marriage socially recognized. This makes for a significant expenditure for which enough savings are necessary that are not easily accumulated.

An inexpensive alternative to costly individual ceremonies is to join the community wedding function in order to just officially formalize the existing union and legitimize the already begotten children. In recognition of their social mandate to marry as well as to alleviate their impoverished economic predicament, these mass ceremonies are generally organized by governmental authorities for social welfare and to boost the dwindling population of the tribe.

'DHUKUA' SYSTEM IN JHARKHAND

In Jharkhand also the abovementioned custom commonly prevails among the tribes of Oraon, Munda and Ho, with subtle yet discernible differences. These tribes reside in Gumla, Khunti and other neighbouring districts of their settlement. Here also, the custom mandates a lavish and expensive feast of rice and meat or *hadiya* (rice beer) which most couples can ill-afford and are circumstantially forced to live-in because the village elders do not bless a marriage until a feast is hosted. So, they select their mates and move-in together and start raising their family without the prudish sanctity of marriage. Instead of being addressed as wife, the girls are branded with the title 'Dhukni' which, in local parlance, refers to a woman who has entered the household without marriage.

In the *Dhukua* system, as it is called in local parlance, the female partner becomes every bit like the legally wedded wife and merges as a privileged part of the man's family but somehow is still viewed as a second class citizen, with her children treated as social outcasts. In some villages, children of *dhukua* couples are not allowed to participate in religious rituals or get married. This peculiar predicament is partly because of the absence of a feast to formalize the marriage and a consequent lack of social acceptance, and also because they have no official documents to prove their conjugal relationship or paternity for the children and, hence, are denied their rights as a married couple under law.

To remedy the situation, social activists, non-governmental organizations and governmental authorities often organize awareness camps and mass weddings but enthusiasm from *dhukua* couples is luke-warm for such efforts regardless of whether they follow the traditional tribal religion of Sarna, Hinduism or Christianity. This is because village elders do not socially approve of this method of marriage and believe that a wedding needs to be celebrated amidst family and friends. They maintain that every couple somehow marries, sooner or later, on their own and it is rare that any couple ends up without solemnizing the marriage with family and friends present for the ceremony. Hence, outside intervention in community customs is despised. It is wisely said, customs seldom die.

A TRIBAL CUSTOM OF DIVORCE IN CHHATTISGARH

The freedom of women and gender equality in India is a hotly debated subject in society as well as the courts. The usual lament is that it exists in geographical patches and social islands, though the general mindset is still biased towards patriarchal superiority and full of gender prejudices. A univer-sal attitude of freedom and genuine equality is missing. That said, the situation in certain parts of India is good. One such example is the tribal community of Chhattisgarh.

Tradition has it that the tribal women of Chhattisgarh enjoy vast freedom in many aspects. For example, they take their own decisions and do not depend on anyone, not even their parents, to choose their husbands. Further, they have full freedom to desert their spouses and remarry another man without being questioned by the elders of the family and tribe. Moreover, to acquire or formalize the divorce, they do not have to go to a court. All they need to do is to break their glass bangles in the presence of the husband and the marriage is considered dissolved. Incidentally, this custom has been recognized by the Courts.

THODA MARRIAGE RITES IN NILGIRIS

Thodas are a small community living in the Nilgiri Hills located in Tamil Nadu in south India. It is believed that this community has sprung up from a few gravely injured soldiers of Alexander, the Great, who could not be comfortably transported back on return of the armed forces to Greece. Some of them married locally out of necessity and procreated. They engage in small agricultural activities. This community still retains some of the Greek customs, for example, they do not lock their houses and don't even fit any devices for this purpose on their doors.

They also retain an unusual wedding ritual. In this ritual, the groom touches the forehead of the bride with the toe of his right foot and the marriage is deemed solemnized. A community elder was questioned whether the ritual will be considered fulfilled if such a 'touching of the toe' happens accidentally, for instance, in a case where a girl trips and her forehead is perchance touched by the right toe of an eligible young bachelor passing by. The answer was in affirmative; the two are then customarily married. However, in case of any ineligibility or dispute, the elders decide on a case to case basis.

SNIPPETS

TYING A KNOT FOR A DAY IN AMSTERDAM

In Amsterdam, there is a custom where boys and girls tie a knot for a day with complete marriage rituals and vows of 'I do' by both. It is a festival of children's wedding celebrated at the NEMO Science Museum in Amsterdam. On this day, children are ceremonially dressed and married, but the customary symbolic marriages are deemed dissolved at sunset.[35]

SWAYAMVAR BY SWAZILAND RULER

In certain countries of Africa, men from the royalty choose their mates in a *swayamvar*-like practice similar to that of selecting bridegrooms by women of nobility in ancient India. The parameters and the method of selection, though, are different and slightly bizarre to our mindset. For example, the ruler of Swaziland, King Mswati, aged 37 years, got married for the 13th time in this manner. His bride was chosen from among 4,000 topless women at a traditional gala dance where she was selected and declared as the dancing queen. The chosen bride had just finished school and was only seventeen years old.[36]

MARRIAGE OF KUMARI DEVI IN NEPAL

Nepal has a custom of installing a living deity to protect the kingdom and its population. The living deity is

---

[35] A pictory, 'Knot for a day', *The Times of India*.
[36] 'Dancing queen', *Hindustan Times*, 28 September 2005.

selected from girl-children of Sakya community through a rigorous selection process and enthroned in the *Kumari Ghar*, a temple at Bhaktapur. She lives there alone and away from the family. She is then believed to possess spiritual powers and is worshipped and revered as any other idolized deity. People seek her blessings with faith and believe in them as much as those of any other deity in a temple.

However, her reign as *Kumari Devi* comes to an end on the onset of puberty, when it is believed that her spiritual powers defect her and she can no longer act as *devi*. At that stage, she is symbolically married to a fruit or a flower or any other similar object and she abdicates her status as the *Kumari Devi*.[37] This is because the *Devi* has to be in pre-pubertal age, a virgin and unmarried. These criteria are sacrosanct and cannot be defied or violated. Hence, the performance of symbolic marriage for abdication of the *Kumari* status.

SUDANESE MARRIAGE RITUAL OF JIRTIK

Solemnization of marriages in Sudan includes a special ritual of *Jirtik*. This requires newly-weds to indulge in a milk-spitting competition. The one who spits right on the spouse is the winner. This indicates and determines who will become head of the household, a coveted position, indeed.[38] The belief and its attendant speculation is indeed adorable.

---

[37] 'Search for a deity: Nepal's fruity wedding', *Hindustan Times*, 4 March 2008.
[38] 'Ripley's *Believe It or Not*', www.ripleys.com

YOU MAY NOW KISS THE BRIDE

In areas of rural China, death of an unmarried man is not considered auspicious. Therefore, there is an unusual custom as per which some families whose unmarried son dies, purchase a dead woman's body, even if the body is in the grave, from within the community; and bury both of them together as a married couple.[39]

ACEHNESE MARRIAGE RITUAL

Acehnese tribals have an unusual marriage custom where the couple feed each other. Aceh is a province of Indonesian archipelago, located at the northern end of Sumatra. Aceh is treated as a special autonomous district with the status of *propinsi* (province) and is called *'Daerah Isti Menra'*, meaning abode of peace. It is predominantly inhabited by conservative Muslim people who are fiercely proud of its traditions and is generally a prosperous area.

One of the wedding customs of the Acehnese, the tribals of the island of Aceh, is for the wedding couple to feed each other by putting some sweets in each other's mouth with spoons.[40] Such an affectionate custom of simultaneous feeding of sweets may be commonplace today, but imagine the vintage of the tradition, social modesty of the olden times, undue emphasis on shyness on such occasions and the practice of bridal veil among Muslim communities for such a liberal practice.

THE LOVE MORSEL

According to a Scandinavian belief and a local tradition, if a boy and a girl share and eat from the same loaf of

---

[39] Submitted by Gulliane Meyer, Orlando, FL, 'Ripley's *Believe It or Not'*.
[40] Narrated from a Pictory (picture-story) with a Reuters report.

bread, they are bound to fall in love; and in fortunate eventuality, may marry each other. One can only admire the imagined certainty and implicit belief in the consequences of this simplistic and innocent action of a young couple, even if unintended.

BEATING OF THE GROOM AT HIS WEDDING

It is believed that Peru, a Latin-American country, has an unusual custom where the groom is beaten up at his own wedding. It may be commented in a jocular vein that in India, though the groom is spared from this ordeal during his marriage ceremony, yet in contrast, he, in a way, gets virtually beaten during all his later wedded life.

TOAD MARRIAGE TO PROPITIATE RAIN GODS

Another type of ceremony to propitiate the rain god is held at Khochakandar, a village 365 km north of Kolkata. The ceremony is called 'the wedding, at ₹5,000'. It is held to propitiate the rain gods and to end a dry spell. Such a 'Monsoon Wedding' was held in June 2005 and some 400 people cheered and blew conches, the band played music and priests solemnized the marriage. The ritual requires a traditional Hindu wedding ceremony between two giant toads designated male and female. After the ceremony, women apply vermillion streaks on the 'bride' toad and there is a lot of joyous merrymaking.

GROOM NOT PERMITTED TO JOIN HIS OWN MARRIAGE PROCESSION

There is a custom among the Mysorean Lambadi tribe, living in southern India, where male members of the family or male friends were not allowed to attend weddings. Thus, celebrations to bring the bride to in-laws' house were an all-ladies affair. This taboo was so strong and strict that even the bridegroom, being a male, was not permitted to join the celebrations and was excluded from his own *baraat* (wedding party).[41]

MARRIAGE OF TREES

In a village in the state of Odisha, there is a different type of wedding ceremony. The distinction is that at this wedding, the bride and the bridegroom are both trees, *peepal* and *banyan,* respectively. A knot is tied to bound them together for performance of the ceremony. A presumable motive could be addressal of environmental concerns and conservation of trees that have always benefitted and supported the life and living of villagers and forest-dwelling communities.

WASHING THE FEET OF UPPER CASTE PERSONS IN MARRIAGE FUNCTIONS

In the Puri district of Odisha there is a custom of washing the feet of the upper caste persons by the lower caste people during auspicious occasions, in particular washing of the feet of the bridegroom at wedding ceremonies. It is an age-old custom that is still being continued.

Sometime back, in irreverence to this custom, four barber families of Bhubanpati village revolted against this practice of washing of the feet of *brahmans* at weddings. This refusal was in consequence of a resolution

---

[41] 'Ripley's *Believe It or Not*' 6-1, c. 2003 Ripley Entertainment Inc.

passed by *All Orissa Barbers' Samiti* that had resolved and ordained its members never to render the 'feet cleaning service'.

Their defiance was quelled by the upper caste that imposed a fine of rupees one lakh on the four barber families for refusing to wash the feet of brides and bridegrooms at weddings. When they failed to pay the penalty amount, the upper caste persons assaulted them with sticks and iron rods and even spat on them. In the mêlée, one Dalit woman was stripped and the male members of the families were beaten up and allegedly one old man was dragged. They were all driven out of the village. The matter has been reported to the police.

3

HUMAN SACRIFICE WITH SAFETY MEASURES

Sacrifices and Penances

In Hindu theology, blood is considered a powerful agent or a vitalizing force to refurbish the pristine productive strength of the Mother Earth and restore its endemic fertility. This concept was acknowledged and imbibed by the followers of the Shakti cult, and devotees of *devi* (female deity) among *Shaivites*. Initially, the cult ordained of *narbali* (human sacrifice) or compensatory human sacrifice, and consequent spilling of blood on the ground was considered essential for recreation of energy and revitalization of productive powers. It was believed that goddess Kali drinks blood for strength and prowess. Sameway, to re-strengthen the creative power of the Earth, enhance its fertility and sustain its procreative capacity, blood must be spilt on the Earth. It can be said that beliefs are never tested on the template of logic.

This practice of human sacrifice continued for centuries, almost in all old civilizations and tribal societies; it still exists, worldwide, in isolated pockets of totemic religion and in sporadic performances by the devout, though sometimes stealthily. With the passage of time, compassion dawned and the chilling experience of selection of a human for *narbali* and his sacrificial execution was compromised in intent and content. Human sacrifice was replaced by animal sacrifice; one idea being that animal sacrifice would also provide edible animal meat to be distributed as *prasad,* fit for human consumption. Besides, sacrifice of a horse at Ashwamedha Yagna had religious sanction and yielded glory to the king. But today, even animal sacrifice is resisted to prevent cruelty to animals and propagate *ahimsa.* Some temple organizations and shrine trusts have relented and started accepting offerings of coconuts, kaddu (gourd), etc., which are broken by hitting on the ground in symbolic sacrifice.

It is believable that, globally, animals like camels, cows, pigs, sheep, goats and even chicken, fowl and fish have been offered for sacrifice in due deference to the religious custom and spiritual belief as also for their abundant availability in the region.

Animal rights activists, all over the world, have resisted such practices of torturing animals, by organizing public protests and moving the court for legal remedy, in places where such practices have prominently existed and persisted. The success of their efforts has been mixed. Nevertheless, in India and some other Asian countries, animal sacrifice has given place to an innocuous custom of breaking of coconut, gourd, cucumber or similar other hard food items or even smashing of pots filled with milk.

KAMAKHYA TEMPLE IN GUWAHATI: A HOLY *SHAKTI PEETH*

Assam is considered to be the land of *Shaktism* and Kamakhya temple of Mother Goddess Kali is the most important centre of *Shaktism* in the world. Thus, the worship of Shakti has been prevalent in Assam from time immemorial. In fact, 'Ancient Assam was a very important seat of *Shaktism*. Kamarup, an ancient state of Classical period of the Indian subcontinent has been recognized as the principal centre of Shakti cult with its chief temple at Kamakhya.'[1] Therefore, this temple is supposed to be the original progenitor of *tantrism* and has shrined ten different forms of the *devi* such as Kali, Tara, Surashi, Bhubaneswari, Bhairavi, Chinnamasta, Dhumavati, Bagalmukhi, Matangi and Kamala.

Chronicle records show that Kamakhya temple, in the past, observed the custom of *narbali* or human sacrifice to appease the Mother Goddess. The Assam Research Society Journal of the year 1933 mentions that living persons were sacrificed at Kamakhya temple until the reign of King Gaurinath Singha

---

[1] H. K. Barpujari, 'Comprehensive History of Assam', cited from Dr Tapati Baruah Kashyap, 'Ambubachi: a prayer to Mother Goddess', *Assam Times*, 23 June 2008.

between the years 1780 and 1796. More recently, documents were discovered, which reveal that human sacrifice at the hallowed temple was revived 80 years ago by *Shakta* priests, but was again discontinued following British intervention. However, for the past few years a select group of *tantriks* gather on Ashtami night of Durga Puja and make a symbolic sacrifice of six-foot tall effigies made of flour, at midnight. This form of sacrifice is a closely guarded secret and no outsider is allowed to witness it.[2]

Kamakhya temple atop Nilachal Hills, also known as Kamarup area, near Guwahati is a landmark in Hindu pantheon for devotion and receiving blessings. It is one of 51 *shakti peeths* or seats of Shakti followers, each representing a body part of Satti, Lord Shiva's companion, who avenged the insult to her husband, by despoiling the *yagna* of her father, Daksha. The temple's sanctum sanctorum houses the *yoni*, the female genital, symbolized by a rock and a rock sink filled with water. As mythology goes, Satti, the daughter of Daksh, married Lord Shiva out of her own choice, though her father did not think high of the naked *vairagi devta* with snakes round his neck and who was always in the company of strange saints and *tantrics* and the lowly people.

Once, Daksh performed a *yagna* and invited all gods and goddesses, except Shiva. His daughter, Satti, on reaching the *yagna* venue was surprized and shocked to see the presence of so many gods and goddesses but not her husband, Shiva. She could not tolerate such affront to her husband. She was highly enraged, and to disrupt the proceedings and to foil the benign effect of the *yagna*, she jumped into the *havan kund* fire. The ceremony was stopped, but by this time Satti was half-burnt. The news reached her husband who in anger

---

2 Rahul Karmakar, 'Revival of ritual in Assam temple', *Hindustan Times*, 19 October 2007.

came and carried away his dead wife, Satti, in semi-burnt condition and started running amuck over the mountain tops. This was resented by the gods who were also scared of Shiva's rage, which they apprehended could turn into a *tandav* (a fierce dance of death) and cause a holocaust in the universe.

The gods approached Vishnu for a solution. The need for reaction was urgent and Vishnu, with his *sudarshan chakra*, cut Satti's body into parts which started falling as Shiva jumped from hilltop to hilltop on the mountains till the entire body that had been cut had fallen out of his arms. Having lost the body, Shiva was filled with remorse; his anger subsided and his temper cooled; an apocalypse was prevented and the gods sighed with relief. It is said that wherever the parts of Satti's body fell, such places came to be known as *shakti peeths*. There are a total of 51 such shakti peeths, and in most of such places temples were built, including Naina Devi temple for Satti's eyes, Kamakhya temple for Satti's yoni.

Kalika Purana is the most informative treatise on Kamarup-Kamakhya that glorifies the goddess, Satti and eulogizes the *Shakta tantric* cult at the temple. According to this text, believably, the genital organ of the *devi* (Satti) fell in this part of Nilachal. Thus, goddess Satti is worshipped in various iconographic representations including in the form of *yoni* symbolizing the creative principle. Therefore, 'this temple is unique and different from other temples of the *devi* (Satti) as it enshrines no images or idols of the goddess. Within the temple there is a cave, in one corner of which stands a block of stone on which the symbol of a *yoni* has been sculptured'.[3] All of this is engulfed by a tank of spring water.

---

[3] Banikanta Kakati, 'The Mother Goddess of Kamakhya', cited in Tapati Baruah Kashyap, 'Ambubachi: a prayer to Mother Goddess', *Assam Times*, 23 June 2008.

Mother Goddess in the form of *yoni* has been deified by different ethnic groups of the north-eastern region of India. From pre-historic times, *yoni* worship has been prevalent in Assam (and other adjoining areas) under the belief that it would increase fertility. Pertinent examples are as follows: Worship of *yoni* at Buri Goshani temple by the Jaintias; worship of goddess Kamaikha by the Khasis; Khammakha worshipped by the Bodos, Kechaikhati worshipped by the Chutiyas and Deoris, goddess Tamai worshipped by the Rabhas, Mother Goddess, Phajaw, worshipped by the Garos and goddess Haramdi as well as Mother Goddess, Kalika, worshipped by the Tiwas. Worship of these tribal goddesses bears ample testimony to the fertility cult as also the Shakti cult of Assam.[4]

According to legends, the sanctum-sanctorum of Kamakhya temple is a natural cave with a spring that also has a rock cut in the shape of *yoni*. Over the centuries, Kamakhya has acquired importance as an ancient centre of Shakti cult where *tantrics* and *sadhus* from different parts of the country as well as from neighbouring countries like Nepal, Bangladesh and others, also make a pilgrimage to the temple in obeisance of the goddess and to exhibit their *tantras* and display body control.[5] This holy place is considered the most important centre for the study of *tantra* in the world.

Apart from *Shaivite tantrics*, Kamakhya is visited by other devotees like Sanyasins, black clad Aghoras, the Khadebabas, and Baul singers of Bengal, who participate in Devadhwani Nritya after Mansha Puja ceremonies. Kamakhya temple is well-known for seeking blessings. The faithful confide their wishes to the goddess who grants them in spiritual benignity

---

[4] Nirmala Prabha Bordoloi, 'Devi' cited in Tapati Baruah Kashyap, 'Ambubachi: a prayer to Mother Goddess', *Assam Times*, 23 June 2008.
[5] Samudra Gupta Kashyap, 'Kamakhya temple gears up for its grand show', *Indian Express*, 21 June 2006.

and motherly mercy. These wishes are believed to come true. However, being a Shakti temple, it gets offerings of goats on certain days and, after sacrificial slaughter, meat is distributed as holy *prasad*. Nowadays, fish offerings are also made.

It is also pertinent to mention that Devi Durga is the epitome of supreme power or Shakti and from time immemorial Devi Durga has been worshipped as the sublime spirit and the mother of supreme energy of the universe. Since energy is considered feminine in Hindu religious philosophy, so this supreme energy symbolized by Devi Durga is the symbol of universal motherhood and considered as the source of ubiquitous energy. In Hinduism, Divine Mother is the first manifestation of Divine Energy and thus represents power, omnipotence, omnipresence, love, intelligence and wisdom. Shakti, the life force, therefore, is latent yet immanent, and is manifest in every aspect of human life and living force.

The Kamakhya temple on Nilachal hills in Guwahati was reconstructed in the year 1565 by the Kochi Rajbonshi royalty; but descendents of the royal family do not visit the Kamakhya temple. Legend has it that the goddess used to dance in the temple while the *pujari* (priest) would worship and say prayers with his eyes shut. Nara Narayan, the last ruler of the undivided Koch kingdom of Kamata, on learning this, became curious and highly desirous to see the activities going on in the temple. With the help of his brother Chilarai, a revered General of Assam, he convinced the then priest, Kendukoli, to allow them to watch the goddess's dance.

Ultimately, the priest relented and thus, they secretly watched the goddess dance. The goddess sensed the happening, was furious and was incensed by the breach of trust by the priest as well as the voyeuristic misadventure of the royalty. As a result, the goddess punished the priest and cursed the offend-ing duo and their descendants with doom if they ever visited the Kamakhya temple. Ostensibly, the curse still prevails and the only ones that refrain from visiting the temple are the descendants of the medieval Koch royalty.[6]

BAIDA—HUMAN SACRIFICE WITH SAFETY MEASURES

The ritual of *Baida* at Rohru, near Shimla, is originally an act of human sacrifice as *narbali* under the direction of the *gram* (local or village) *devta*. It is also known as Narmegh Yagna and is performed in supplication and to appease the virulent powers of the *devta*.[7] For the ritual of sacrifice, a local resident is chosen, generally from the lower caste and the chosen one is put to the venerated sacrificial test. If he comes out alive from the ordeal, he is then elevated in status to be considered and treated as a Rajput, however, he is not truly equated with real-born Rajputs. Lately, however, with government intervention, a symbolic sacrifice is offered as an act of swinging on a rope from one hill top to another. As the traditional ordeal was dangerous, it is now conducted with safety nets in place and other precautions.[8]

The locals believe and have faith in magical powers of the *devta* and in awe, obediently comply with his dictates. Elders narrate that in certain moments the *devta* possesses the *pujari's* body and listens to the villagers' woes and administers remedial justice. Solutions declared by him are to be complied without demur. Some declarations are benign development measures that are welfare-oriented like building a short road or constructing *chaupals* and temples.

Occasionally, the *devta* loses his temper and it is then that the villagers have to supplicate and pacify him. For example,

---

[6] Refer http://www.thehindu.com/todays-paper/tp-life/celebrating-the-goddess-who-bleeds/article24235989.ece

[7] 'Symbolic Act', *Hindustan Times* (Delhi Edition).

[8] Chetan Chouhan, 'Rites or wrongs' in the Off Track column. From newspaper clipping. Publication details not available.

for years he has been strongly urging for the demolition of encroachments by villagers and as punishment, offenders have to feed the entire population to a religious meal with non-vegetarian course of cooked sacrificial goat. As a concession, serving alcohol is optional but only a few take such a chance or risk. The *devta's* hold is so strong in people's mindset that the local populace in Himachal Pradesh and neighbouring Uttarakhand will go to any extent, even conduct a secret human sacrifice, to appease the wrath of the powerful deity.

THE CUSTOM OF SANTHARA

Jainism commands that life be lived according to four tenets: *Kama, Artha, Dharma* and *Moksha*. *Moksha* is the spiritual culmination of a fully lived life and it comes through death, which can be attained in many ways. Death may come by accident or through natural biological attrition of the physical body or by invoking *santhara*, a holy practice of systematically abandoning the body through voluntary fasting unto death, achieving consequent purification of the soul.

Jainism ordains *santhara* for Jain monks and *sadhavis* of *Gondal Gachh Sthanakvasi* sect of Jains but, at times, ordinary mortals also adopt this spiritual practice because of an intense desire to voluntarily end one's life by giving up ingestion of food or water and purifying the soul by purging old *karmas*, preventing the creation of new sins and 'remaining indifferent to death' and thus, attaining *nirvana*. This holy practice of *nirvana* through fasting was first introduced by a monk in the year 1790.[9]

Santhara (also known as *sallekhana*) is a spiritual decision taken when a person so feels and is convinced that life has served its purpose and one must strive towards attainment

---

[9] 'Fasting sadhavi attains "nirvana"', *The Times of India*, 16 November 1992.

of *Moksha*. Thereafter, it is Him (the God) and me. Such a celebrated death bestows an iconic status within the Jain community but for family members, coming to terms with such a situation and the bereavement is difficult to cope with. Nevertheless, the person embarking on *santhara,* after making his decision to tread this path, takes permission from the *guru* and the family members, who look after the person during the fasting period. Thereafter, the person entertains no persuasion; it is a tryst between the vow-maker and Lord Mahavir Swami; family members do not interfere with a person's *santhara* and only look after the person during the *santhara* fast.

Most of such deaths are gradual and peaceful and there is no crying involved. One family, having undergone this experience, confided, 'He made us promise we would not mourn his death by shedding tears. He asked us not wear white during his funeral.'[10] We abided by his instructions but it was hard not to cry. Anyway, we were happy for the spiritual elevation of the departed soul. We were also reminded that the Jain belief warns 'that mourning a *santhara* death is equivalent to holding the soul back from *Moksha*'.[11] For us, that would have been deplorable.

A *santhara* death is a celebration where the dead body is draped in a white cloth and put into a decorated palanquin either in a sitting position or in lotus position, in contrast to the lying position prevalent in Hinduism. This position on the pyre symbolizes that the person would attain *Moksha*. Thereafter, the mortal remains are taken to the cremation ground in a grand procession of literal rejoicing with mourners attired in bright and colourful clothes. The body is cremated as per usual Hindu rituals.

---

[10] Mansi Choksi and Hemali Chhapia, 'The fast road to moksha', *The Times of India* (Crest Edition).
[11] Ibid.

Lately, there has been a discernible increase in the number of *santhara* deaths and these have attracted increasing publicity in the media. Though, *santhara* is mainly prescribed for Jain monks (*sarewade*), yet ordinary but religious Jains are also increasingly adopting this practice. As a result, this age-old spiritual custom has courted controversy raising the question whether the practice of *santhara* has a place in modern society and polity. Human rights activists have dubbed it as a social evil and treated it as equivalent to suicide under the Indian penal law. Indian Constitution also grants a fundamental right to life under Article 21 and its voluntary termination is a breach.

The Jains, on the contrary, maintain that *santhara* is an act of pure volition after rational thinking. It is a decision taken with a sound mind and religious intent. It is a conscious choice of a person with full knowledge to voluntarily go on a spiritual journey after understanding the inherently painful and flawed nature of earthly existence that may be terminated volitionally or by will of God. Therefore, it cannot be termed or compared to suicide which is an immature, emotional and hasty action in disregard of consequences. Though, there is only a thin line between suicide and *santhara*, the latter is removed from the negativity of suicide because of its holy nature and spiritual purpose of attaining *Moksha*. In case the law-makers had thought otherwise, they could have enacted a law similar to that of banning *sati-pratha*. However, this has not happened and the practice of *santhara* survives.

The preamble to the Constitution of India also assures to all its citizens, liberty of thought, expression, belief, faith and worship. In furtherance to this, Article 25 of the Indian Constitution guarantees that every person in India shall have the freedom of conscience and a right to profess, practice and propagate religion. Moreover, Article 29 goes further and declares that any section of citizens having a distinct culture shall have the right to conserve the same. If any law comes in conflict with these constitutional rights, it will have to yield.[12] Hence, the practice of *santhara* finds adequate protection under provisions of the Indian Constitution.

It is further advocated that *santhara* is merely a practice of giving up food in the name of God like any Hindu *vrat* or religious fast; and obviously, no one can force anyone to eat against one's desire and if they are not hungry. It is true that the practice is generally opted by old people and allowing them to suffer without medical assistance, food and water is inhuman under any civilized society or social values. This argument, howsoever valid, can be tilted to state that the individual has sufficient time to change his mind and revoke *sallekhana* due to unbearable physical pain or resurgence of love for kin or a rekindled desire to enjoy wealth and possessions. The decision, either way, is entirely personal and voluntary with no coercion to or resistance against. Incidentally, undoing *santhara*, once having undertaken the vows, may incur social ignominy and ostracism within the community.[13] But this is no law; only a social norm.

THE PRACTICE OF *KARWAT*

The Hindus have also, in the past, followed a practice similar to *santhara* among the Jains. The practice was called *Karwat* and was performed about seven centuries ago. Hindu philosophy speaks about four *ashrams* or stages of life and if each part of life is lived morally and religiously well, it leads to *Moksha* or *Mukti*, that is, salvation and riddance from the cycle of birth and death. Average life of a person is considered to be 100 years. The first part of life is *Brahmacharya* and it starts at the time of birth and lasts till youth (25 years

---

[12] Hemali Chhapia and Mansi Choksi, 'Is santhara against the law?' *The Times of India* (Crest Edition).
[13] Ibid.

of age). This is the period of childhood fun, for studying and preparing for a vocation in later life. The next 25 years belong to *Grahastha ashram*, which is for marriage, to beget children, for professional advancement and for faithfully looking after the family. In short, it required living like a perfect household being who is honest to the vocation and devoted to the family.

The third stage of life is *Sanyas ashram* that lasts for the next twenty-five years. In this stage of life, a person is expected to duly perform and progressively complete his worldly responsibilities. During these years, the individual attempts to accomplish unfinished tasks and wind up one's duties towards their family, profession and society. They, thus, gradually withdraw from vocational, familial and social bonds so as to move towards a retired life of rest and respite. Accordingly, they mentally and emotionally prepare for renunciation of worldly affairs with a sense of achievement on having performed their part well and as best as possible.

The last stage of life is *Vanaprastha ashram*, when a person retires to the jungles to live alone with himself and survive for himself. In seclusion and with non-existent profane stimuli, mind and effort are devoted to overcome temporal vices and exercise control over the human urges. This is the time for an honest introspection of the self and an evaluation of a lifetime of deeds leading to resultant repentance or impenitence or satisfaction. The next step is meditation and self-realization; to be one and merge with God to attain the ultimate *Moksha*.

To attain *Moksha* people preferred the areas around Varanasi, more popularly known as Benares in olden times. Holy books maintain that Varanasi was established by god Shiva and it happens to be the first habitation created on the Earth and is haloed with Shiva's aura. There is also a belief that any person who breathes his last in this sacred *nagari* (town), their soul goes to Vaikunth, which is equivalent of the 'Heaven' of westerners. For spiritual consolation, as per *Skand Purana*, *Moksha* is assured if one embraces *mrityu* (death) around Lord Vishwanath's temple in Kedarkhand, near Varanasi. This conjunction of blessed death and sacred place, in other words, assures *Moksha* or salvation or liberation from the cycle of rebirth.

At this stage of renunciation and anticipation of the end of physical life, the endeavour is to acquire complete control of faculties, to understand the purpose of life, mission for the self and to establish communion with God. Some spiritually lucky ones get bestowed with this realization too easily and much sooner than others. Some fail to mentally overpower vices of the faculties and stray away from the chosen path of salvation from human bondage. Both categories of mortals may, in their own way and effort, find and realize that just living a mortal life any further has neither divine grace nor spiritual meaning nor temporal purpose. They may, thus, prefer an end to physical living.

In such cases of revelation, the enlightened souls go to Shiva's Araa (a cutting saw mill) located in Varanasi and get themselves cut into two halves from head to the crotch and, thus, end their worldly life in humble submission and divine devotion. This practice is called *Karwat* and was once exalted as a celebrated voluntary end to life by the blessed souls. This custom finds mention in a verse of saint Kabir, who lived in Varanasi around 13th century AD. This verse is included in Sri Guru Granth Sahib (SGGS), the holy book of the Sikhs. In a loving mood, Kabir remonstrates to God, *'Karwat bhala, naa karwath teri.'*[14] In a gist, it can be translated to mean that

---

[14] Raag Asa, Bhagat Kabir Ji, *SGGS, ang* (p. 484). SGGS has standardized pagination in all editions.

it is more acceptable to me to die in the manner of *karwat* rather than endure your turning away from me.

With the passage of time, this custom lost its sublimity as a method of release from human bondage and fell from salutary grace. This method of dying came into disrepute and has been equated with suicide and consequently discouraged during the Mughal reign and the British rule. Perhaps, Shiva's *ara* also went into disuse and wasted away. No wonder, this custom of *Karwat* does not seem to exist anymore, the location of Shiva's *ara* is not known and Benares has no memory of this incident in history.[15]

THOOKAM FESTIVAL IN KERALA

At the Elavoor temple, near Kalady in Kerala, every year, on 24th April, which is the tenth day after the Malayalam new year, 'the thookam (hanging) festival is celebrated'. It is possibly a carryover of the ancient practice of human sacrifice performed here in days of yore. This ritual probably belongs to goddess Kali's *narbali* sacrifice or Shakti cult of *Shaivism* and, in the present day, has been mitigated to symbolic suffering.

As per the ritual, a devotee who wanted to fulfill a vow, engaged a professional 'sacrificial' man by paying him a hefty sum of money to undertake the ritual on his behalf. After recitation of several *mantras* and performance of preceding rituals, two huge iron hooks pierced through this man's bare flesh on his back and this naked man is pulled up on a con- traption resembling a manually operated crane. He dangles up there, in mid-air, blood dripping, while devotees wheel him around the temple in circumambulation three times.

Lately, however, better sense has prevailed and a towel is worn around the waist by the 'sacrificial' man. No one is

---

15 Based on interviews with a few priests in Varanasi.

sure if the wish invariably materializes or fails despite tantric rituals. Nevertheless, public awareness and literacy has led to the decline of this practice and social organizations are spearheading the movement to stop this barbaric ritual of 'thookam'. It is no longer held regularly.

STONE PELTING FESTIVAL OF UTTARAKHAND

The annual Bagwal festival of stone pelting is held on the day of Rakshabandhan at Barhi Devi temple at Devidhura village in Champawat district of Uttarakhand.[16] Men from four clans of Devidhura village namely, Walik, Chamyal, Gaharwal and Lamgharia, don plain turbans of four different colours, namely, white, pink, orange and yellow, respectively. Participating men reach Barahi Devi temple for this customary event. When the ritual starts, the men start throwing stones at each other rather indiscriminately and at the same time use shields to protect themselves from being hit. When some blood has spilt, the ritual is stopped and the event is declared as over.

Origin of the festival goes back to a mythological story. Lakshman Singh Lamgharia, patron of the temple narrates that it is believed demons were troubling the four clans of Devidhura who then prayed to their patron goddess, Barahi Devi, for help and protection. In kindness, the goddess agreed but demanded that a human sacrifice be invariably made to her every year. The agreement was religiously obeyed without remorse and a human sacrifice was offered as promised.

One year, when a man was about to be sacrificed, his mother prayed to the goddess for mercy. The benign goddess relented but stipulated an alternative condition. The goddess now ordained that once a year, people from the four clans would

---

[16] Prem Punetha, 'Apples, peers new "rocks" in stone-pelting festival', *The Times of India* (Chandigarh Edition), 28 August 2018.

hurl stones at one another till the blood spilt on the ground was equal to the blood of one human sacrifice. The concession was well accepted by the clans and the revised practice continued as a tradition.

In view of the injuries caused to hundreds of people and the inhumane nature of the custom, in the year 2013, the High Court of Uttarakhand intervened and took notice of this practice, and since then stones have been replaced by fruits like apples and pears to reduce casualties and injuries. Thus, in the year 2018, on the day of Rakshabandhan, six quintals of fruits were made available within the precincts of the temple and the event of Bagwal was played for about eight minutes in the afternoon. This year, 112 people sustained minor injuries and the deity now stands propitiated for one more year.

STONE PELTING FESTIVAL OF HIMACHAL PRADESH

'Pathar ka Mela' is held at Halog which was once the capital of a princely state called Dhammi. It is situated about 25 km from Shimla town. The *mela* is organized on the day after the festival of Diwali and is intended to ring in good times, as a symbol of hope and devotion. It is also called *'Patharon ka khel'* or the stone-pelting festival that has been traditionally carried on by the Khunds, a warrior community of Himachal Pradesh. No outsiders are allowed to take part in the ritual. Conventionally, women do not participate in the *khel* but make for good spectators and enthusiastic on-lookers. The audience maintains good decorum and there is no hooliganism, except cheers from the crowd when blood is drawn for ritualistic *tilak* to be applied to the deity.

For the game, two teams are formed; one from the royalty of Dhammi called Halogis along with members from the clans of Katedu, Tundu and Dhagoi. The opponent team is called

Jamogis who hail from a nearby village called Jamog. The ritual starts with the respective teams starting their procession with drum beats to reach a circular structure near Sharda Devi temple, where a queen of Dhammi royalty had committed *sati*. The Halogi procession starts with prayers and chanting of drums from the temple of Narsingh Devta, whose seat is inside the Dhammi palace. Jamogi team also embarks on this mission in a similar fashion to meet at the appointed place and offers prayers to *sati mata* before the fight begins.

The venue of the game is a circular structure on both sides of which the teams take position, generally at a reasonable distance of 150–200 m. The participants do not use any protective gear or shields. Stones are normally showered up in the air and not directly at the members of the opponent team. This tradition is a celebration of camaraderie and devotion that entails joy, and getting hit during the ritual is considered auspicious. Thus, as it gradually becomes a constant hail of stones, no participant wishes to escape or scramble for shelter. The game is played on till a player bleeds enough to offer blood that can be drawn for applying '*tilak*' on the goddess Bhadra Kali for appeasement and propitiation. Then the red flag is raised and the *khel* stops. The locals believe that it is due to divine intervention only that no serious incident of major injury or death has ever occurred.

To find the exact origin of this ritual or festival, sociological research may be needed, but locals claim that it has its origins in human sacrifice or *narbali*, a practice which has been followed for many centuries to appease goddess Bhadra Kali in the princely state of Dhammi. Once, a kind-hearted queen, perturbed by the cruel custom, ordered its dissolution and instead offered to commit the act of *sati* by herself. The place where she performed *sati* is the location of Sharda Devi temple. Thereafter, human sacrifice was put to an end and as an alternative, the ritual was replaced by '*Patharon ka Khel*' or '*bhed*' in local parlance.[17] This contest is held annually for a symbolic *tilak* of blood to be smeared on the forehead of the deity[18] as token of sacrifice.

There are, however, other explanations for this custom and one of them appears more credible: According to another legend, a woman from Halog village was engaged to a royal member of the neighbouring princely state of Rangoili. But due to mutual animosity, residents of the neighbouring Jamog village poisoned the royal prince's mind just before the marriage could take place. The distraught woman burnt herself on the pyre of her fiancé in the tradition of *sati* near the circular structure. At this, the enraged villagers on both sides fought with stones. This practice is perpetuated and residents of Halog and Jamog villages participate in this fight of resentment and revenge, though the purpose is now ostensibly intended to ring in good times and seek protection of the deity.[19]

ANIMAL SACRIFICE DURING DURGA PUJA

Hindu mythology can boast of a pantheon of gods and each god is different from the other and is unique. Lord Rama was *maryada purushotam* (the upholder of social norms and traditions) while Lord Krishna was just the opposite (the upholder of rights and truth in utter disregard of the methods to enforce such rights and truths). Lord Shiva saw no difficulty in being godhead and a husband. Lord Hanuman represents *bhakti* (devotion) and Lord Ganesha bestows *riddhi* and *siddhi* (prosperity and attainment, respectively).

---

[17] Surekha Dhaleta, 'Festival of stones to appease the goddess', *The Times of India*, 28 October 2011.
[18] TNN report, 'They get "stoned" day after Diwali', *The Times of India*, 25 October 2014.
[19] Neha Sharma, 'In Himachal, people pelt stones to ring in good times', *The Times of India*, 12 November 2017.

Goddess Durga represents *shakti* (power) which she used to kill *asur* (demons). The Shakti cult worships the divine female principle, the immanent power of the absolute, in forms such as Durga, Kali, Lakshmi, Tripurasundari, Bhairavi and other local variations of these female deities.[20]

Durga Puja is famous in Bengal and is popularly celebrated in many forms and with myriad rituals. Apart from decorating pompous and extravagant *pandals* for carrying out the celebrations, Durga Puja represents Durga's *shakti's* victory of good over evil. In *devi* worship, power is concentrated in the blood and blood has been a symbol of reproduction and regeneration and fertility. This *puja* is, thus, related to blood and demands sacrifice to rejuvenate the powers of the mother. Hence, animal sacrifice has been practised by Shakti Cult believers from times immemorial. It is pertinent to mention that only male animals are offered for sacrifice and female species are spared this ritual.

Apart from Bengal, Durga Puja is held with equal fervour and pompous celebrations in adjoining states also. For example, Odisha is another state full of Durga devotees who are quite into the ritual of animal sacrifice on the occasion of Durga Puja to propitiate the goddess. It is estimated that 'lakhs of goats, sheep, buffaloes and cocks are sacrificed during the *puja* across Odisha'.[21] The practice mostly prevails in villages. In the past, animal sacrifice was a community affair to collectively appease the deity. Lately, however, due to compassion for animals, some believers have taken to offer cucumbers, gourds and coconuts to appease the deity, but mostly, 'Bali relates to the economy (and faith) and man's cruelty has not come down.'[22] A legal enactment, The Prevention of Cruelty

---

[20] Avani Bansal, 'Lord Shiva through a feminist lens; few gods would withstand it as well as he does', *The Times of India*, 8 July 2019, p. 16.

[21] Sandeep Mishra, 'Lakhs of animals sacrificed', *Hindustan Times*, 17 October 2002.

[22] Ibid.

to Animals Act, 1960, prohibits animal sacrifice, however, the law is not always followed to the letter due to the religious sentiments of devotees.

AT TEMPLES IN NEPAL

Virtually closed to the outside world for centuries, the tiny, land-locked Himalayan state of Nepal has retained ancient religious practices and cults with curious religious trends from India and Tibet. The Nepalese society is religious and traditional with ingrained tolerance, self-imposed rules and social taboos governing its rural life style. Hinduism with its myriad sects and deities dominates its beliefs and proclivities. *Sanatanic Puranic* Hinduism is the dominant religion of the kingdom of Nepal, its royalty and its populace; so are its festivals and celebrations.

Thus, with the majority of the population of Nepal professing the Hindu faith, the country has majorly followed the practices of the *Shaivite* sect. People are religious and ritualistic and have followed the traditional practices for centuries. One such practice is of *bali* or animal sacrifice, as a religious ritual and offering to the local deities in the hope of a harmonious life and increase in prosperity. Prayers are offered for this purpose and animal sacrifice is specially performed at many *Shaivite* temples that exist in the kingdom.

There is the temple of Dakhin Kali which is dedicated to the deity Kali, the warrior goddess. The temple is located in the forested canyon, about 20 km off Kathmandu city. This temple maintains an age-old practice of bi-weekly sacrifice of goats, chicken and ducks. The sacrificial offerings are made every Tuesday and Saturday at the temple. Perhaps to everyone's satisfaction, and as a general taboo, no female animals of any kind are offered for religious sacrifice.[23]

---

[23] 'Nepal retains ancient rituals', *The Statesman*, 22 October 1992.

Another shrine with a similar practice of *bali* (offering an animal for sacrifice) is the temple of Gadhimai. This temple holds the world's biggest animal sacrifice event in Nepal at five-year intervals. This practice has been continuing for over 300 years; and for generations, believers have sacrificed animals to propitiate the goddess to grant them a better personal life and welfare of the community.[24] The devout have never ever doubted the efficacy of their sacrificial offerings, which are made under a spiritual obligation, with accompanying religious devotion and personal humility.

The number of animals killed at the Gadhimai festival, every five years, has been escalating, turning it into a massacre of innocent and helpless animals in return for unquantified betterment or unknown benignity. This has aroused resentment of animal lovers across the globe, who treat the killing of animals as ruthless and unnecessary violence. They have advocated replacing sacrificial violence with peaceful worship and symbolic sacrifices. In India, however, there has lately been a gradual but growing acceptance of symbolic sacrifices in the form of breaking cucumbers, gourds, coconut, etc., on the ground, in place of customary animal sacrifice. Many devotees also feel that the time has come to transform this old tradition and give it a new identity and modality.

The crescendo of opposition to this ritualistic mega-sacrificial event was very high in the year 2015, and in acknowledgement of this resistance movement, Nepal's Gadhimai Temple Trust announced a formal decision to place a ban on animal sacrifice and urged devotees not to bring animals to the festival for the purpose of sacrificial slaughtering. The Trust's decision of imposing such a ban has also possibly been influenced by the ruling of India's Supreme Court in the year 2015

---

[24] Vishwa Mohan, 'Nepal temple bans animal sacrifice', *The Times of India*, 29 July 2015,

to prohibit movement of animals from India to Nepal for the festival.[25]

The cumulative effect of both these triggers will possibly ensure that the festival around October in 2019 will be free from bloodshed and gore, or at least on a low key, and will save millions of animals from cruel torture and unnatural death. Thus, Gadhimai festival in 2019 will, in all probability, ensure a momentous celebration of animal life and at the same time, herald a tremendous victory for compassion. Animal lovers look forward to a slowdown of this event with bated breath. But at times, ingrained beliefs and cultural strangle-holds keep lingering and generally take time to unshackle the mindset. Patience should be the hallmark.

KHARCHI FESTIVAL OF TRIPURA

The royal family of Tripura celebrates an annual seven-day Kharchi festival at old Agartala, the erstwhile capital of the princely state of Tripura and situated about 13 km from the present city of Agartala. The festival was started by King Trilochan, the first king of Tripura. This is a popular festival for the populace and participation of people transcends caste and community and as such it has a universal character. The festival, thus, symbolizes peace, harmony and fraternity among the people of Tripura.

The rituals start with devotees taking a sacred bath at Kharchighat on *Shukla Ashtami*, sometime in July, every year. The ceremonial worship commences with a holy dip of idols (only the head) of fourteen Hindu deities, namely, Hara, Uma, Hari, Maa, Bani, Kumar, Ganesh, Brahma, Prithi, Ganga, Abdi, Kamesh, Agni and Himadri in the river Howrah. Then the *puja* (worship) is performed by the *raj chintai* (head

---

[25] Ibid.

priest) according to Hindu scriptures by chanting of *mantras* addressed to the fourteen idol-heads of the gods. Thereafter, begins the sacrifice of 108 goats by the assistant priests with concurrent chanting of *mantras*.[26]

The unique features of this festival are as follows: First, the festival starts with the august Guard of Honour to the uncrowned *raj chintai* and not to the king of Tripura. The second unique feature is that after the festival the idols of deities are kept locked in a room throughout the year and taken out again during the festival. The third unique factor is the sacrifice of 108 animals, which was started by the first king of Tripura, Sri Trilochan. The culture of sacrifice of animals to pray for welfare of the community is a common practice in eastern parts of India, among the people practising and believing in *Shakta* cult of the *devi*.

In Tripura, there is another temple called Mata Tripureswari Mandir, which is a *shakti peeth*. At this temple, one goat is sacrificed every day as part of the rituals that were performed since over five centuries ago. Interestingly, funds for this sacrificial goat are borne by the state exchequer because this ritual was protected under the terms of merger (pact) of Tripura into the Indian Dominion at the time of partition of India in the year 1947. In litigation, it was argued before the court that the tradition has been observed for ages and animal sacrifice is an integral part of worship in the Mata Tripureswari Mandir. Its discontinuation would, thus, hurt the sentiments of the devotees and believers of this tradition and the ingrained beliefs of the people must be respected. This plea was in line with the judgement of the Orissa High Court which ruled that killing of animals for religious purposes cannot be construed as an offence under the Prevention of Cruelty to Animals

---

[26] Newspaper report dated 10 July from Agartala, 'Seven-day traditional Kharchi Festival of Agartala.'

Act, 1960. However, in variance with this judgement, the High Court of Tripura, while disposing of a petition on a similar subject had decided, 'Aiding Tripureswari temple with funds to sacrifice 1 goat each day from government money does not fall within the ambit of secular activity. It is the state's duty … to eradicate all ill practices to bring reforms in the society.'[27] Popular sentiments will, of course, dilute its enforcement and only strong political will can prompt a bold step in the suggested direction. Any coercive action should be taken with sensitivity and sagacity.

RITUAL IN A CHURCH: TOSSING A GOAT FROM THE BELFRY

A small village named Manganeses de la Polvorosa, located about 60 km north of Zamora in Spain has a tradition of tossing a live goat from the church tower to honour the town's Patron Saint. Only if the animal walks away from the fall can celebrations start in honour of Saint Vincent. The actual origin of this practice is unclear, yet one popular account maintains that it began after a local priest's goat fell from the church belfry and was saved by the people. The faithfuls believe that the animal was saved because the priest used to routinely give goat's milk to the poor.

However, animal rights organizations in Spain opposed such cruel treatment of the animals. The church resented the opposition claiming that a net is spread below the belfry for the safety of the animal. The activists explained that quite often the young persons throwing the animal are careless and sometimes the animal does not precisely fall into the net; or the young persons holding the net are drunk and take the task too frivolously such that the animal gets injured and is barely able to walk away.

---

[27] Sandeep Mishra, 'Killing animals for religious purposes not an offence', *The Times of India*, 28 September 2019, p. 7.

The government, after due consideration, imposed a ban on this practice in the year 2000 and has imposed a fine of 500,000 Spanish pesetas (equivalent to USD 5000) per goat thrown. Another organization offered one million Spanish pesetas for the development of the town if the people of the town stopped this practice of goat throwing from the belfry. However, the youth of the town were adamant and in no mood to accept enforcement of the ban. In defiance, they even threatened to throw the mayor and the parish priest down the belfry, that too, without the nets.[28]

ANIMAL SACRIFICE BY SANTERIANS

Santeria is a faith that originated in the Yoruba tribe in Nigeria and came to America via Cuba. Its believers were transported to Cuba as slaves nearly 400 years ago. They arrived into United States during the fifties and sixties of the 20th century and have settled mostly in south Florida since then. Their number is estimated to be at least 60,000, but since they are scattered, the number could be more. The followers congregate at the Santeria church of Lukumi Babalu Aye.

Santeria means 'the way of the saints' and is a blend of Roman Catholic and African religious beliefs, closely related to the Haitian voodoo cult. Santeros, the priest of Santerian church, asserts that they have an age-old custom, integral to their religion, of ritualistic sacrifice of ducks, chickens, doves, goats, sheep and even turtles. This ritual has been a central part of the religion for 4000 years and forms the core of rites performed at the time of birth, marriage and death. Another ritual of this religion is the sacrificial ritual involving slaughter of 13 goats, every time a new priest is initiated or anointed. As part of the religious ritual, the Santerians 'cut

---

[28] 'Church ritual with animals opposed', *The Statesman*, 26 January 1992.

animal throats, bleed them on a sacred altar and then splatter each other with blood'.[29]

In the year 1987, the predominantly Hispanic city of Hialeah near Miami banned the ritualistic slaughter of animals by enacting a law to address the concern that the animal carcasses are left at roadsides, which creates nuisance and could also spread disease. It was also argued that it offends America's sense of civic propriety and love for animals. The prohibition was upheld by two different courts. American Society for the Prevention of Cruelty to Animals contended that such a practice 'is quite simply outside the cultural norms of this country' while civil liberties advocates, supporting the ban, argued on the matter of 'the methods of slaughter, (contravention) of hygiene laws and children being traumatized by the spectacle of animals being killed'.[30]

The Santerians appealed to the Supreme Court and pleaded that the ritual is integral to their religion and has been in practice for nearly 4000 years and thus 'the ban represents an infringement of their right to freedom of worship under the first amendment to the American Constitution'. They also contended that the carcasses are not abandoned but actually cooked and eaten. As for the alleged trauma of children, they argued that television programmes and videos are bloodier and gorier than their rites.[31]

Fearing judicial interference in religious matters and greater regulation of religious practices by civil authorities, and enactment of similar laws in other cities also, many religious denominations like Seventh-Day Adventists, the Mormons, Evangelical Lutherans, Jews, Baptists and several Catholic

---

[29] Ben Macintyre, 'In sacred war on the chickens', *The Statesman*, 17 June 1992.
[30] Ibid.
[31] Ibid.

groups have signed 'friend-of-court' briefs in support of the Santerian appeal for upholding of constitutional rights and repeal of the Hialeah ban in the Supreme Court. However, the final judgement on the fate of the case is not known.

THE RITUAL OF PENANCE IN MALAYSIA

Hindus, following the *Devi*-cult, consider self-torture a method of penance and self-purification. Despite the visible agony and pain of self-torture, the devout indulge in it with abandon and believe that faith is the alleviator of pain. This happens on the festival of Thaipusam generally celebrated in the southern states of India by the *Shaivite* Hindus. It is celebrated in the month of January and is dedicated to Lord Murugan, who is particularly revered by the Tamil community in South India. British rulers had taken ethnic Tamils to Malaysia as labourers for work. These *émigré* Hindus, on migration, carried with them their beliefs and rituals. There are now about two million descendents of this community in Malaysia.

On the festival of Thaipusam, in Malayasia, massive crowds of Hindus throng to the temples in Batu caves, Penang, Ipoh and in other cities. The devout perform the rituals of penance by piercing dozens of needles, a little bigger than sewing needles, into their chest, back and arms. Some hang lime fruit from the hooks pierced into their body in true devotion. Many display their religious 'fervour by carrying heavy ornate metal structures called Kavadis, affixed to their bodies with sharp metal spikes that are hammered into the skin.... Others pierced their faces with tridents or hung multiple hooks and chains from their body in an act of penance'.[32]

---

[32] AFP report, 'Malaysian Tamils defy virus fears to mark Thaipusam', *The Times of India*, 20 February 2020.

The more faithful devotees visit Batu cave temples and indulge in more severe penance. It was seen that some had spear-shaped steel rods, one metre long and about 1 cm thick, struck through one cheek and coming out of the other, and a few devotees inserted the rod into their tongue also. Some devotees had smaller rods going through their lips. The less adventurous ones just carried pots of milk on their head for atonement which were eventually smashed as offerings. Some shaved their heads bald, bathed in a stream at the foot of Batu caves and climbed the 272 steps to the temple inside a limestone cave, which is about the size of half a soccer field.[33]

Much to the bewilderment of the locals and western tourists, the ritual goes on in full view of the public. Some physicians who examined and investigated the piercings, found that in the process of insertions, no blood had been shed and the devotees claimed that they had no feeling of pain during the process of insertion and even after the insertion. Many of them seemed to be lulled into a trance due to the sounds of chanting and beating of drums. The devotees do apply a paste mix of burnt cow-dung, milk and sandalwood on their bodies. This paste is smeared on the skin at the time of piercing and once again when the hook is drawn out.[34] Its anesthetic effect is yet to be chemically established but the belief stands.

A foreigner, Carl Bell from Australia, now a freelance journalist, who participated in the ritual this ritual commented that the westerners look at this spectacle from a physical, practical and scientific point of view instead of viewing religion and belief as a transcendental and holistic experience. He claimed that through faith, the practitioners get elevated to a different level of consciousness where there is no feeling of pain, the faculties get numbed and the body ceases to

---

[33] 'The rituals of penance', *The Statesman*, 22 January2 1992.
[34] Ibid.

exist as a physical entity capable of experiencing pain.[35] In short, unflinching faith in and ardent devotion to the ritual of penance is the answer to this enigma of torture, tolerance and painless observance.

SNIPPETS

CUSTOM OF QURBANI AMONG MUSLIMS

Among the Muslims also, the concept of *qurbani* or animal sacrifice exists, though in a different context having a different meaning and a different motive. Shariah law approves of sacrifice and it is said in the Holy Quran, 'What is sacrifice? Sacrifice is the nourishment without which the tiny seeds of Iman, faith, will not grow into mighty leafy trees; provide shade and fruits to the count-less caravans of humankind' (Quran, 14–24–5).[36] Hence, animal slaughter of goats and sheep, as well as sacrifice of camels and horses, has religious sanction and is observed as a social ritual on the festival of *Bakr-id*.

HOLY COMMUNION CEREMONY: A SYMBOLIC SACRIFICE

The Christians also observe a custom of symbolic sacri-fice, known as Holy Communion, with offerings of bread and red wine in the churches. It represents the spirit of sacrifice of Christ, the Lord for humankind. The bread represents His body and red wine symbolizes His blood. After the ceremony, the consecrated items are distributed as benediction to the believers. They also partake of it voluntarily and individually on visit to the church on special occasions. The late comers partake individually.

---

[35] Ibid.
[36] Refer Sacred Space column on Editorial page of *Times of India*, 21 August 2019.

KAPPAROT RITUAL OF THE JEWS

Orthodox Jews perform a ritual called Kapparot on Yom Kipper day (Day of Atonement) to atone for past sins. As per this custom, Jews in Jerusalem swing a chicken above the head of their eldest son, in strong belief and fond hope, to transfer the sins to the fowl. Rituals are built upon their own logic and carry a strong hold over the mindset of believers.

BUDDHIST PURIFICATION BY FIRE

Buddhists monks in Japan undertake an annual ordeal of 'walking on fire'. As per this religious rite of purification, a monk walks bare feet across a smoldering belt prepared on the ground. The ceremony for this practice of asceticism is conducted at the foot of Mount Takao in north-western Tokyo. This annual event of purification is also marked to herald the advent of spring season. In the year 2006, this ritual was held on 12th March (Sunday). Hundreds of Buddhist priests and other believers participated in this purification ceremony.[37]

NIRVANA THROUGH SELF-TORTURE

Ranipur Khirki is a small village on the periphery of Patna in Bihar. According to the ancient myths and legends long embedded in their psyche, the people of this village strongly believe that self-torture is a way to *nirvana*. The legend behind this custom relates to the mythical character of Savitri who was married to Satyavan. Savitri was faithful to her husband and when Satyavan died, she begged Yamaraj, the god of

---

[37] AP report, 'Blistering Barnacles', *Hindustan Times*, 13 March 2006, 10.

death to revive her dead husband. Yamaraj relented due to her heart-rending pleading and brought Satyavan back to life. Thousands of people gather to pray in deep frenzy which does not stop short of extreme forms of masochism to appease the gods to get the final *mukti*, that is, freedom from the bondage of perpetual cycle of life and death.[38] Here, though the purpose is spiritually benign, the method is ritualistic and masochistic.

FESTIVE SPIRIT AND PENANCE

'*Uda Parva*' is a festival celebrated in Odisha. During this festival, the devout pierce their body parts with fishing hooks made of iron for piety and penance. They also observe fasting for self-purification for seven or thirteen or twenty-one days, before performance of the ritual, depending upon intensity of devotion and faith.[39]

---

[38] 'Moksha...The masochistic way', *Indian Express*, 20 April 1993.
[39] Extracted from report, 'Festive Spirit' published in *Hindustan Times*.

4

FEAST TO THE MONKEYS
Of Stratified Societies, Festivals and Prasads

This chapter attempts to cover three aspects of society which are obliquely connected. First part covers stratification of society that prevailed in India on the basis of caste and creed. An effort has been made to research global parallels of similar instances of social stratification in different religions and societies, which independently and on the basis of their own thought process lived by the rules of social classification, presumably, for harmony and betterment of society. These systems of allocation of avocations have worked well with conviviality and cordiality in the West since the landing of Noah's Arc after the Deluge.[1]

This has been achieved because of equal respect to all vocations and honest acknowledgment of the value of every person's contribution to the overall well-being of society. But the bane of such a caste-pyramid system in India was the strict and impervious hereditary acceptance of parental avocation. Merit and capability had no recognition in society; even prodigies among *shudras* remained downtrodden. Secondly, the gentry at the top of the pyramid attracted high esteem with condescension and disrespect reserved for the bottom layers of the pyramid. Notwithstanding its original appropriateness, the caste system now seems outright discriminatory and disrespectful to individual merit.

The second part of the chapter discusses festivals. In India, festivals were specifically allotted based on the caste system. The festivals had to be celebrated as per a prescribed style and demanded a proper routine of observance. It was, thus, convenient for society because each caste had its separate space for celebration without intrusions or conflicts. Incidentally, the caste system did not interfere with the adoration of *gram devtas* or local deities because there was no philosophy rationalizing worship. The system of festivals worked well, but with passage

---

[1] Deluge, according to a Biblical story, is that great flood that engulfed the world and all living species perished except those saved in the Arc of Noah.

of time, intermingling began with mutual interests and benefits. Today, strict separation in festival celebrations is hard to find and all celebrations are treated as common *melas*. Other secular festivals have also been discussed to reveal social evolution in different communities. Some festivals from abroad have also been discussed for a global view of this 'allotment of festivals' phenomenon.

The third part of the chapter discusses the kind of items distributed as *prasad* at temples, shrines and *gurudwaras*. Common sweets and flowers are well known *prasad* items, but at certain religious places unusual items like different kinds of meat, alcoholic drinks, *bhang sharbat*, etc., are offered to the deity and after consecration, are distributed to the worshippers. Thus, motivation to partake of these benedictions may vary from the divine to the profane based on the shades of devotion. This implies that one may take a small quantity of alcohol-*prasad* with devotion whereas another may ask for it repeatedly to get drunk. Other unusual *prasad* items are butter from the *pindi* of the idol or thread rendered sacred and shared in small pieces as sanctified *prasad*. Faith appears to be the strong, common pillar of sustenance of such cognate practices. Further, it is faith that evokes respect of the believers for the *prasad* items.

KSHATRIYAS, THE RULERS AND BRAHMINS, THE KING-MAKERS

Hinduism, technically, is not a religion in the sense of Semitic religions of the West, which are centred around a singular divine figure and monotheistic beliefs. On the contrary, Hinduism is a medley of diverse social customs, cultural traditions, elaborate rituals, societal norms, mystical illusions, metaphysical conjectures, divine visions and celebratory festivities with a multitude of regional variations, philosophical connotations and varying interpretations. One such custom or tradition, with varied norms for different societies, is the caste system in India. There are, however, different lines of thought about the origin of this system of social order.

Rishi Manu[2] is popularly believed to have introduced a system of a caste-based society or '*varna* division' for the Indo-Aryan inhabitants in India and this societal division of population still persists, at least to some extent, despite serious efforts to neutralize this concept and its legacy. Manu had divided the society according to the avocations prevalent at the time; the different castes were as follows: brahmins, kshatriyas, vaishyas and shudras, in that order of precedence and importance. It was a societal pyramid of relevance and respect, as also of command and obedience. Manu's Dharamsastra, popularly called Manusmriti and academically referred to as the rules of Manu, propounded a closed, hierarchical and segmentary social order. The tiers of societal placement were impervious, insular and unbreachable. The castes were, thus, hereditary and stratified; their respective privileges were enjoyed and the relative status, restrictions and condemnations were endured.

It is also contended that the caste system originated in the later Vedic periods because Rig Veda, which is the first, oldest and most important of the Vedas, refers to many occupations in society but does not allude to any stratified caste system as such. It is, however, in the Yajur Veda and the Atharva Veda that about 66 castes are mentioned to comprise four *varnas* namely, brahmin, kshatriya, vaishya and shudra. Later, Puranas refer to about 150 hybrid castes or *jatis*, which at the present time in India, can be estimated at over 5000 *jatis* or sub-castes.

Interestingly, *varna* in Sanskrit means colour and this system is possibly indicative of the Aryan ethnocentric view and colour consciousness. Aryans from Central Asia were fair complexioned and distinguished themselves from brown

---

[2] Sage Manu is believed to be svayambhua yet considered to be spiritual son of Brahma. Being the first man (*manav*), he is attributed to be the progenitor of humanity.

coloured natives and dark-skinned Dravidian ethnic groups and created an implied assumption of superiority and ethnic exclusivity. Thus, the Aryan stakeholders perpetuated the caste system and created a social hierarchy, with the Aryans at the top of the hierarchal pyramid, to elicit respect and demand observance of the social status.[3]

As per another philosophical thought from other sacred Hindu scriptures, it is believed that the *varna* system in India is much older and was originated by Brahma, the creator of the Universe. It is stated that Brahma established this system when he peopled the earth. The brahmins were created from his head or brain and possessed spiritual nobility; the kshatriyas or *rajahs* and warriors issued forth from his shoulders and arms and were strong in physique; the vaishyas came from his belly and were adept in meeting the daily needs of the society; and shudras were derived from his feet and seemed best suited for performing requisite errands and services for all other *varnas*.

It may be easy to understand the oblique allegorical significance of this legend and distinctly trace the relative importance or attach degrees of subordination to the different castes[4], yet there is a fallacy in understanding the true import of the caste system. For a body to live well and harmoniously, all functions and roles are equally important and indispensable. It is also believed that since the 'creator-body' from which all castes originated and came forth was one and the same, hence, all castes derived the same genes, which implied equality in status and importance. Inequality and the concept of graded

---

[3] Hakeem Abdul Hameed, ed., *Islam at a Glance*, (New Delhi: Vikas Publishing House, 1981), 94–95.

[4] Dubois, *Hindu Manners, Customs and Ceremonies*, 47. Incidentally, the word 'caste' has been derived from the Portugese language and is used in Europe to designate the different tribes or classes. Interestingly, it has become popular and common in India almost for the same purpose.

respect were possibly absent from the original idea, which had doctrinal approval, and unnecessarily crept in as a product of history, politics and power play.

In India too, each caste had a task cut out for it and was ordained to deliver best results. But the professions were tiered in hierarchy and graded in their importance with descending order of dignity and respect. The brahmins were the educated class, with the right to acquire knowledge and were expected to be proficient in Sanskrit *mantras*. As teachers, they would disseminate requisite education to the entitled castes only. They were destined to fulfil the performance of functions of spiritual and priestly duties and show the way of salvation to their fellow-men. This was the elitist caste that was most revered for its knowledge and wisdom and it generally managed the priesthood and temple affairs. They also acted as high priests for important religious ceremonies of the state as well as functioned as advisor to the reigning king and the nobles.

However, not each and every member of the caste-community can be equally learned and proficient in the hereditary profession, therefore, brahmins, who could not learn Sanskrit with ease or remember by rote the Vedic *mantras* to be recited at special occasions or were not adept in ceremonially conducting specific rituals, were called 'Omi-brahmins' who would just repeatedly chant 'AUM, AUM' and meditate in the name of God. They were, thus, assigned to preside over less important ceremonies and manage other mundane affairs of the temple.

The next caste in priority and importance was Kshatriyas. They were endowed with physical force and were destined to undergo the fatigues of war. This warrior class were the subaltern rulers, obeyed the king and defended the frontiers of the country. Their role was administration of the state and defense of the national boundaries and offensive operations in pursuance of annexation of neighbouring territories to expand national dominion and extend the frontiers of the state. They were trained soldiers and chieftains manning the armed forces for the reigning king. Thus, their numbers and strength were determinable and could only be improved in numbers by increased procreation within the caste. Other methods to create and maintain a formidable force was by improving their fighting skills or equipping them with more lethal weaponry or better accoutrement. This was the governing or the ruling class.

Vaishyas were the next rung of society and had a duty to sustain the society with commercial facilities and availability of daily-need products and fulfilment of common societal requirements. In short, their duty was to provide the food, the clothing and other bodily necessities of man. Thus, this caste comprised of agriculture farmers, traders and merchants. A few members of this caste were also producers of goods. They ensured availability of all types of household, community and state requirements and were involved in value-addition to the wares on sale. Their motivation was profit and at the same time, to promote economic growth in the state for betterment of the society.

The base of the pyramid consisted of shudras who were lowest in hierarchy but not the least important in their contribution to the society through their avocations and societal functions as well as by their demographic numbers. Their ordained lot was general servitude and hard labour in the fields. They were expected to provide for all types of services that were wanted for the comfort and convenience and cleanliness among the upper classes as also of the society.[5] It was a service-provider class and could not climb to or upgrade to a higher caste despite prodigious wisdom, extra-ordinary learning capabilities and noteworthy competence in skills of the higher castes.

---

[5] Ibid.

Indeed, it has sometimes happened that persons, born outside of the brahmanical order, have been highly endowed with spirituality and meditative capabilities, despite being denied the privilege of education and learning. But these persons were not granted permission to listen to or recite religious Sanskrit texts. Some such enlightened souls from lower castes have attained sainthood and have composed their own *'vani'* or spiritual poetry in their respective native languages. Some such verses of poetry from the lower caste saints, denigrating the caste system and upholding equality of human beings, have been respectfully included in Sri Guru Granth Sahib, the holy book of the Sikhs. The examples are many but a few acknowledged saints like Kabir, Ravidas, Namdev, Dhanna, *etc.*, may be quoted here.

The pyramidal hierarchy was strait-jacketed and insular. Crossing the caste barriers to reach an upper caste was taboo and prohibited and, at times, even attracted harsh sanctions and decapacitating sentences to the adventurous. Shudras were, thus, generally a repressed class, most insulted, mostly shunned and had nothing to boast about to satisfy their ego or restore self-respect. The purpose of this definitional allocation was to create generational bonding and early grooming in the respective caste-wise cultures and duties to be eventually discharged for a life time. Repression of lower castes was then justified in many ways. No one could forsake its bounden duties and had to perform the same in the interest of maintaining social order and healthy metabolism of society.

Thus, *'dharma'* as duty and *'maryada'* as social order, were the strangle-hold of this sort of regimented and claustrophobic caste lines of social duties and societal demarcations; and caste boundaries gradually sharpened and persisted for many centuries with virtual brahmanic autarchy wielding near-absolute power. Inter-caste mingling and marriages were strictly prohibited and were considered a taboo and deemed to be a dishonour that could even result in honour killing of the rebels. Hindu society smugly lived with this caste arrangement that suited different communities in different ways. In fact, beneficiaries became proponents of the system and acted as the instruments of enforcement of the practice and its continued perpetuation. No wonder, benefits and privileges tended to get institutionalized and were zealously protected by stakeholders.

Thus, what started as social reformation and a societal structuring process in the overall interest of the society and its harmonious working, intended for prosperity for all, started degenerating and engendered patterns of social inequality in what is now a pervasive caste system prevalent in the Indian sub-continent. Throughout its history, independent variables in the context of social, cultural, legal and political systems have contributed to this collective social transformation. There occurred a conflict between the doctrinal ideal and the complex social phenomenon of castes that caused a degenerative mutation. The result of this repression has been continuing for centuries now.

However, lately, mechanisms for the emancipation of the lowest caste have been set in motion by constitutional protection, legal enactments and social engineering but the process appears rather slow and generational. Fortunately, the process began in earnest after India achieved independence and the results seem to be promising.

THE SIKH PERCEPTION OF SOCIETY

Sikhs are a small community. They exist as a separate and distinct religious denomination that originally draw from the state of Punjab in North India and have since spread from this region to different parts of the country. This religious minority is the follower of Sikh *gurus* who preached about a classless, casteless fraternity of Sikhs, which believed in equality of all men and women in the society. Guru Nanak's social philosophy is contained in his verse, *Brahmin, khatri, shud, vaish; Updesh chaun varna ko sanjha,* which means that he has the same duty to teach all *varnas.* This was the Sikh social reform introduced into the then divided society which had acquired negative characteristics of a caste system (this covers a period of two centuries starting from the 15th century.). This institution of casteism needed reformation and a change of image, which believed in equality without discrimination. 'Equality without discrimination' was the loud slogan of the Sikh *gurus.*

Thus, Sikhs subscribe to a different concept and connotation of a social system and structuring, and practise no caste differentiation; after baptism all baptized individuals belong to a single, unified community, where everyone is considered equal and treated with dignity and as belonging to one religion with no classification based on caste or *varna.* This type of social system was promulgated with the preachings of Guru Nanak, the first guru of the Sikhs, in the 15th century. Guru Nanak started to spread the message of universal humanity and inclusive equality that transcended the barriers of caste, creed, race, region, language and, even, gender in the Indian sub-continent. This was a social revolution with different moorings and motivation.

The thrust of the Sikh gurus was against discrimination or domination of any kind that generates atrocities among humankind. Therefore, his followers, generally called Sikhs (loosely meaning pupils), though came from diverse backgrounds, castes and religions, yet were considered equal, made equal and treated equal, within the Sikh community and outside. The recognition of the fundamental principle of equality of mankind by the Sikh fraternity marked a great leap forward from the prevailing beliefs of impervious stratification, unequal rights and tiered duties ascribed to the Hindus as per the caste system, indicating a person's differential social status, economic standing and political role.

Guru Nanak propagated ultimate oneness of all gods, prohibited idol worship, preached equality of all humans irrespective of religion or other distinctions, advised the tenets of good deeds and taught the Sikh religion's spiritual doctrine of *naam japo, kirat karo and wand chhako* meaning recite the name of the God, earn ethically and share with the needy. The Sikh philosophy of 'sarbat da bhalaa', meaning welfare of all in the Universe, is a unique slogan, which is a part of Sikh prayers repeated every day. Thus, in a way, it promises a just and humane world order with assured values of life, equality of humanity and dignity of mankind. This message had universal reach and mass appeal.

As a result, many individuals became Guru Nanak's followers and believers in the Sikh religion even in the foreign countries that he visited during his four sojourns in the four geographical directions; the countries, in particular, included Afghanistan, Saudi Arabia, Nepal, Bhutan, Tibet, China and Sri Lanka, to mention a few. Lately, however, the Sikh faith has reached the West including Europe, United States and Canada; transcending racial diversity, the 'White Sikhs' are significantly visible there. There are also 'Yellow Sikhs' in China and a small number of 'Black Sikhs' of African ethnicity, concentrated in a couple of countries in the African continent. Today, emigrant and locally converted Sikhs inhabit almost all parts of the world.

The general impression of Sikhs is that of a warrior community or a martial race, but in reality, this identity formed due to a circumstantial role that was thrust upon them by the repression of the Sikhs and Hindus by the Mughal rulers in India. However, the Sikhs practise all avocations and adeptly perform all sorts of activities including *sewa* or menial services at *gurudwaras*, which is reverentially exalted in many ways and those voluntarily performing such activities are held in high esteem.

All Sikhs, rich and poor, high caste or low caste, including non-Sikhs from lower castes, as well as people practising other religions sit together in rows, with no distinction or discrimination or segregation whatsoever and honourably share the *langar* (free meal) served at Sikh gurudwaras. In a dedicated spirit of service to humanity, *langar* is served with due humility and offered with utmost dignity and respect to all those sitting in *pangat* (congregation in rows) and eating together.

To specifically reiterate, the status of women within the Sikh community is of equality or perhaps a shade better. The Sikh gurus preached that women cannot be lowly because even kings are begotten by them. The sacred verse espousing this view goes like this: *so kiyon manda aakhiye, jit jammey rajaan*. Thus acceptance of principle for all in the Sikh religion is indeed laudable and worth emulating.

STRATIFICATION OF SOCIETY: GLOBAL PERSPECTIVE

Interestingly, caste system has prevailed in other ancient civilizations also, except that, the caste system in the other ancient civilizations accorded the same consideration and sensitivity to all castes. In the West, the caste system was a consequence of the Great Flood that deluged the earth and turned it into a vast global desert. The entire world perished and after the disaster, the human survivors in the Noah's Ark, with the other birds and beasts, landed in the plains of Sennaar and re-inhabited the barren earth. In due course, they started procreating and indulged in other activities they were best at like agricultural cultivation or manufacturing implements for collective survival and living. Moses mentions of social stratification and a caste system prevalent at the time of restart of the settlements.[6]

---

[6] Ibid., 47, 100.

A tiered avocational distinction and societal classification into castes has existed among the ancient Egyptians also, where 'the law assigned an occupation to each individual, which was handed down from father to the son. It was forbidden to any man to have two professions, or to change on his own. Each caste had a special quarter assigned to it, and people from a different caste were prohibited from settling there'.[7] Despite the official allotment of avocation and the residential segregation, 'all castes and all professions were held in esteem: all employments, even of the meanest kind were alike regarded as honourable'.[8] The contribution of every caste and its calling was deemed to be towards achieving social harmony and general good of society at large. The society was sensitive and valued dignity of labour with equality among all, and there was no prejudice attached to any caste.

Islam, basically, believes in the concept of *tauhid* or unity of god as monotheistic belief. This 'theological doctrine delineates major policy implications both for perception and, more significantly, for the structuring of human society.... By refutation of duality or multiplicity of god-hood, Islam sought to unify humankind through obeisance to an integral, indivisible, impersonal... God of all the Universe'.[9] This Islamic social system was a radical breakthrough in human civilization 'against the backdrop of social patterns obtaining in pre-Islamic and non-Islamic civilizations'.[10] The message of Islam was clear and emphasized 'equality of men and their distinction based on piety and noble deeds rather than the accident of birth and the accumulation of wealth'.[11] In summation, Prophet Mohammed's exhortation was, 'Bring

---

[7] Ibid, 31.
[8] Ibid.
[9] Hakeem Abdul Hameed, ed., *Islam at a Glance*, (New Delhi: Vikas Publishing House, 1981), 90–91.
[10] Ibid., 92.
[11] Ibid., 93.

me not your genealogies but your good deeds'[12] that will be judged by motives.' A famous *hadith* amplifies this thought in the following words: 'God doth not accept faith if it is not expressed in action, and doth not accept action if it does not conform to faith.'[13]

This belief emanated a clear resonant affirmation of a new nexus of social relationships assuring fraternity and equality, which led to the creation of an egalitarian polity in the early phase of Islam. The Islamic social order was, thus, doctrinally integrated, inclusive and definitive but socially open and pervious with no labels whatsoever. Nonetheless, Islam has a different version of caste system which is not intrinsic to society but imposed by external circumstances and extraneous pressures. With the passage of time and birth of ethnic groupings, hierarchical pressures, sectarian considerations, movement of people to other lands and political ascendency, the core message of Islam, propagating equality and distinction based on piety and noble deeds rather than accident of birth or accumulation of wealth, became obscure.

The first religious divide led to the formation of two sects: Sunnis and Shias. Further, expediency led to social stratification and political gradations. The *Quraish*, the then aristocratic tribe of Prophet Mohammed, divided itself into two major streams of Hashimites and Umayyads. Soon enough, Sayyids gained importance as descendents of the Prophet. Ashrafs were descendents of the Prophet's daughter, Fatima, and became the new nobility. Last in the social ladder was Ajlaf, which literally means rabble or riff-raff.[14]

The gradations among Muslims became more pronounced and proliferated by contact with the Indian caste system. Muslims acquired new *zats* or *biradaris* (professional groupings), for example, butchers became Qureshis, weavers

---

[12] Ibid., 91.
[13] Ibid., 92.
[14] Ibid., 95–100.

became Ansaris or Momins, commercial communities became Ismailis, Khojas, Bohras, etc., and mercantile Muslims of Tamil Nadu came to be known as Labbas. Khans, as Muslim kshatriyas, got elevated because of political clout and authority. In a way, this self-acquired superiority still attaches to them and it gains them respect among the Muslims. Be that as it may, ethnic groupings with gradations, *zats* and *biradaris* and other assumed elevations, do vitiate the original spirit of the caste-less and class-less fraternity of Islam.

CASTE TAG ON HINDU FESTIVALS

Interestingly, Sage Manu, while establishing his concept of societal functioning order and allocating caste-vocations in the Hindu society for a harmonious social order and to ensure conflict-free living, laid down certain ground rules of behaviour and class interaction and segregation. These rules enforced the practice of endogamy and hypergamy in marriages; avoidance of inter-caste dining and inter-caste social gatherings; restriction on food, drinking and smoking, i.e., a brahmin could consume only satvik food whereas kshtriyas could eat meat, and shudras could drink alcohol and/or smoke; distinction in social customs, conventions, etiquette, clothes, appearance and speech; differences in rituals and other social privileges or disabilities; and closed-caste cohesion and occupational association. Further, with the concept of 'pollution' associated with sudras, the possible perviousness in the social order was completely sealed for upward mobility.

In consonance with the abovementioned caste restrictions and social disabilities, Manu also earmarked special festivals for celebration by each of the four castes or *varnas*. These varied according to caste accomplishments and societal purpose of respective community. So, each caste celebrated its designated festivals, allocated by Manu, based on vocational proclivities and enjoyed the festivities with religious commitment and emotional fervour. Their special festivals were in-house for the caste and restricted thereto for celebration and enjoyment. Other festivals did not concern them for observance and festivity and thus 'others to the festival' remained only incidental or peripheral to or indulged in only symbolic participation on the occasion, more in the sense of fair than solemn celebration.

Perhaps, the purpose behind this allotment of specific festivals to each caste was to create exclusivity and insularity in society. At the same time, it was intended to foster inclusive positivity, create cohesion, nurture kinship, promote specific functional aspirations and to permit free play of celebratory instincts of each caste. This created a sense of empathy and led to mutual sharing and caring within the fraternity. Understandably, this could generate social harmony and keep each caste tied firmly to their roots in the interest of and for the welfare of entire populace. Community order and cumulative betterment were the primary aims of the concept and for its enforcement.

As per Manu's allocation, brahmins got festivals relating to worship of gods, to display the performance of religious rites and for practice of spirituality. Their share included festivals like Rama Navami, Janmashtami, Ekadashi, Saraswati Puja, Guru Poornima and the likes. These festivals attracted persons from other castes to attend the religious rite. They were permitted to visit the temples to pay obeisance and to seek blessings of the deity. The worship and bestowal of boons was regulated by the brahmin sorority.

The kshatriyas were allocated the festival of Dussehra, which celebrated the occasion of victory of Lord Rama over the demon, Ravana. This was apt for the warrior community to rededicate itself, with commitment, to emerging and ensuing victories. The caste members celebrate the occasion by performing ritualistic sacrifice of animals and enjoy feasting on the animals' meat. This, in a way, provided them bodily strength to be prepared for martial duties in defense of the nation and to be fit to undertake wars to annex more territories for their king.

In a similar gesture, the Gorkhas of Nepal,[15] display strong kshatriya qualities and indulge in heavy feasting on meat on the day of Dussehra. They worship Lord Pashupati Nath and at the temple dedicated to the god, near Kathmandu, they perform a ritualistic sacrifice of animals, praying for the happiness and prosperity of the Nepalese community. It was reported that in the year 2014, nearly 5000 animals were ritually sacrificed on the day of Dussehra.

The vaishyas were allocated the festival of Diwali. It is a festival of the traders, who worship Goddess Lakshmi, who is the bestower of wealth and material benefits as also higher profits (*Shubh Laabh*). Thus, this festival rightly suited the temperament and aspirations of this caste and is celebrated with great rejoicing, fervour and solemn devotion. Nowadays, this festival has been voluntarily embraced by all castes and even non-Hindu communities. It has, thus, assumed a secular character with a prolonged period of celebrations and exchange of goodwill gifts.

Further, shudras were allotted the festival of Holi in its varied forms. Over a period, this festival got debased in character and method of celebration, promoting 'free for all' and 'all is fair' attitude during the celebrations. This 'all is fair' license is resented by certain communities but the festivities have persisted despite the disrepute. This festival also furthered a 'forgive and forget' philosophy for past animosities and grudges and encouraged starting afresh with a clean slate. It strived for catharsis of negativity and ushered positivity for the ensuing year. Even then, total cleansing of the buried ill-will in the heart never really happened. It is also relevant to know that upper castes also have started celebrating Holi but differently and ceremoniously; yet mostly in similar style and with same purpose.

---

[15] Nepal, up until a few years ago, was the only proclaimed Hindu country in the world.

DIWALI: ONE FESTIVAL, DIFFERENT REASONS TO CELEBRATE

Diwali (or Deepawali) is one festival of India that is universally celebrated by almost all communities of India; though the festival may be celebrated with different beliefs, different motivations, different perspectives, different manner, different solemnity or in a different manner with different rituals. In different parts of India, it may even be observed by different names; yet the religious fervour in observance of the occasion and the exuberant grace in the festivities, nevertheless, remain solemn and celebratory.

Frankly, this festival of lights and fire crackers, even among the Hindu community, carries a different meaning and differentiated importance and celebrates varying perspectives based on community beliefs or caste affiliations. Apart from these variations, regional distinctions are based on affection for a particular local deity and the myths and popularly held beliefs surrounding his/her worship. But ultimately, all diversity metamorphosizes into the common festival of Diwali.

In North India, Diwali signifies Lord Rama's homecoming from the fourteen-year exile imposed on him by his father, King Dashrath's wishes, arising out of the uncomfortable predicament forced upon him by his wife Kaikeyi who wanted her son with Dashrath (Bharat) to sit on Ayodhya's throne. It also denotes the return of Rama to his native city of Ayodhya after killing Ravana, the king of Lanka (present Sri Lanka). Rama's return was marked with salutary lighting of lamps, bursting of firecrackers and general rejoicing among the people of Ayodhya.

While Rama, Sita (Rama's wife) and Lakshman (Rama's brother) were in exile, Ravana had abducted Sita and refused to let her go with honour; as a result, a war ensued between Rama and Ravana. Rama defeated Ravana and rescued Sita. Diwali is, thus, celebrated as triumph of good and defeat of evil. However, people of a village in Uttar Pradesh believe that Mandodri, the wife of Ravana, was from their village; hence, they treat Ravana as a 'virtual son-in-law' and have subdued observance coinciding with his death.

In South India, Diwali has an altogether different connotation and significance; it celebrates the destruction of the tyrant demon Narakasura by Lord Krishna and Satyabhama. Among the trading communities of Gujarat, Goddess Mahalakshmi rules the festivities. For them, Diwali involves worship and propitiation of the deity of wealth for the growth of business and family prosperity.

In the eastern parts of India, in the states of Assam, Bengal, Bihar and Odisha, Diwali involves conducting *puja* for Mother Kali, again in joyous celebration of victory of good over evil, in the unique style of *Shakta* cult. Goddess Kali is the creator of the entire universe and can devour any entity at her will; in other words, she creates and destroys *maya* at her volition and design. As a fierce deity, she sucks the blood of evil doers and for that reason she wears a necklace of fifty skulls of the *rakshasas* and is dressed in red robes.[16]

According to the Nirukta Tantra, she has beautiful, long tresses which are symbolic of *maya*. She is considered superior to the primal energy of Brahma, Vishnu and Shiva. She is omnipotent and omniscient and has no beginning or end, thus, is eternal. Goddess Kali takes on various forms, like Lakshmi in Vaikuntha, Radha in Gokula, Sati on Mount Kailash or Chamunda in the Himalayas. Kali Puja is invoked on *amavasya* and devotees pray for freedom, knowledge and wisdom.[17]

---

[16] Acharya Mukul Bikash Mishra, 'The Mysterious Goddess Kali' in Meditations column.
[17] Ibid.

Diwali, in fact, is not a one-day festival, but a celebratory season for the Hindus that starts a few days before the day of Diwali and continues for almost a week after Diwali. Some of the ancillary functions and rituals of Diwali, which differ with change in geography, are briefly described hereinunder.

Bengalis celebrate Kali Puja one day before Diwali. But for Maharashtrians, it is an elaborate five-day affair with continuing festivities and offering and consumption of traditional sweets like *karanji, chakli and laadu*.

In North India, Bhaiya Dooj and Vishwakarma day are also important events. On Bhaiya Dooj, which is celebrated on the second day after Diwali, sisters, particularly the ones who are married, visit their brothers and present gifts to them and apply *tika* on their forehead to renew their sibling bonding and filial love. Vishwakarma is believed to be the primal artisan and craftsman, omniscient and omni-practical in respect of every type of work and material creation. This day, in his remembrance, is devoted to cleaning and worship of tools of work; artisans do no labour or paid work on this day.

For Kashmiris, Diwali comprises two main occasions, namely, Dhantryodashi and Sukhsuptika. Dhantryodashi falls on a day before Diwali and is associated with acquisition of gold jewellery or a precious possession or even household utensils; while *Sukhsuptika* means to sleep with worriless happiness. The latter is one of the oldest rituals practised by Kashmiri pandits and it also finds a mention in the Nilamata Purana.

Trading communities like *gujaratis* and *marwaris* specially mark the day after Diwali as the beginning of the New Year. They usher in the year with 'Chopda Pujan' in which new account books for the new year are worshipped and marked for *shubh laabh*, meaning good profits. For these communities, Dhanteras that falls two days before Diwali, and Govardhan Puja are also important.

One of the last days of celebration of the Diwali season is celebrated as Chhat Puja, geographically observed in Bihar and adjoining areas, and by *biharis* wherever they are settled. It is primarily a rite of worship performed by women, who stand in water and pray to the setting sun, in the evening, on the sixth day after Diwali. The prayer includes an offering of water to the sun. The worship of the setting sun marks the uniqueness of this festival, because normally among Hindus, and generally even around the world, it is the rising sun that is worshipped, physically and metaphorically, but on Chhat Puja, prayers are offered to the setting sun.

The last *puja* of the season is performed fifteen days after the day of Diwali, on a full-moon night, known as '*Boita Bandhana*', and is celebrated by the Oriya community. It is an age-old tradition where symbolic ships sail in a water body and prayers are held for their smooth and safe voyage. This is reminiscent of the times when Odisha had great maritime relations with eastern countries across the sea; when mothers used to see off their sons who were going on board ships into the high seas for trade with Indonesia and Thailand, and prayed for their safety and well-being.[18]

Diwali also celebrates the power of three goddesses, namely, Lakshmi, Kali and Saraswati. There are various legends associated with these deities and the festival of Diwali. A few are narrated hereinafter.

In a mythical tale, on the new moon night or *amavasya* of the month of *Kartik*, Goddess Lakshmi was incarnated during the churning of the ocean of milk (*Kshirsagar*). The churning was done by *devtas* on one side and *rakshasas* on the other side. Thirteen other items were also pulled out of the ocean;

---

[18] Nivedita Khandekar, 'One festival, a myriad way to celebrate it,' *Hindustan Times*, 7 November.

amrit, a nectar that immortalizes the drinker, a pot of liquor that intoxicates the drinker, a ruby and a horse called Erawat, among other things.

As per another legend, Vishnu, in his fifth incarnation as Vamana, rescued Lakshmi from the prison of King Bali, and this provides the believers another reason to celebrate Diwali.

Another legend, more popular in South India, mentions that Lord Krishna killed Narakasur on the eve of Diwali, that is, Narak Chaturdashi. Lord is believed to have slain this demon king to rescue 16,000 women from his captivity. Lord Krishna returned home in the wee hours of the next morning when some women got together and gave a massage to Lord Krishna with scented oils and gave him a good bath to wash away all the filth and blood from his body. Since then it has become a custom in South India to take oil bath before sunrise on this auspicious day.

According to another legend from Mahabharata, the Pandavas returned to their kingdom after completing the exile of 12 years on the day of Diwali. They had to undergo this exile as a condition imposed by the Kauravas, after being defeated by them at a game of dice. Their subjects celebrated the return of the Pandava brothers and their wife, Draupadi, by lighting earthen lamps in their welcome. Another small, historical fact related to Diwali concerns the coronation of one of the greatest Hindu kings, Vikramaditya, on the day od Diwali.

Jains, all over India and abroad, celebrate Diwali as the anniversary of liberation and attainment of eternal salvation by Lord Mahavir, the twenty-fourth *Tirthankar*, from the cycle of life and death, during the Swati Nakshatra. It is the day of *nirvana mahotsav*, that is, enlightenment of Lord Mahavir or the day he attained *moksha* (emancipation), which coincidentally falls on *amavasya* (no moon) night. 'Thus, Jains do not mourn the death of Lord Mahavir but celebrate his emancipation from life', asserted a *muni* of the *Sthanakwasi* sect of Jains. The community also marks this occasion by reading the Uttaradhyayan Sutra, the last message of Lord Mahavir, for fifteen days.[19] The Upanishadas also preach *Tamsoma Jyotirgamya,* which means 'to illumine our life from darkness'. This is the core essence and the spirit of Diwali.[20]

For Sikhs, Diwali is special for three historical reasons. First, in 1577AD, on this auspicious day of Diwali, on the request of Guru Arjun Dev, the fifth Sikh guru, a highly revered sufi saint, Mian Mir, laid the foundation stone of Sri Harmandir Sahib, now popularly known as Golden Temple, located in Amritsar. This project of the construction of Sri Harmandir Sahib and the *sarovar* (holy tank) around it, was completed in about three decades. This site is considered the holiest of all Sikh shrines. Incidentally, it has been internationally rated as the cleanest religious place in the world with the highest footfall.

The second important historical reason that makes this day important is Bandi-Chhod Divas (freedom from bondage day). Much later, Guru Hargobind, the sixth guru of the Sikhs, was imprisoned in the Gwalior fort by King Jehangir, at the insistence and persuasion of local rulers, as a perceived threat to the Mughal authority. In fact, the young guru's father, Guru Arjun Dev had already been tortured and martyred in Lahore in a conspiracy by the local rulers and with the approval of Jehangir. As a result, there were protests in the Punjab and many petitions were made to the king, but to no avail.

But later when Jehangir fell sick, he was advised by his sooth-sayers to set Guru Hargobind free because he is a god's man, so as to get back his health and fitness. Orders were accordingly conveyed, but Guru Hargobind, out of compassion,

---

[19] Ibid.
[20] Swami Chaitanya Keerti, 'The real spirit of the festival of lights', Meditations column.

refused to leave the prison, having seen fifty-two other small-time Hindu rulers illegally dispossessed of their lands and arrested and kept in penury. Permission was given that anyone who can hold on to the guru's robe (chola) and get out with him, will be set free. It was a cunning ploy by Jehangir's courtiers, who knew about the exit from the prison being narrow. On the other hand, Guru Hargobind requested for a special robe with fifty-two tug lines (tassels) of varying lengths. It was stitched to order and, thus, the illegally imprisoned rulers held on to the tug lines and came out in single file and were set free. This event of 'release of the bound' that happened on the day Diwali is now traditionally observed as Bandi-Chhod Divas (release from confinement day) by the Sikhs in general, and is particularly celebrated at Sri Harmandir Sahib, Amritsar.[21]

The third historical reason is the remembrance of the martyrdom of Bhai Mani Singh. Sikh history records that Bhai Mani Singh wrote, as dictated, the final version of the Guru Granth Sahib as recalled from memory by Guru Gobind Singh in 1704 at Damdama Sahib. After completion of this task, Bhai Mani Singh was directed to assume the management of Sri Harmandir Sahib in the year 1708. In the same year, King Aurangzeb died, and in those days, celebration of Diwali by anyone, was banned by the Mughals.

In the year 1737, Bhai Mani Singh specially obtained permission from Zakaria Khan, the Mughal governor of Punjab, to allow Diwali celebrations at the Golden Temple on a Zakia payment of ₹5000 as religious tax, to the state. He later learnt of a plot hatched by Zakaria Khan to kill the Sikhs gathering in the temple on this occasion. This was sheer deceit. To prevent this massacre, Bhai Mani Singh sent word in secret to the Sikh *sangat* (devotees) to stay away. This frustrated

---

[21] Renuka Naraynan, 'Festival of India', *Indian Express*. Later published as part of book titled, *Faith: Filling the God size hole*, Penguin Books, India, 2003.

Khan's plan, and infuriated at his failure, he sentenced Bhai Mani Singh to death and ordered his execution by cutting of his body, joint by joint, at Lahore Fort.[22] Bhai Mani Singh's martyrdom is solemnly and poignantly remembered on Bandi-Chhod Divas with dignified pride and grateful remembrance.

As such, it can be said that the Sikh celebration of Diwali relates to the release from human bondage in the cycle of life and death, in symbolic sync with Guru Hargobind's release from the fort of Gwalior. The flames of the lighted lamps represents burning away of the human ego and baser desires. It, thus, creates, at the same time, a yearning in the purified soul for sublime emancipation and to merge with god for salvation and eternal bliss.

LA TOMATINA FESTIVAL OF SPAIN

Spain can boast of a unique festival called 'La Tomatina', which is held in the town of Bunol. It is an occasion when people throw tomatoes at each other in a gesture of fun-fighting and frolicking about in the red pulp beneath their feet. Revelers literally paint the town red. For this purpose, the organizers of the annual La Tomatina festival toss 145 tons of over-ripe tomatoes into the streets from six large trucks, which the crowds quickly convert into a sea of pink and red. Some revelers, to protect their eyes from unintended harm, wear goggles, while some buildings are draped in tarpaulin to save the walls from being ruined by the splashes of red and other discolouration. The joyous crowds, pelting tomatoes at each other and soaked in pulp, present a scene worthy of modern art.

Memory recalls that the La Tomatina festival originated from a spontaneous bust-up amongst villagers in the year 1945.

---

[22] Ibid.

Possibly, it was a year of a glut in tomato production beyond economic sales. The festival was banned for some time in the 1950s during the dictatorship of General Francisco Franco. However, the custom revived in the 1980s and gained quick popularity across Spain. It has since survived and draws large crowds of Spaniards as well as foreigners for the customary revelry and relaxation, covered in tomato pulp. In the year 2019, the town hall of Bunol distributed more than 20,000 tickets to watch and participate in the festival.

MOTHER MARY'S ROSARY

It is not uncommon to see wrinkle-faced grandmothers praying with a rosary (mala), a string of beads, in their hand and reciting religious words in a repetitive nature. This happens irrespective of religion or geography. The Christian rosary or *vinati* (a string of beads) is roughly comparable to what a *mala* is to Hindus, Buddhists and Sikhs and *tasbih* or *misbaha* is to Muslims. The only difference is the number of beads in the string: *Vinati* has fifty beads; the Hindu *mala* has 108 beads plus one *meru* bead in the centre; the Hindu *simarna* (a smaller version of a *mala*, normally worn on the wrist when not in use) has 27 beads plus one *meru* bead; and the Muslim *tasbih* may have 33 beads or 99 beads plus one.[23]

The rosary is an aid to prayer to recall religious beliefs with focus and concentration for private or collective prayers. It, thus, becomes 'a good example of a physical act triggering memory and bringing to mind central ideas of the religion'.[24] All the prayers by virtue of their reflective character

---

[23] There are smaller versions of these. The smaller *mala* is called *simarna* and has 27 plus one beads, it needs four repeats to equalize one *mala* recitation. The smaller *tasbih* has 33 plus one beads and needs three repeats. The beads of *tesbih* are made from *zaitun* (olive) wood and each bead is engraved with Allah or Mohammed.

[24] Douglas Davies, 'Introduction: Raising the Issues' in *Worship*, eds. Jean Holm and John Bowker (London, Pinter Publishers, 1994), 4.

and meditative concentration have, in common, a tranquil or calming effect on the mind of those who pray with them. Repetitive recitation leads believers to a spiritual experience with god and impels them to do good deeds and strive for universal peace and brotherhood.

The month of May is the traditional time of prayers with the rosary for the catholic Christians all over the world. It is called the month of May devotions. During this month, children and elders, all gather in front of the grotto of the Virgin Mary, usually in the courtyard of a church, and recite the rosary together. These recitations in prayer are, both, the means of reaching god and produce a deep love for god. Rituals, sincerely followed with devotional faith, can lead to an exalting spiritual experience.

The rosary is a simple yet profound and meaningful prayer device through which one recites prayers including the Hail Mary, the Blessed Virgin Mary, and the Mother of Christ. It is recited repeatedly with devotion, beseeching Mother Mary to pray for the believers to God for mercy, grace and good life on the earth and also, thereafter. For devout Christians, meditation, in the holy names of the Blessed Trinity (Father, Son and Holy Spirit) and the remembrance of the Virgin Mary, renews in them deep faith and a missionary spirit that makes them more loving and compassionate to others, specially the poor and the afflicted. It is also believed that Christian mysticism is rooted in wordless prayer. Whatever be the belief of the people, it deserve veneration.

However, in the modern times and for the millennial generation that loves technology, the Vatican has launched a new wearable device that allows the ease of a 'click of the mouse' to pray. This device will be part of a digital network, creating 'virtual pilgrim communities'. In fact, this 'click-to-pray-e-Rosary' bracelet contains a 'smart cross' that uses Bluetooth technology to transmit prayers, track health information and deliver religious messages on your phone.[25]

The e-Rosary consists of ten black agate and hematite rosary beads and also a smart cross that stores data from the connected app. It is activated by making a simple sign of the Cross. According to the Vatican announcement, the device is positioned as a tool for learning how to pray with the rosary for peace in the world. It is priced at 99 euros.[26]

Besides, a reflection on the joys, sorrows and the final triumph of Jesus Christ in twenty contemplative scenes of his life, with the aid of a string of beads, leads the 'meditator' to inner transformation and spiritual elevation. Thus, Christians have a firm belief that a true believer in the rosary is bestowed with divine mercy and is never left unaided by the lord. Many have been granted their wishes while many others have experienced the power of the Divine through the traditional rosary when recited with full faith and true devotion.

UNUSUAL *PRASAD* ITEMS

Prasad is the sanctified edible or inedible item that is ritually distributed to the devotees at a particular temple or shrine, every day or on auspicious occasions. We are all familiar with *laddoos* (a confectionery), *peras* (a milk based product), sugary *batashas* or sugar-coated puffed rice or wheat-based preparations made with pure *ghee* (clarified butter) or milk, which are normally distributed to the devotees visiting and paying obeisance in the temples. Apart from these items of confectionery, fruits of different kind are also offered at various shrines, either cut-up into pieces or as a whole and

---

[25] Vatican news report, 'Vatican launches click-to-pray eRosary wearable', *The Times of India*, 18 October 2019.
[26] Ibid.

are distributed as *prasad*. In certain shrines, flowers and petal are also distributed as *prasad* to the devotees.

The Sikh practice is to distribute '*Karah parshad*' after *bhog* (benediction), among visitors who come to a *gurudwara* (Sikh temple). This preparation is also sweet and is made from wheat flour, sugar, clarified butter and water, which are all cooked on high flame while chanting or reciting *Gurbani* from the Sikh scriptures. It is sanctified by cutting a piece of the sweet with a small iron sword (kirpaan) and is thereafter, distributed hot to the congregation. The Muslim dargahs are usually offered *churma* which is prepared using flat Indian breads made of wheat flour (chapati), roughly sheared and sweetened with jaggery or sugar.

These are the usual offerings made to the pantheon of gods, on specific days, among the Hindus in temples or Sikhs in gurudwaras or Muslims in dargahs and seem so customary, natural and obvious. But this generality and familiarity disappears in the face of distribution of unheard of *prasads* including mutton meat, fish meat or liquids like liquor or *bhang sharbat* or a piece of butter taken from an idol or even a piece of cotton thread that has been rendered auspicious. A few instances of unusual *prasad* items that different shrines are known for distributing, are narrated in following paragraphs.

COTTON THREAD AS *PRASAD*

Nanda Devi, or Maa Nandu, as she is popularly known as, was the daughter of Vasudev and Devki, the birth parents of Lord Krishna. She was killed by Kans, the cruel king of Mathura, under apprehension of a premonition that she could be a cause of his death. After this beheading, she was reborn as Nanda in Kulsari, beyond Kinner river in Uttarakhand. She married Lord Shiva whose abode was on a hilltop. Her *doli* was taken to that hilltop and Lord Shiva and Nanda got married there. A temple, known as the Nanda Devi temple, was established there to celebrate Nanda and her marriage to Lord Shiva. The temple is located in present-day Uttarakhand.

In this life, Nanda had seven sisters, who are symbolized as seven hilltops surrounding the Nanda Devi temple.

Each year, to honour her memory, the villagers, in symbolic celebration of her marriage to Lord Shiva, take Nanda's *doli*, (palanquin for the bride) in the form of a pilgrimage, from her maternal home in Kinner to her in-laws' home at the Nanda Devi peak. The procession, while on the pilgrimage, passes through several places. The pilgrimage also halts at several places, prominent among them being the temple of Maa Bhagwati and Yama Dwar. The last stop of the pilgrimage is at Mandoli. On the way, the procession crosses Bedi Paavan Kund, a small water body where a *rakhshas* (demon) was killed by drowning in it.

While returning from a trip to her in-laws' house, Nanda expressed a desire to bathe in the small Bedi Kund lake. But the lake had no covering or surrounding shelter to prevent unwanted persons to see her while she bathed in the lake. She asked the ladies accompanying her to wind a cotton thread (*mouli*) around the lake through which no one would be able to see Nanda bathing in the lake. The women complied and wound the thread around the lake enabling Nanda to have her bath, as she desired. The ladies considered this thread to be auspicious and filled with miraculous powers and each of them partook of a piece of the thread. With the passage of time, this act of the ladies dividing the thread among them developed into a traditional religious practice. Today, the thread is traditionally tied round the lake as a ritual and later unwound and distributed in small pieces as *prasad* to the devotees.[27]

---

[27] Narrated from an episode seen on *epic* infotainment television channel, India.

PRASAD OF LIQUOR

Strangely, there are a few Hindu temples devoted to Lord
Shiva and a few Muslim Dargahs, where devotees make offerings of liquor. The liquor, after benediction, is distributed
among the devotees as *prasad*. One such temple is the Kaal
Bhairav *mandir* in Ujjain. There is another shrine devoted to
Shamshan Baba in Gaya, where devotees make an offering
of alcohol to the deity along with the regular offerings of
flowers, incense and sweets.[28] Other temples, where liquor is
offered to the deity, are the Bhairav *mandir* behind Purana
Qila in Delhi and Kali Devi Mata *da* Mandir at Patiala in
Punjab. At these shrines, and some others, offerings of liquor
are accepted by priests and deemed to be consecrated by
the deity.

Even according to Christian customs, liquor, particularly red
wine, sanctified by god, is distributed to the devotees along
with bread; although, the intrinsic meaning accorded to this
gesture is different from the Hindu custom of offering liquor
to a deity. In Christianity, such distribution of wine is generally said to be for deification of the sacrifice of Jesus Christ.

Lately, many religious-minded Hindu devotees have looked
down upon this devotional offering of liquor, but faith sanctioned by religion and the stranglehold of custom have prevailed among the believers.

For instance, Shiva and *tantra* are inseparable and bear a
divine and symbiotic relationship. *Tantriks* are his most
devoted followers and they regularly visit different temples
devoted to Lord Shiva. *Tantra* comprises of five rituals, often
referred to as five 'M's. These are as follows: *madyra* (liquor),
maans (meat), *meen* (fish), *mudra* (gesture) and *maithun*

---

[28] 'Amen (HIC)!' *Hindustan Times*.

(copulation). Lately, except open offering of liquor in certain temples, the other rituals are selectively and symbolically performed and only at select *tantric* centres.

Intoxication is associated with Lord Shiva and, in folklore, he is often depicted in a state of perennial intoxication or possibly, meditation. He is the embodiment of stillness that emanates dynamism and allows for the universe to manifest. This stillness permits him to remain in *vairagya* or remain detached, which in turn enables him to be passionate and dispassionate at the same time—deeply involved in the household life yet untouched by it as an ascetic. This seemingly contradictory image is the core of his existence and an expression of freedom of life.

In *Shaiva* philosophy, intoxication is a lubricant of life that reduces friction and tension while engaging with the world and permits us to experience exuberance without stress. Yet, Shiva is not a consumer of cannabis. He is the essence of cannabis, the very source of intoxication or intoxication personified.[29]

BHAIRON DEVI TEMPLE AT DELHI

Delhi has two Hindu temples dedicated to Bhairon Devi. One temple is located in north-east Delhi and the other is located in the back-end of Purana Qila. Strangely, in one of the temples dedicated to the deity, devotees make an offering of milk, while in the other temple at *Purana Qila* dedicated to the same deity, liquor is the preferred offering, particularly on Sundays.[30] This unusual tradition has been preserved till date. This temple is also famous for another legend that marks it

---

[29] Sadhguru Jaggi Vasudev, 'Shiva: Stillness, Exuberance and Intoxication', *The Times of India* (Chandigarh Edition), 20 February 2019.
[30] A Flash Fact titled 'Bhairon Mandir' in *Hindustan Times*.

as a site where the mighty Bhima of Pandava dynasty offered worship to the deity.[31]

The concept of Bhairav is associated with different kinds of *tantricism*, one aspect of which is personified by *aghoris* (inhabitants of cremation grounds). But, exactly, how *aghoris* relate to Bhairav worship, is not clear. Nevertheless, *aghoris* are infamous for reveling in unclean surroundings, smearing their bodies with filth and even their own faecal matter; and their diet is obnoxious. It is generally the unburnt flesh of half cremated bodies or, if available, flesh of children whose dead bodies are thrown into the river for '*Jal-Pravah*'. They remain dirty, unwashed, unkempt and seem to be infected by insects, with flies buzzing around them. They eat excreta and drink urine, sometimes from a skull used as a utensil. Despite this despicable way of living, *aghoris* are highly regarded and feared for their occult powers, which they may use for good or evil.

The relationship of Bhairav worship with the *aghori* cult and practice is obscure. However, the legend says that the *tantric* who was the first *bhairav* tried to seduce a goddess and was cursed by her into becoming her lowest slave. There are several versions of this legend which cannot be authenticated either. A superior notion of *aghoris* links them to Bhairav worship as celestial messengers and also as carriers of the souls which are destined to suffer in the afterlife.[32]

Recently, a cult has grown around the concept of Bhairav that is neither *aghori* nor *tantric*, but akin to the mystic association with Shiva. The followers of the cult are called Bhairavs, who are believed to be messengers of Yama, the god of death. Traditionally, it is considered a worthy service to appease them with liquor to escape suffering at their

---

[31] A report by RVS, 'Strange Sunday ritual', *The Statesman*.
[32] R. V. Smith, 'Strange Sunday story', *Hindustan Times*.

hands after death. Another sect devoted to Lord Shiva is the
Bholenath Babas sect. They are dressed more like *sadhus*
(saints) but wear a turban-like head gear with a plume of
peacock feather; they are generally seen on specific days
of the week or month when they go from house to house, collecting alms. Their uniqueness is that they do not stand still
even while pausing to receive alms or to bestow a blessing.
They play and ring brass bells. They and also keep themselves
girded around their waist as though like a warrior of Shiva or
a *sadhu* with a stern mein.

A STONE IDOL THAT DRINKS LIQUOR

A stone idol of a deity, installed at Bhawani Mata *mandir,*
accepts offerings of liquor and is believed to drink two and a
half cups of liquor from every individual offering. This temple
is located near Bhawani village that is situated about 16 km
from Merta in Nagore district. The temple has a plaque with
'Samvat 1700' engraved upon it, indicating that it was built
in the year 1700 (as per the Samvat calendar) and is believed
to be about one thousand years old. It is a fine specimen of
ancient architecture. The main gate of the temple faces west.
The temple houses idols of two different deities. One of the
deities is Brahmini Devi, who does not accept any offering
of liquor from the devotees, while the other deity is Kalka
Devi, who drinks two and a half cups from a bottle of liquor,
offered to her by the devotees. Every year, on Ram Navami, a
big celebratory fair is held and huge masses of devotees throng
the temple with their offerings, either to make a wish or to
offer their gratitude on fulfilment of a wish made previously.

Not very far from the temple is a liquor shop selling English
and Indian brands of liquor. Devotees purchase liquor from
this shop to offer to the deity. Some enthusiastic devotees
offer self-made liquor. The *Devi* makes no distinction or

discrimination on this basis. However, as per the ritual, the *Devi* accepts the offering of liquor only from the hands of her *pujari* (priest) and drinks from a special copper cup, which has no holes in it. The priest opens the bottle to fill this cup and when he puts it close to the lips of the deity, he either closes his eyes or looks away from the idol of the *Devi*, while she drinks the liquor. He repeats the process two more times. In the second instance, the *Devi* only drinks half a cup and leaves the rest. As such, the deity is known to drink only two and a half cups of liquor from each offering and no more. The *pujari* pours the left over drink back into the bottle and returns the bottle to the offerer as *prasad*, which he can either drink by himself or share with other relatives and friends. It is no mystery that the entire ritual takes place in full vision of the offerer as well as the other devotees present at the temple.

Sometimes, devotees, out of uber faith, insist on offering the drink in the cup by themselves, which at times is accepted by the *Devi* and the cup empties of the drink in it, however, occasionally the cup remains full. It is so interpreted that such refusal by the Devi occurs in respect of devotees lacking in true devotion and unflinching faith in the powers of the deity; it is also believed that the deity insists on the offerings being procured using self-earned resources obtained by performing a rightful vocation and practicing ethical business practices. Such occurrences of refusal to accept the offerings are indeed rare.

There are multiple beliefs about the temple coming into existence and its history. Many accept that the temple is ancient, but due to a curse had been resting unfrequented and dilapidated in the jungle. It is believed by some that it was discovered, constructed and reinvented about 200 years ago. Legend has it that once a group of dacoits, after committing a dacoity, ran to hide into the ruins of the temple. The king's forces, searching for them, reached the ruins and laid siege to the place. In order to save their lives, the dacoits started to pray to the idol of the Devi with full faith and true devotion in the hope to escape capture. It is then, that the Devi, in her mercy, caused a miracle and all the dacoits suddenly grew moustaches and beards to give them the physical appearance of saints. The king's soldiers believed them to be real saints performing their prayers, and left them unmolested. Relieved, yet imbued with devotional sentiments and remorse, they used the looted money for the reconstruction of the temple.

With the passage of time, this temple has become a place of pilgrimage. Residential and other arrangements have been made by a Jain-Oswal family of Merta for the pilgrims travelling to visit the temple. It is believed that elders of the Jain-Oswal family had migrated to and settled in Merta after partition of India but could not prosper here economically. So, they decided to return to Pakistan and applied for Pakistani citizenship. Around that time, a scion of the family got afflicted with leprosy that could not be cured. The family was distressed, tense and anxious. During one such stressful night, the father of the child, who was also the head of the family, had a clairvoyant dream in which the *Devi* told him to abandon his decision to re-migrate to Pakistan and remain in India, where everything will be well again.

Convinced of the boon bestowed to the family in his dream, the head of family gave up the idea of re-migrating to Pakistan. As expected, his son soon recovered from the illness and the family business started flourishing. The family, thus, became devout believers of the powers of the Devi and started diverting a part of their business profits for the development of the temple complex. The family also took to organizing annual fairs near the temple complex at its own expense. Though the Jain family is a teetotaler and no one in the family drinks liquor, yet all the members of this family religiously offer two and a half cups of liquor to the Devi to propitiate her and seek her continued blessings.

MUSLIM DARGAH AT BHOMA IN THE PUNJAB

Another, even more elaborate and more visited shrine, where liquor is distributed as *prasad*, is a Dargah on the outskirts of Bhoma village in Amritsar district of Punjab. This shrine is built in the memory and on the tomb of a Muslim *faqir*, Baba Rode Shah, and every year, in either March or April, a fair is held near the shrine. The uniqueness of this Dargah is that it accepts offerings of liquor bottles of foreign, Indian or locally brewed varieties. The liquor is sanctified by offering a prayer and is later distributed as *prasad* among the devotees and visitors. Of course, the male visitors consume the *prasad* to their heart's content, while female devotees ingest only a few drops of the *prasad* as a sign of reverence and in the true spirit of consuming a *prasad*.[33]

The Dargah has heavy footfall and pilgrims flock to it from as far as Jammu and Kashmir, Himachal Pradesh as well as Haryana. They tell of a peculiar experience and a different expectation. According to some devotees, the *prasad* at the shrine does not intoxicate them or even make them tipsy. On the contrary, it serves as a benediction and helps them realize their desires and dreams. The belief is, indeed, strong and the faith, unflinching. The devotees praise the Baba in glowing terms and are determined to perpetuate the tradition. Lately, however, dubious devotees also throng the place for the pleasure of free liquor.

The legend has it that the Baba had a love affair with a girl of questionable character. When he realized the truth and futility of the experience, he renounced the world and came to the

---

[33] 'Curious mix of liquor and benediction', *Indian Express* 13 April 1993.

place where the Dargah is now located, and lived here till he died. He breathed his last in March 1924. The Baba was a recluse and spent a lot of time meditating. In due course, he attracted disciples and would offer them liquor as *prasad*, so that they could forget their worldly worries. This tradition faithfully continues till date, albeit on a large scale. Interestingly, the Baba never consumed liquor himself. The caretakers proudly maintain that in the history of the shrine, despite the distribution of liquor as *prasad*, there have never been any ugly fights among the devotees.[34]

KAAL BHAIRAV TEMPLE AT UJJAIN

Kaal Bhairav is the presiding deity at a small but famed shrine in Bhairavgarh, near the temple town of Ujjain in Madhya Pradesh. This black stone temple is located right in the middle of a Hindu cremation ground, on the bank of the river Kshipra. This god is believed to be high spirited and to never disappoint anyone. The stone statue of the deity is worshipped by devotees who make an offering of liquor to the god. Such an occurrence is routine in this shrine. The liquor may be of any kind, quality, variety or brand, and is solemnly offered by the devotees to propitiate their favoured god. *Tantriks*, devotees, visitors, tipplers and free-loaders, all throng the temple for their own respective interests such as performance of rituals, curiosity in miracles or for the free liquor distributed as *prasad*.

The ceremony starts when the *pujari* (priest) sitting in front of the deity pours the offering of liquor in a stainless-steel dish, and then offers his prayer to the god, chanting *mantras* in Sanskrit and performing *tantric* rituals. In the middle of the prayer, he quietly picks up the saucer full of liquor and places it near the slit that forms the lips of the statue. The

---

[34] Ibid.

plate is then tilted just a little bit and gradually the liquid starts vanishing, no matter how many times such offering is made. The priests claim that the deity can, within a couple of minutes, drink as much as a quarter of a bottle of liquor.[35] Incidentally, the fascination of Kaal Bhairav for liquor may be traced back to his mythological background recorded in the tales of Ashtha Bhairavs. He is said to be the *dwarpal* (doorman) of Maha Kaleshwar, the lord of death.

This practice has been going on for hundreds of years and the phenomenon has yet to find a scientific explanation. Rationalists consider the claims incredible and harbour their doubts since an ordinary devotee fails to achieve the same miracle that the *pujari* achieves. The rationalists believe that there has to be a cavity somewhere in the idol, though priests repudiate such suspicions vehemently, yet permit no investigation of the idol, claiming such an action would mean disrespecting the god. No wonder, miracles have their own divine logic and mystic explanations.

Some locals and a baffled senior journalist, Suresh Mehrotra, recollect an investigative effort during the British rule in India—'The entire temple was dug up during the British period to find out whether the liquid flowed into any cavity or tank. But the mystery remained unsolved.'[36] The miracle of divine and mysterious powers of Kaal Bhairav are, indeed, devoutly believed in.

PRASAD OF BHANG SHARBAT

Bhang sharbat (cannabis syrup)[37] is believed to be a favourite drink of Lord Shiva and is consumed as *prasad* during

---

[35] N. K. Singh, 'One For The Lord,' *India Today*, 31 July 1994, 24.

[36] Ibid.

[37] To prepare *bhang sharbat*, *bhang* (cannabis) is ground to a fine quality paste, mixed with sugar to taste and is consumed for mild intoxication and frolic.

the *Barah Chhappan* festival celebrated at the Shiva temple, located beyond half a dozen crematoriums on a hilltop in Jodhpur, Rajasthan.[38] According to a popular belief, Shiva, the lord of ghosts, begins his annual journey from his mythical abode at Mount Kailash (in the Himalayas), accompanied with his associate ghosts and spirits. The journey continues till the wee hours of morning, and the ghosts remain busy with their master, while his devotees can enjoy themselves at the festival.

This happens when the clock strikes exactly 12.56 in the afternoon, that is, *barah chappan* in Hindi language. Hundreds of Shiva devotees gathered at the Jambreshwar Mahadev temple in Jodhpur commence Shiv-*bhakti bhajans* and gulp down litres of intoxicating cannabis (bhang) *sharbat* as *prasad* blessed by Lord Shiva. Thus, this annual function is partly a religious festival and partly a fun-filled revelry. Each year, about a dozen such *bhang* binges are held to commemorate this event in the months of *shravan-bhadrapad* (monsoon season). There is no fixed day or fixed location for the celebrations. The celebrations depend upon convenience and inclination of the devout donors and are held in different temples in Jodhpur and in other parts of Rajasthan also, although such mass participation by tipplers is unique to Jodhpur.

Inquiries about the origin of this event revealed that there is no mention of such religious mandate in Vedic texts or folklore, but locals attribute such celebrations to their culture and customs. Another annual festival where free *bhang* is distributed occurs at the Ram Deora fair near Pokhran in Rajasthan. People drink this traditional drink for its medicinal value or its tranquilizing effect or for sheer fun. Opium and bhang are quite commonly consumed in Rajasthan. In fact,

---

[38] Rohit Parihar, 'Timed for Tipplers,' *India Today*, 28 November 2005, 10.

the excise policy of the state Government allows auction of cannabis vending machines, and Jodhpur alone has six wholesale and 18 retail outlets for cannabis.

PRASAD OF BUTTER FROM AN IDOL

Brajeshwari Devi temple in Kangra is one of the *shakti peeths* in the country. This temple has a tradition of making an idol out of butter during the annual festival of Makar Sankranti. Devotees make offerings of ghee and this ghee is converted into butter by a specific technique involving washing it 108 times in holy water and purifying it by chanting *mantras*. The process of converting ghee into a requisite quantity of butter takes about a week. The sanctified butter is then applied on the *pindi* (body) of goddess Brajeshwari Devi and this process requires 20 priests and about 12 hours to complete. The butter-idol weighs 17 quintals and is, thereafter, decorated with dry fruits.

The legend has it that the goddess was once injured during a fight with demons and the gods treating her injuries, applied butter to her wounds and, thus, she was healed. The day her wounds fully healed happened to be the day of Makar Sankranti. In commemoration of the miraculous healing, the devotees make the butter-idol. The butter remains on the *pindi* of the Goddess for one week. Thereafter, the butter is removed from the *pindi* and distributed as *prasad* among the devotees. It is believed that the sanctified butter so removed from the *pindi* has miraculous healing powers and is good for treating chronic skin ailments and joint pains.[39] Pilgrims from all over the country throng the temple to watch the process of conversion of ghee into butter and its application on the idol and to collect *prasad*.

---

[39] S. Gopal Puri, 'Pilgrims queue up for glimpse of butter idol', *The Times of India*, 15 January 2012, 5.

SNIPPETS

PRASAD OF MUTTON

There are certain temples in India as well as some in other countries, where a ritual of sacrificing animals is performed by the devotees on certain occasions. This ritual is specially performed at Kali Mandir in Kolkata and Kamakhya Mandir in Guwahati. After the ritual, the sacrificed animal's meat is distributed as sanctified *prasad* to the devotees and visitors. This is one of the five *tantric* rituals that includes indulging in meat-eating. However, this practice is on the decline.

PRASAD OF FISH

The primary vocation of the Koli tribal community, settled on the west coast in Maharashtra, is fishing. While worshipping their tribal deity, Mumba Ayee (Mumbai mata), the Koli's make an offering of fish to her from their daily catch, which is later distributed among the devotees as *prasad*. This practice has been prevalent for over a century.

Similarly, Kamakhya Temple in Guwahati also accepts offerings of fish and after consecration and prayers, distributes the same among the visitors as *prasad*. This is an accepted ritual of *tantric* worship.

Fish is offered to and blessed by the deity, before it is distributed to the devotees as *prasad* at the Varahi temple in Odisha also.

A FEAST TO THE MONKEYS

The Niko temple in Lap Boori is located about 110 miles north of Bangkok in Thailand. The area is abound with monkeys that prance around freely. In fact, it can be called a republic of monkeys that live there with pride and authority. They are generally orderly and peace-loving but resent threatening gestures and unnecessary intrusions. Humans may visit the precincts of the temple, however, only peacefully and unobtrusively and entirely at the will and pleasure of the monkeys. Incidentally, the temple has paintings of the Tibetan monkey mascot, of 'the proverbial three wise monkeys; in which the three monkeys cover their eyes, ears and mouth, with their hands as a sign of not seeing, hearing or speaking anything bad, respectively. This image of the three monkeys with the three virtues was popularized by Mahatma Gandhi in India. The Tibetans treat monkeys as 'Boddhistava'.

Yuang Putt, possibly a Buddhist, is a resident of this area and owns a hotel there. Every year, he arranges an expensive feast, costing the equivalent of nearly ₹120,000, as a treat for the monkeys living around the local temple, also called Kala Mandir. The monkey-feast is properly and decorously arranged as if for high society clients. Tables are laid out properly with dishes and, also, with folded napkins. No wonder the monkeys really enjoy the delicious offerings served in plates including diet Pepsi cans as substitutes for water. This event has since become very popular and a great tourist attraction. To witness this strange feast, tourists come from far off places and take photographs of the feast for capturing memories.[40]

Irrespective of the high costs and vain décor of the crockery, accessories and dishes for the monkeys, Yuang

---

[40] Translated and stylized from *Hind Samachar* (Urdu Newspaper), 15 January 1993.

Putt believes that by feeding the monkeys annually, in a royal manner, he is improving his hotel's business and family's prosperity as well as the general welfare of the locality. The nexus between the feast and prosperity appears to be tenuous, however, increased tourism could be one reason. No wonder, perceptions and belief count far more than facts and finances.

5

HURLING OBSCENITIES IN FRONT OF A DEITY
Celebrating with Abandon

Religion and religious practices are sacrosanct and naturally evoke spontaneous veneration, high solemnity and utmost devotion to the presiding deity of the temple or shrine. The devout bow low or even prostrate themselves in overt displays of religiosity and reverence. Hence, obedience to god is normal and induces predictable responses. In this manner, accumulated wisdom of men long gone is perpetuated by the living who are cognizant of the significance of the cultural patterns they preserve or modify in altruistic rationalizations.[1] Disrespectful posture, irreverent behaviour and irreligious conduct at such pious places is an outright taboo and highly condemnable. Thus, taboos are a means of social control that 'bring about conformity, solidarity and continuity of a particular group or society'.[2] Taboos are also a method of social training and social prohibition where defiance may invoke community condemnation or social ostracism.

Despite such cultural constraints and societal strangleholds, there are certain practices associated with some shrines that are socially repugnant and outright blasphemous like singing vulgar songs or hurling obscenities in front of the deity or worship by women, in the nude, in Renukemba temple or women abusing an opponent with expletives. A plausible explanation can be derived from the psycho-cathartic import of acts in the extant social milieu of domination of women. The repressed women could spit out pent up resentment to start another year of harmony and peace on a clean slate.

This chapter narrates some such irreverent and unusual practices that happen to be rooted in the theistic faith, cultural tradition and social values, which were prevalent during the

---

[1] Joseph Roucek et al., *Social Control*, (New Delhi: Affiliated East-West Press Pvt. Ltd, 1956), 7.
[2] Kimball Young, *Sociology*, (Cincinnati: American Book Company, 1942), 898.

time when these practices were common and rampant in the society; and thus, need not be validated on the template of modernity, logic or rationality. Religion has its own realm of practices and a different grammar for their observance. No wonder, divinity remains incomprehensible to human faculties and can only be experienced through utmost devotion and meditation.

FESTIVAL OF ABUSES BY WOMEN

Two villages in Sangli district of Maharashtra perpetuate an age-old, bizarre event of hurling abuses by womenfolk of these villages, against each other. This annual event falls one day after the religious worship of Nag Panchami. At this festival of abuses, womenfolk from the respective villages of Sukhed and Bor in Khandala tehsil stand on either side of the canal running between the villages and hurl abuses at each other regardless of who is at the opposite end of the canal.[3]

According to the legend handed down the generations, a village *patil* (head of the village) married two wives, one from each of the aforementioned villages. The wives did not get along and often swore at each other. One day, when both of them were washing clothes on either side of the canal, a quarrel started between the two and both of them drowned. This enraged both villages. The event of abuses is held annually to commemorate the jealousy and bickering between the two *soutens* (concurrent wives of the same man). The police have tried to put a stop to this quaint practice but have not succeeded so far.

A plausible reason for social sanction and customary acceptance of such a practice could be the catharsis of pent-up emotions of bitterness and grudges in these women, once

---

[3] 'Police stop festival of abuses', *The Statesman*, 7 August 1992.

a year. In olden times, women were generally repressed in the society and would suffer a lot of mental torture, emotional abuse and carry around the burden of wounded pride. This caused a buildup of resentment and frustration in them, which in the prevailing claustrophobic social environment, they could neither freely express nor swallow. This caused accumulation of unreleased ill will and asperity against those in power, wreaking such indignity that constantly irked the mind. It must have been terrible to withstand and bear such treatment. Vengeance was a natural reaction but could not be carried out due to their highly dependent position in the family and their lack of gumption to resist or rebel.

The milieu was certainly delicate and loaded against the women. They would often and quite naturally blame their native conditions for their pitiable plight and sorrowful state of living. Perhaps, this ritual was invented, developed and promoted to indulge in cathartic expression to expunge cumulated malice and harboured animus. Having spewed out this pique and anger, and spitted out acrimony in the form of abuses hurled on each other, the womenfolk would feel comforted and at ease to bear another bout of repression for one year before they got to release the anger in the form of abuses again next year. It was society's own home-grown release mechanism to maintain sanity and domestic peace in the villages. In the light of this, the ritual, indeed, appears ingenious and workable and has been practised by many generations of women in these two villages. But for how long, with growing gender parity and escalating freedom for women!

CHOICEST OBSCENITIES IN FRONT OF A DEITY

Customs and practices carrying the sanction of religion, even if strange, are hard to kill or change, because in face of criticism, the protagonists often quote in justification, passages from holy scriptures, even though out of context.

The Bharani festival of Sri Kurumbha Bhagwathi temple in Kodungalloor on the Malabar Coast, situated about 40 km from Thrissur, in Kerala, is one such example. Every year hordes of drunken devotees descend on the temple and chant choicest obscenities in front of and within the earshot of the *devi* and, that too, to propitiate the goddess. The irony is obvious.

Again, Kavu Theendal ceremony is the ritual of singing ribald folklore. It generally falls in the month of March or April. In the year 1993, the festival fell on 25th March. The content of the songs are vulgar lyrics, handed down from generation to generation. The lyrics pertain to lurid sexual acts and pornographic descriptions of the female genitalia, often accompanied by the raunchiest gesticulations.[4] Imagine all this and more, happening within the precincts of a temple of worship, which is supposed to be a pious place, and to top it all, to propitiate a female deity!

Interestingly, this devotion is not a male preserve, and thousands of devotees including women, oracles and children reach the temple for celebrations. The annual festival of Meena Bharani opens with a ritual of dancing by oracles of both genders; the male oracles are distinguished by their red-lion-cloth attire, carrying swords and *chelambu* (insignia of the deity). Their dance, in front of the sanctum sanctorum, reaches a frenzy to the traditional beating of the copper-thatched roof of the temple with sticks while devotees throw turmeric powder on the dancers. Pepper and coconuts are conventional offerings to the deity.

Another controversial ritual associated with Bharani festival is Kozhikallumoodal.[5] This literally means covering a flat

---

[4] 'Gradual decline of "religious ribaldry"' *The Statesman* (Delhi Edition), 19 April 1993.
[5] Ibid.

stone with red silk cloth to sacrifice cocks and hens on it. This was the other part of Kali pooja related to animal sacrifice and bloodletting to propitiate the deity. The stone is a little distance away. However, this practice of animal sacrifice has been banned by the government since 1956. Nowadays, the stone is still covered with a red silk cloth, however, the cocks and hens are merely tied and placed on the sacrificial stone but not killed. The animals are not sacrificed but collected, live, and later auctioned off by the temple authorities; the proceeds are utilized for temple improvement.

The reasons for this ironical ribaldry, animal sacrifice and solemn worship, that occurred all at the same time and at the same place and got social acceptance and later transformed into reverential observance, are interesting yet intriguing. It is hard to comprehend or believe in the element of faith associated with such religious ribaldry and animal sacrifice, both from the mythological and the historical perspectives, discussed below.

The mythological point of view justifies this unholy custom by gaining support of the Kali cult. The legend has it that goddess Kali was reborn as Kannagi. The story goes that Kodungallore was once the capital of Chera king, Chenguttavan (Chera is the clan of rulers like Chola or Lodhi, etc.). The Nedunchuzhiyan, king of Madurai, got Kovalan, the lover of Kannagi, executed, by foisting on him false charges of stealing a *chelambu*, a golden bracelet of the deity. Kannagi was enraged at the injustice by the king and she set Madurai aflame for having been unjustly deprived of her husband, Kovalan. Believably, she was, thus, denied marital bliss and, therefore, she reveled in ribaldry and associated vices. Thus, the deity Kannagi, worshipped in this temple, is an incarnation of Kali and the annual celebration commemorates the victory of Kali. According to a popular belief, goddess Kali likes the liquor, the animal sacrifice, blood and gore as well as the smutty songs.

The historical perspective maintains that the temple was earlier, a Buddhist shrine. When the Aryans landed in India, they spread their stranglehold over this land and annexed the ready-made shrines. But the Buddhist monks refused to vacate this particular monastery and cloistered inside chanting their holy prayers. To chase them off, the Aryans executed an ingenious plan. They engaged people from northern Kerala, mostly from the lower castes, gave them as much liquor as they wanted and, thereafter, asked them to scream such obscenities that would drive out the chaste Buddhist monks from their monastery. Their plan really worked. The present festival is said to commemorate this event. This explanation appears more credible and plausible because some of the Buddha engravings in the temple give credence to this possibility.

Despite the sanction of the religion and customary acceptance of this ritual, it is ironically weird. Lately, it's acceptance may be declining due to the rational mindset of the modern generation and the efforts of some social reform organizations and a regional Rationalist Society to abolish the practice. However, the religious sanction and customary tradition still maintain a stranglehold over a small number of devotees. Governmental efforts are also afoot but traction in compliance is weak. In 1954, the government banned singing of obscene songs in public places but enforcement of the same was minimal. Since 1992, stricter action is being taken and police arrests those shouting smutty things in public. As such, pornographic ritual was confined within the temple precincts.[6] More earnest and sincere efforts are required for a complete elimination of this vulgar practice.

---

[6] Ibid.

WORSHIP OF DEITY IN NUDE BY WOMEN

An annual ritual of 'worship in the nude' by women takes place at the temple of goddess Renukamba near the village Chandraguthhi in Shimoga district of Karnataka. It falls on Magh Purnima during February or March and hundreds of women who take a vow to perform this *puja* participate in this ritual. This worship is performed only by women; the men participate in the ceremony as helpers or spectators. Generally, people come from all over Karnataka and adjoining states of South India to witness this event, which is locally called Sri Renukamba *jatre* (fair). It goes on for five days and is well-known and has been popularly celebrated for over a century.[7]

Goddess Renukamba is a local deity and is worshipped in this area, and is considered to be an incarnation of goddess Durga. Women vow to perform this ritual, called 'Bethele Seva' in Kannada, if their prayers get fulfilled. The worshipping families take this pilgrimage to the craggy hills of Malnad and visit the temple during those five days and camp there while the women perform nude worship. The ceremonial worship starts early in the morning before sunrise when women congregate at river Varada, about 6 km from the temple, take a bath in the river and then run nude to the temple, either in groups or all together. Their family members carry their clothes that they wear after offering prayers to the deity at the temple.

The legend has it that Sage Jamadgni and his consort Renuka lived in this area. One day when Renuka was bathing in the Varada river, she was distracted by the good looks of a youth. Jamadgani sensed this through his yogic powers and ordered his son, Parashurama, to behead Renuka. While fleeing for her life, Renuka dropped her clothes and escaped into a cave

---

[7] Ravi R. Prasad, 'Nude Worshippers dodge police', *Indian Express*, 6 March 1995. Also refer *Hind Samachar* (Urdu), 12 February 1993.

where she merged with God. The worshippers started nude worship, Bethele Seve, in sympathy for the predicament of the goddess and in atonement.[8]

In fact, it is a week-long festival that involves various other rituals also. A religious procession of the presiding deity Renukamba, in a caparisoned chariot, is taken around the village by the gathered pilgrims. Then there is Ookali Aata, which is a ritual of playing with colours, comparable to the festival of Holi celebrated in North India. There is a day of donations called Thula Bara. On this occasion, devotees offer coconuts, equivalent to the weight of the offering person, to the temple. These coconuts are auctioned and the proceeds are used by the temple.

This ritual has been in controversy for about three decades. In 1985, there were clashes between the supporters and the antagonists as regards the nature of the ritualistic worship and the police had to intervene. But sentiments were so strong that some police officials were stripped completely by the supporter and were forced to worship the deity. As a result of this, considering it a law and order problem, the Karnataka government imposed a ban on the nude worship in 1987 and since then elaborate arrangements are made to prevent the ritual. In pursuance of this order, the District Magistrate of Shimoga has promulgated a prohibitory order under the Karnataka Police Act, 1963, curbing this event.[9] But despite all this, devout worshippers sneak in and camp at the temple many days in advance and hundreds of women still indulge in nude worship, despite the prohibition. Certain communities have vehemently protested against the governmental order banning the worship. It is truly a matter of faith and tradition; sentiments in favour of the practice still linger and urbanized civic rationality may not be the right course of action.

---

[8] 'Devotees favour nude worship', *The Statesman* (Delhi Edition), 18 March 1992.
[9] 'Nude fair banned', *Hindustan Times*, 2 March 1992

WORSHIPPING FOR RAIN IN THE NUDE

From times immemorial and all over the world, rain dances have been performed to propitiate the rain god or gods with the hope and faith that the period of drought will end and result in a downpour. Well, this practice must have been successful most of the times, else people, duly disillusioned, would not have continued with it. The wise say, faith can move mountains, and here, it sure brings rain to the parched lands with the benignity of the worshipped god.

There is a tribe in India, which performs a rain dance that is quite unique. They are the Rajbansis of Cooch Behar who actually originated from Sikkim, but came and settled as the sole inhabitants of the inhospitable stretch of land called the Terai, on the India–Nepal border. Their local deity for daily obeisance is Hudum Deo, who is also worshipped for protection and prosperity of the tribe, and in particular for bringing seasonal rain. The rain dance of Rajbansis is intended to propitiate the local deity, Hudum Deo to end the drought. But this dance is different from other rain dances in many ways; firstly, it is performed only by women; secondly, it is performed in the nude; and thirdly, it is considered unlucky for any man to witness it.[10]

Despite this curse, one English traveler, in 1927, decided to see for himself this uncommon dance, believing it to be a 'once in a lifetime opportunity' for scientific curiosity and to leave his sociological research notes for posterity. Whatever be his motives, it was a decision fraught with risks and danger, but Augustus Sommerville, the adventurer, could not care less. He planned his action discreetly and found out the day, the exact time and place of the event. To watch the dance, he hid

---

[10] P. J. O. Taylor, 'Dancing for the rain god in the nude', *The Statesman*, 16 December 1994, 5.

and ensconced himself safely and snugly at a high vantage point, atop a huge Peepul tree for a good view of the clearing in the jungle where the ceremony was to be performed.

Soon after midnight, around 20 women, mostly young girls, accompanied by some older females, carrying drums and cymbals, appeared in the clearing. In the middle of the group, they put the idol of the deity, Hudum Deo, the rain god of great repute in the area. The idol, made of mud and painted a bright red, was placed, with reverence, in the centre of the clearing. The proceedings then paused until the moon was fairly overhead. Once the position of the moon was favourable, the older women started playing the music. They started with a steady beating of drums in a syncopated rhythm, punctuated at regular intervals by a sharp clang from the cymbals. Overall, it was a pleasant symphony.

The start of the music was a signal to the young girls, who sprang to their feet, stripped off all their clothes, and in the nude, formed a circle round the idol. They soon began to dance and, then, started singing in accompaniment, in a wild plaintive chant. At first, the dancers' movements were slow and graceful and they clearly seemed to be pleading to their god for a favour, no doubt, of rainfall. But soon the music grew louder, faster and more compelling. With this, the dance movements grew wilder and swifter and the chanting lost its plaintive tone of supplication. Gradually, they worked themselves into a fury. Their hands were swung around their heads, their bodies, gleaming in the moonlight, twisted and contorted and like dervishes, whirled round and round.

The respectful pleading with the god now ceased, instead, the girls heaped vituperation and abuses on him, accompanied by spitting and hissing. The chant now changed to songs of obscenity till, in a final burst of fury and frustration, they fell upon the clod of mud which so far was considered a revered idol, breaking it to pieces and scattering the pieces in all directions. This was clearly the climax, for the music ceased thereafter and the performers dressed themselves decorously, but dejectedly, and quietly returned to the village.

Hudum Deo, the venerated deity of the village is worshipped all year-round and is expected to perform its duty as the rain god and bring copious rainfall to the area. So long as this happens, the god is duly respected, popularly loved, heartily worshipped and held in high reverence. But when he fails in his duty and the drought conditions continue, his idol is taken outside the village and disgraced. Should rain fall during the dance or even if the sky becomes overcast, the repentant god is brought home amid rejoicing and dancing to be reinstated and reinstalled with due apologies and every mark of respect.[11]

In the end, the English peeping tom, Sommerville, says that throughout the ceremony not a single male was visible, but he was aware, and probably, so were the dancers, that the whole population of the village, as curious spectators, hidden behind every tree and bush in the clearing, had stealthily witnessed the entire ceremony. The curse seemed notional and acted as a deterrent to save this solemn performance from becoming a public event fueled by curiosity of human beings.

THE RAINMAKER OF LUGBARA

A similar ritual, though slightly different from the Rajbansis of Cooch Behar, is performed by the Lugbara tribe in Uganda, Africa. The basic social unit of the Lugbara society is based on patrilineal segmentary lineage system, where a unit is co-terminus with minimal lineage of three to four generations. The genealogically senior most person is the head of the clan

---

[11] Ibid.

and is addressed as 'Elder'. They have a structured social system that engenders harmonious relationships in which every self, unfolds naturally, in its fullness without external constraints or distortions. This community can boast of unity and harmony, egalitarian solidarity, natural life activity and prosperity and well-being of all.[12]

The most important ritual of Lugbara is the 'rainmaker' or 'rainchief'. The latter term equates to the Lugbara term *opi-ezo*, which is not a causal agent of rain, but is viewed as the manifest representative of *Adroa*, the symbol construct of solidarity and harmony. 'Essentially, he is not controlling rainfall as such; rather he is ensuring the proper relationship between Divinity and man...'. The rainchief has symbolic paraphernalia in the form of ritual stones shaped like male and female sexual organs that he manipulates to create union of the organs. He hides these stones in a bush, the realm of the natural.

The initiation ceremony of the rainmaker is strange in that he is pelted with insults as a ritual of separation from normal society and is, thereafter, prohibited from cutting his hair and nails. Anthropologists suggest that the ritual of heaping of insults involves 'the elevation of an individual's social status' and makes for 'a procedure by which both liminality (undifferentiation) and communitas (solidarity) are symbolically emphasized'.[13] Consequently, the rainmaker then moves out of the hierarchical social world of inequality of status and ordered constraints. His passage is, therefore, deemed to be a transformation from a differentiated to an undifferentiated order. In a similar strain of undifferentiation, the rainmaker,

---

[12] John Middleton, 'Prophets and rainmakers', in *The Translation of Culture*, ed. T. O. Biedelman (London: Tavistock Publications, 1971), 179–201.
[13] K. S. Bose, *A Theory of Religious Thought*, (New Delhi: Sterling Publishers Pvt. Ltd, 1991), 43.

after his death, unlike other men, is buried at night and lying on his left side. Besides, due to his exalted status, his corpse is not subjected to ritual insults as is the case with the other men.[14]

CELEBRATION AT SHAMSHAN GHAT

Kashi, also known as Benaras, in Uttar Pradesh, is the land of Lord Vishwanath. As per the *shastras*, it is the very first town established on the globe by the god of Hindu pantheon, Lord Shiva. A death in this town is not only a tragedy or a cause for grief, but also a reason for celebration because it is believed that those who die here, attain *moksha* (salvation from rebirth). Apart from this consolatory belief, tradition-ally, *nagar vadhus* (courtesans or sex workers) gather at the Mahashamshan Nath temple, a little off of Manikarnika *ghat* on the seventh night of Chaitra Navratra to propitiate the lord of the cremation ground. They pray and perform in front of this deity, annually.[15]

The event begins in the evening and the first dance is performed inside the shrine and is devoted to the lord in propitiation of the well-being of all. Thereafter, the audience, mostly comprised of locals and a sprinkling of foreigners, joins in and the dancing continues to the beat of garish and loud music till midnight. At that time, a customary *aarti*, known as Shayan *aarti*, is performed to put the deity to sleep. All this *dhamaal* takes place on Manikarnika *ghat*, where it is said that the funeral pyre never dies out. So, the celebrations go on against the backdrop of death and wailing mourners, with embers of freshly lit funeral pyres rising into the dark sky.

The knowledgeable ones narrate that it is a tradition, which is five centuries old. The legend has it that Sawai Raja

---

[14] Ibid, 45.
[15] Binay Singh, 'Kashi crematorium jig for the Lord of Dance', *The Times of India*, March, 2015.

Man Singh of Amber, Rajasthan, got the Man Mandir *ghat* built near Dashwamedh *ghat* in 1585 AD. He also got the Mahashamshan Nath temple renovated. *Nagar Vadhus* had performed at the inauguration of the refurbished temple. This tradition has lived on for centuries and has perpetuated itself. Strangely enough, Manikarnika *ghat* is also known for celebration of a strange type of Holi, which is played with funeral pyre ashes on the day after Rangbhari Ekadashi.[16]

CELEBRATION OF GAALI-BAZI AS AN ART-FORM

Gaali-bazi is a street corner tradition unique to Jaipur, where witty repartees in local slang regale those hanging around *paan*-shops at street corners. The form of *gaali-bazi*, prevalent in Jaipur is called *Dhudhadi*. These informal street gatherings were later formalized into schools that have existed from the time of the reign of Sawai Madho Singh (1835–1880 AD). Interestingly, *gaali-bazi* finds mention in Tulsidas' Ramcharitra Manas also and was traditionally performed during the festival of Holi by elderly men in the family.[17] It was believed to be a private affair and an engaging time pass, at a time when there were few means of entertainment.

There was a time when Jaipur had 25 such independent schools, which have now reduced to 11. Each school has a leader called the *Ustaad* and his followers, between 5 and 50 in number, are called *Khalifas*. The first such formal gathering was organized by the Dayajwal family in Jodhpur, which later shifted to Jaipur and settled down in *Maaliyon ka Chowk* in the Topkhanadesh locality. The family, after migration, continued the tradition and it became so popular that other schools like *Khunteton ka Raasta* or *Kishanpol*

---

[16] Ibid.

[17] Meenakshi Sinha, 'Where abuse is an Art form', *The Times of India*.

Bazaar Chowkri also sprang up.[18] *Gaali-bazi* is a home-grown art form and its session starts around 10 pm and the congregation generally lasts for four to six hours, but sometimes continues all night, with singing of satirical and witty songs in sync with music. The session starts with a prayer to Lord Ganesha, with the *Ustaad* sitting on a *chowki* (a raised platform) and his *Khalifas* sitting at a lower level. Now-a-days everyone is welcome to join and enjoy the performance, though participation is not allowed. This is because participation required the skills to instantly compose a poem in retort to the opposite party and involves spontaneous singing. This requires creativity and the capacity to deliver instantaneous critical commentary. The poems sung are in *hasyaras* (fun/wittiness), *shingarras* (sarcastic praise of beauty/fashion) and *cholbaazi* (teasing) style.

The *Ustaads* contend that the word *gaali-bazi* is made up of two words, *gaali* and *bazi*; *gaali* stands for 'gaaliya' meaning what has already been sung and *bazi* stands for competition. Therefore, such gatherings are primarily used as a medium to spread social awareness and reforms, where the participants sing songs full of sarcastic humour and taunts, covering topics ranging from communal harmony, drinking of liquor, festivals of olden times, corruption, fashion, films, traffic and present-day inflation. Further, through songs, they make satirical comments on social practices and beliefs and touch upon issues of superstition, sex, environment and polity.[19]

Considering the activities of these congregations, this art-form surely acts as the nuanced conscience of the society and plays a role comparable to that of today's media. It is made clear that in these sessions there is no intention to insult any people, any community or any organization. The songs are subtle without

---

[18] Ibid.
[19] Ibid.

any specific mention of names or references. This way the targeted audience gets a hint that he is hit, yet without making him feel embarrassed or insulted in public. No wonder, old traditions have intrinsic wisdom and common sense.

LICENTIOUS KING GETS THE BOOT

There is a fort in Sandhana village, about 15 km from Yamunanagar in Haryana (India), which takes the boot every year during 'Kapal Mochan' fair for the evil deeds of its once-upon-a-time occupant, during the ancient times. This is a mandatory ritual for those attending the festival at Sati Mata *mandir* that commences on Kartik Poornima, falling around the months of October or November according to Hindu Lunar calendar. Concurrently, a fair is held in Bilaspur area of Yamuna Nagar district that goes on for five days. Participation in the festival of *Kapal Mochan* is believed to be incomplete without the devotees performing the ritual of kicking the walls of the fort, though people primarily throng this festival for seeking blessings of the goddess bride known as Sati Mata.[20]

The legend has it that King Jarasandh ruled the Assandh area, in present Haryana state, during the times of the *Mahabharata*. He was known to camp out of his capital for a licentious life and one such camping place was the fort at Sandhana. On visits to this fort, he would swoop down on weddings and kidnap the bride for the night. Once he abducted a brahmin's daughter, but she managed to escape from his clutches. She cursed the king and afterwards took 'Jal Samadhi' to end her life. According to the *mahant* of the *mandir* situated on the bank of the main pond, the curse has since prevailed. There are, thus, three tanks or *sarovars*, namely, *Kapal Mochan*,

---

[20] Manveer Saini, 'Shoe ritual at KapalMochan fair', *TNN report* in *Times of India* (Chandigarh Edition), 24 November 2018.

Rin Mochan and *Suraj Mochan,* where pilgrims take a holy dip. In the year 2018, it is estimated by the district administration that nearly eight lakh devotees visited the *Kapal Mochan* festival that commenced on 19th November 2018.[21]

In keeping with the legend, every year devotees take a dip in the tank and then kick and throw shoes and stones at the fort that used to be licentious king's temporary rest house, which has since tumbled down with age and now exists only as a non-descript mound. Some men, women and children, while taking part in the ritual, get so carried away that they begin to abuse the king and use expletives while kicking and beating the mound, perhaps in belief that the king lies buried there. Further, those who are unable to come, send their shoes and stones to be hurled at the fort with equal anger and disgust. According to the temple priest, who narrates with deep conviction, this act gets the devotees a pardon from Sati Mata for all wrong-doings and sins committed by them in their present life as well as their previous lives. Thus, this visit to the *Kapal Mochan* fair blends spirituality, salvation and vengeance for evil deeds.

SNIPPETS

HUNTING FESTIVAL FOR WOMEN

The tribal women in Jharkhand celebrate the festival of 'Jani Sikar'. This festival upholds an old tradition of hunting by women.[22] During the days of festival, the women go on a prowl to hunt animals and enjoy a feast of the animals hunted by them for night's dinner.

---

[21] Ibid.
[22] Extracted from report, 'Hunting Fest' published in *Hindustan Times.*

Whether men are permitted to join the feast, is not known!

CHITHIRAI THIRUVIZHA OF MADURAI

Chithirai Thiruvizha is an annual festival celebrated in the month of *chithirai* corresponding to the month of April. It is a two-week long festival of dance and music, the longest celebration held in the city of Madurai in Tamil Nadu. The festival re-enacts the wedding of Lord Sundareswarar (Lord Shiva) and Goddess Meenakshi, Lord Vishnu's sister. Madurai is famous for its Meenakshi Temple, having an ornate exterior architecture with idols of numerous gods and goddesses on its facade.

BURNING AWAY THEIR SINS: IVANA KUPALA

In Kuritsko, situated in Novgorod region of Russia, there is an interesting custom believed to burn away ones' old sins. It is performed during the traditional *Ivana Kupala* which means 'Ivan, the bather'. As per the ritual, people jump over burning campfires and then ritually bathe in a lake or a river. It is believed that performing this rite will purge them of their past sins. Of course, the stranglehold of societal beliefs baffles rationality.

BIDDING ADIEU TO WINTER: THE RUSSIAN STYLE

The Slavic regions of Russia, Belarus, Ukraine and other adjoining countries bid a celebratory adieu to the winter season. This age-old tradition of indulging in festivities as a farewell to winter includes baking and eating traditional pancakes or *blini*, playing snowball fights and burning effigies of Lady Maslenitsa.[23] The festivities are

---

[23] Maslenitsa is not a living person. Effigees are burnt as camp fires while celebrating Maslenitsa. Photo-feature, 'Bidding adieu to winter, the Russian style, *The Times of India* (Chandigarh Edition), 13 March 2019.

observed around the month of March and can be compared to the *Lohri* festival of North India, in celebration and spirit.

The legend has it that in earlier times, Maslenitsa was for the remembrance of the dead. However, with passage of time the fun-loving Russians have transformed this solemn and salutary holiday into a festival of jolly Maslenitsa, observed with fun, frolic and rejoicing.

6

TALE OF PLATONIC LOVE THAT BESTOWS BOONS

Miracles, Myths and Boons

Certain events and occurrences cannot be explained by rules of science, moods of logic or by principles of rationality. These events and occurrences are called miracles, myths or mysteries. In India, miracles are known to occur in religious shrines and other places of faith and people believe in them with devotion and fervour, without scientific inquisitiveness or rational affirmation. Of course, in the age of scientific temper, such happenings are viewed with suspicion and disbelief and deemed devoid of logic or rationality, yet some of these happenings seem evident and real to the naked eye and a layman's experience. Mostly, for occurrences of this nature, apparent facts count far less than perception, devotion and tradition. In such cases, real or surreal, one is really amazed, truly overwhelmed and impelled to spontaneously bow in reverence to acknowledge God's absolute, supreme powers and the expanse of His divine actions.

Mysteries are surely mysterious but cannot be deemed as non-existent. It may have to be conceded that there may be some iota of scientific explanation for many of these manifestations, but a general condemnation of such mysteries as blind faith, is being in denial of God's utter supremacy and His unbounded powers. This would be blasphemous or at least an obstinate abdication of the unknown or inexplicable. Some such instances of apparent disbelief or mysterious occurrences with specific details are narrated in this chapter, which may, with respective permission, be open to scientific investigation and confirmatory analysis for agnostics and rationalists to satisfy their inquisitiveness as well as ego.

Similarly, myth is not falsehood; it is only a different kind of truth. The celebrated mythologist, Devdutt Pattanaik, maintains that there are many types of truth. Some objective, some subjective; some logical, some intuitive; some deductive, some inductive; some cultural some universal; some ephemeral, some eternal; some are based on evidence, others depend on faith. Therefore, myth is a truth that is subjective, intuitive, inductive, cultural and grounded in faith.

Apart from these, there are experiential truths which cannot be described or explained; these can only be personally experienced or enjoyed with involvement. This predicament is often compared to the experience of a dumb person tasting a sweet. He cannot speak of the taste nor express its sweetness in intelligible words; he remains mute and moot in expression, yet his face and body language betray the feeling that speaks a million words and is understandable. Nevertheless, it remains a myth.

Besides the above, there are primal truths that have been true from the beginning, but are foxing and undecided like 'hen first or the egg' riddle. These are undeniably immutable truths but there is no clear answer or a final choice; the dilemma remains. The ultimate truth here is the eternal truth, which could be beyond human comprehension or scientific proof but, nonetheless, is the truth, was the truth and shall remain the truth, forever. Eternal truth never changes nor mutates in any manner or content.

Miracles of god and godmen are unbelievable happenings but do occur sometimes, more so in the domain of religion. These are, most often, defined by suddenness and inexplicability. No one doubts the miracles created by the benign and merciful god in response to human prayers or meditation or concentration or by religious rituals. But many godmen, through the ages, have been suspect and have most often performed clever magic tricks or sheer gimmickry or stark hypnotism for the gullible devout, like 'physicalizing' a material gift article or creating *babhooti* (holy ash) out of nothing.

Rationalists have exposed many godmen by publicly demonstrating their tricks; they have unraveled the chemistry of some of the miraculous acts by observation and analysis of the same. First, some godmen pro claim they can stop a heartbeat or pulse merely by a meditative trance. The rationalists explained that by holding any hard object such as a lemon or battery cell under the armpit, a pulse cannot be felt at the wrist. Second, some godmen avow that they can bend a spoon by staring at it with concentration. In this case, it was found that the spoon was made of bimetals. The strong heat from the lights caused the two metals to expand differently and the resulting imbalance caused the spoon to bend.

Third, it was found that the claim of godmen, setting off *yagna* fires by *mantras*, was merely a sleight of hand; the scientific explanation was that potassium permanganate was scattered over the firewood before the devotees congregated to witness the miracle and a few drops of glycerin were dropped later to set off the fire without striking a match stick. Fourth, some godmen claim that they are able to make *vibhuti* fall on picture frames. The explanation is that lactic acid, sprayed over a picture frame, precipitates into ash when it comes into contact with moisture. It was demonstrated to happen on any frame and not only on a *guru's* photo frame. But many godmen have not permitted any such scrutiny or investigation into their divinely miraculous acts, and contrarily have questioned the caliber of scientists and rationalists.

Again, religious acts are generally wish-fulfilling and known for bestowal of boons on the adherents. In this regard, most religions, including Hinduism, Islam, Christianity, Sikh are all alike. For the purpose, each religion has subaltern deities or *gram devtas* (locally worshipped gods) or revered sages or exalted peers who benevolently grant wishes of beseechers on performance of specific prayers and/or ordained rituals. There are no statistics of successes and failures to measure the wish-fulfilment quotient, yet the efficacy of each shrine travels by word of mouth and is almost invariably believed in amazement as sacrosanct truth. Delhi, alone, has a host of such shrines scattered all over the city, offering alternatives to the wish-seekers, irrespective of the religion. There are other secular traditions also that tend to get transformed with shifting needs of the times and changing values of the society. Accordingly, traditions metamorphosize and develop new observances and novel rites for perpetuation of social virtues and community bonding, for example, deity as a banker at Narrawada in Andhra Pradesh. In nutshell, this chapter is a miscellany of lesser known legends and unusual rituals that are nonetheless interesting and informative.

BHOOTONWALA MANDIR: CONSTRUCTED IN ONE NIGHT BY GHOSTS

In Datiyana village of Simbhawali *tehsil* in Meerut district, there exists a Bhootonwala *mandir* which is believed to have been constructed by ghosts in only one night. This ancient temple is dedicated to Lord Shiva. It is constructed entirely with red bricks and no binding agent like mud or cement, to hold the bricks together, is visible. Further, the temple is estimated to be more than a thousand years old, yet it shows no signs of any kind of wear and tear irrespective of exposure to the elements of nature for such a long period of time. Interestingly, this entire red brick structure has only two black bricks in the centre of the front wall; the placement of the two black bricks is in the nature of Christian cross symbol.[1]

It is maintained that since the ghosts had to return to their ghettos during the day, the temple could only be constructed by the ghosts overnight; therefore, when the sun arose, they had to leave the upper portion of the spire (shikhar) unfinished. The work on the dome and the spire was completed later by the villagers. Since, the addition of the spire and the

---

[1] Ishita Bhatia, 'Bhootowala Mandir: A Temple Made by Ghosts?' *Sunday Express*, 1 October 2017.

dome was done by humans and not the ghosts, it was not considered perfect; in fact, unlike the rest of structure, the spire and the dome are adversely affected by the impact of adverse weather and unfavourable climatic conditions. A couple of decades ago, it was discovered that the spire had developed cracks and there were deposits of algae on it. So, the dome had to be reconstructed in the year 1980.

The temple is believed to exercise benign influence and provide protective support to the village. People have faith that this temple saves them from natural calamities and protects their crops from hailstorm and floods. They shared instances of crops getting severely damaged in adjoining villages due to hail and heavy rain, leading to farmers committing suicide due to the failed crop, however, their village remained unaffected by such calamity. No wonder, faith can cause miracles. The construction of the temple by *bhoots* is a tale handed down the ages by village elders for inducing acceptance of and reverence to the temple in 'as is' condition, with whatever deficiencies.

The villagers muster every reason handed down the generations to vindicate their belief that the temple was built by ghosts in one night. But historians and archeologists disagree with vehement logic. They, however, accept that it cannot be established who constructed the temple, but according to the architecture and style of construction, its origin dates back to the 3rd century AD, that is, the Gupta dynasty period, when brick temples were a tradition. Besides, there are carvings done in the foundation of the temple which also depict the Gupta period. However, a lot of additional construction work, like the spire and dome, as well as renovation, have taken place subsequently in different years. Such subsequent additions do not fully match or integrate with the original style. As regards usage of cement, archeologists argue, it did not exist then and only natural pastes were used to bind bricks together. Science and faith seldom walk together.

CURING PEOPLE OF EVIL SPIRITS

Hussein Tekdi Sharif is a venerated *dargah* located in Jaora village of Ratlam district, nearly 170 km from Indore. This 19th century shrine complex was built by Mohammad Iftikhar Ali Bahadur, the *nawab* of Jaora. At this shrine, *Chehlum*, an observance of mourning, is observed for forty days after Muhharram, with the belief that it can miraculously cure mental illnesses and exorcize evil spirits. A large number of Muslim and non-Muslim devotees gather here on the eleventh day of the *Chehlum*. On that day, the faithful walk on a 15 feet long carpet of burning charcoal and the mere sight of this ritual is considered to relieve people of evil spirits proving that belief in miracles exists.

In January 2012, when the first batch of newly-married men performed the ritualistic fire-walk, people surged to get a glimpse of this auspicious rite, leading to a stampede; in this tragic accident 12 persons including six women were trampled to death.[2] Truly, it was a case of a celebration having gone wrong.

OFFERING COW-DUNG CAKES TO BE BLESSED WITH CHILD

It is a strange, old custom that has continued for centuries in the village Pandori Waraich near Amritsar town in Punjab. The custom is that issueless women throng to the *gurudwara* of Bhai Shallo ji with offerings of cow-dung cakes in their hands or basketfuls on their heads to seek blessings for bearing a child. People swear by these blessings as they return for thanksgiving with new-born child very soon. A *Times of India* reporter, among others, interviewed a devotee on this

---

[2] TNN report in *Sunday Times of India*, 15 January 2012.

subject, and the lady informed the reporter that she had been married for ten years and did not bear any child. Last year I came and wished while making the customary offering to Bhai Shallo ji and you can see for yourself, this year I have come with my new born child. This custom has now turned into an annual fair, which is held around the month of October.

Myth is that Guru Ramdas, fourth *guru* of the Sikhs, founded the town of Amritsar and he assigned the task of construction of buildings and supervision work to his trusted followers, Bhai Budhhaji and Bhai Shalloji. Once during the monsoons, when it rained heavily and continuously, it created a shortage of dry firewood and other heating material to feed the kiln for baking of bricks. This was an urgent necessity because the kiln had been filled and fired. Bhai Shalloji got the ingenious idea to collect cow dung cakes from the households to be used in place of dry firewood. So, he went to the village, Waraich, near the kiln and announced that whosoever will give dry cow dung cakes (one in number or one basketful) will be blessed with a son. Many families donated cow dung cakes either out of devotion or to seek the blessing for a child.

Resultantly, the situation of shortage of dry fuel was tidied over and bricks in the kiln baked perfectly. However, the matter was reported to the *Guru* that Bhai Shalloji had made tall promises, which were far too cheap. Bhai Shalloji was summoned by the *Guruji* to explain; *bhai sahib* pleaded guilty and apologized for his foolhardiness, but at the same time he pleaded with *Guruji* that since he has no dearth of anything whatsoever, in his benevolence, *Guruji* may please sustain the promises, made by Bhai Shalloji out of sheer enthusiasm and necessity, under the prevailing circumstances. The *Guru*, in his divine mercy and spiritual benignity, granted the very boon which comes true even today, that is, four centuries after the incident. The sublimity of the donations did bear fruit for many people and a tradition commenced.[3] Today, centuries have gone past, but this *sakhi* (true folklore) still holds its sway over the devout believers. No wonder, unquestioned beliefs and deep faith, with passage of time, turn into miracles of divinity.

COINCIDENCES TURN OMENS

Sheer coincidences, confirmed by the occurrence of impending or anticipated events, and reinforced by similar past memories, tend to become omens of future happenings. Such premonitions were seen and observed for about a year before the Indian Mutiny of 1857. In fact, there was a prediction that 100 years after the battle of Plassey, the British Raj in India would end. There were widespread omens, which some thought pointed towards this forecast. Some of these omens, portending the Mutiny, are discussed in the following paragraphs.

In Agra, a sheet of blood was seen for several nights; these sheets are considered a bad omen. Further, a comet (jharoo-dar sitara) appeared in the sky, which was said to be inauspicious for the British rulers. In some parts of North India, the *dund,* that is, the headless horseman, was sighted by late-night travelers, on moonless (amavasya) nights. Some of the surprised and frightened travelers swooned and were picked up half-dead the next day and taken to the hospital. Again, this was a bad omen.

In Shahjehanpur, a sepoy picked up a stone to kill a cobra, which was found on the roadside with its hood spread. His Hindu companion stopped him from hitting the cobra, saying that it was a manifestation of Lord Shiva, therefore, was considered deified in Hindu pantheon. Further, a Rajput

---

[3] Retold from stories personally heard.

soldier was prevented by a *sheikh* from firing at a flock of pigeons with the caution that they were deemed 'Sayyids' and respected in Islam.[4]

Around the same time, in Delhi, a white lady was seen outside Kashmiri Gate after midnight, dressed in a shroud. Even if it was an apparition, it was a bad omen. The *seths* (rich traders) of Chandni Chowk dreamt of Devi Chandi (a ferocious goddess) asking for blood while the residents of Jama Masjid saw the 'Mardan-e-Ghaib' (mystical persons) flying atop the *masjid* (mosque). The sentries on duty at the Red Fort swore that they saw the apparition of Aurangzeb on his charger. All these indications foretold of inauspicious events.

Believably, it was not only the Indians, but also some Britishers, who later shared their experiences of having such ominous dreams. A family which was shot dead in church dreamt about their end nearly every night for a week before the event. Only a girl and her mother, Mariam, survived, as was foretold in the dream. As is well-known, the mutiny occurred and before the British forces commenced their assault on Delhi, a lot of bloodshed had happened. The mutineers even insulted King Bahadur Shah Zafar, tugged at his sleeve and called him *budha* (old man) and much worse. The Indians, surreptitiously helping the beleaguered British officers and soldiers with rations like bread or meat, were also killed.

Just as the start of the mutiny was presaged by ill-forebodings, its end was also pre-indicated by good harbingers. A *neel-kanth* (blue jay), a bird sacred to Shivji Mahadev, was seen flying towards the Ridge in Delhi. Another good sighting was of the *jinns* offering *namaz* (Islamic prayer) towards the north, where the British troops were camped. Around the anniversary of the mutiny, one is reminded of these beliefs,

---

[4] R. V. Smith, 'Omens—and the Ridge', *Quaint Corner*, *The Statesman*, 9 May 1992.

which had great psychological effect on the minds of *Delhi-ites*; a few images still linger in their memory, like the white woman, in shroud, stalking Kashmiri Gate.[5]

LEGENDS IN A CAULDRON

There is a huge cauldron placed outside the palace of Jehangir in the Agra Fort. There has been much speculation about its possible or precise use and how it came to be placed where it is at present. Several legends have come to be associated with this antique cauldron and gaps in the legend have been filled by the imagination of fertile minds, to make the conjectures appear plausible and intelligible.

The cauldron is a gigantic vessel. It is five feet high and four feet deep with a diameter of eight feet and a circumference of 25 feet. Undoubtedly, it is huge and has steps outside and inside it for climbing in and out of the cauldron. It seems hewn out of a single rock stone despite its huge size and concomitant weight; its use can, thus, only be a wild guess.

Some believe that the cauldron was used by Bhima, the strongest of the Pandavas, to grind *bhang* for his drink. A man as big as him must have required that much quantity for consumption of this, not so potent, intoxicant-cum-invigorator. Surely, a vessel so big must have been suitable for the needs of a gigantic person. But the myth of Bhima using this cauldron does not stand scrutiny. Had it been used by Bhima, it would have ideally been found somewhere in Indraprastha and not Agra. But the argument can be logically extended that from the time of Mahabharata, it passed into the hands of many rulers till it was acquired by the Mughals for fulfilling their fancy, and placed in Agra fort.[6]

---

[5] Ibid.
[6] R. V. Smith, 'Legends in cauldron', *The Statesman*, 1 February 1992.

Another clue is a small inscription that indicates that the vessel was a bath tub that was presented by Jehangir to Nur Jehan in 1611, when he married her after a long wait and it also seems quite in keeping with the romantic emperors' sentiments. The existence of steps inside and outside the tub supports this conjecture. Another story connected with the bath tub theory, provides that it was filled with rose petals and one morning Nur Jehan was pleasantly surprised to find an oily layer on the water. That is how rose *ittar* (perfume) was made known to the world by the Mughal queen through her discerning sense of smell.

Another plausible legend associated with the tub claims that it was used by Jehangir as a vessel for bulk storage of drinks to be offered to his distinguished guests. The tale narrates that this cup was used to be filled to the brim with liquor and kept in a garden where royal parties were held. The steps outside were used by the *saaqi* to climb up to the edge of the cup; when the drink started depleting, he climbed down the steps inside to reach the receded level of the drink in the cup.[7] The cauldron is very likely a coveted object of ostentatious presentation by a king; but all the folktales have holes in them, which is natural for such primitive historical objects.

A TRIBUTE TO SHEETLA MATA FOR MIRACLES

A village named Kailar had, believably, existed for nearly 3500 years. Though the villagers were poor and backward by modern standards, yet they were happy and content in their lives. The primary settlement of just over 500 people was spread on the north side of a mound and predominantly comprised of Rajput families and Jat farmers. The lower castes occupied the lesser fertile land at the south west end of the mound. There was a Shiv temple in the village towards the west of

---

[7] Ibid.

the mound. Nearby, there was the village pond and a couple
of public wells for designated use by the various castes of the
village. This area has since been acquired by the Chandigarh
Capital Project and re-established, with a few landmarks
intact. On the Kailar mound exists the present-day Indira
Holiday Home of Sector 24, Chandigarh; the Shiv Temple is
still present at its original site.

At the turn of the last century, the small population of Kailar
was repeatedly afflicted by deadly diseases. Doctors and medi-
cines in the area, then, were rare and many deaths occurred.
Troubled by repeated eruptions of the deadly diseases and
considering it a curse, many families abandoned the main settlement on the mound and started living in low-lying lands
around the mound. But this did not help and superstitions
haunted the minds of people. The only solace lay in religion
and propitious prayers. In India, one of the most powerful
curative deities is Sheetla Mata, a mother goddess, who helps
cure and alleviate the sickly conditions of people, in particular, people afflicted by the deadly small pox and its less potent
cousins like chicken pox and measles. In fact, this *devi* is worshipped in many other forms throughout the sub-continent
for her potent miracles that rid the body of the disease and
cleanses entire colonies of the deadly virus.

The legend goes that one village virgin, struck by the pox,
advised the village elders to construct a temple dedicated to
Sheetla Mata who will ensure return of good health. The temple
was established in 1902 and, miraculously, the disease soon
vanished. The temple came to be called Basanti Devi temple.
There are, however, different conjectures as to how it got its
name. According to one version of oral history, the name of
the virgin who proposed the construction of the temple was
Basanti. Another version maintains that the name derives from
the day of *basant panchami,* on which the idol of the goddess
was installed.

The villagers lived happily ever after under the benign munif-
icence of the *Devi* till the construction of Chandigarh town
displaced them and filled up their pond and wells. Fortunately,
Basanti Devi temple still stands, tucked in a fold between the
house of a judge, the local Senior Superintendent of Police
and a strawberry field. Old villagers, settled elsewhere, still
visit the temple on occasion and swear by the curative power
of the merciful Goddess. Possibly, miracles do happen and
these have an embedded place in the human psyche.

A TALE OF PLATONIC LOVE THAT BESTOWS BOONS

It is not a love story but a story of love that was truly platonic.
The Jesal-Toral shrine in the small town of Anjar in Kutch,
Gujarat, tells the tale of a rare association between a dacoit
and a queen. The real story, as documented, dates back to the
year 1526 AD. In that era, Jesal, a young *Kutchi* Rajput, was
a dreaded dacoit of the area. Due to some tiff, his brother's
wife chided him and challenged him that if he was really
brave and a great dacoit, he should prove it by stealing Toral,
an extraordinary mare from the stables of a Saurashtra king.
With a stung ego, Jesal accepted the challenge and vowed to
prove his mettle.[8]

He soon set on the task so accepted and in the process of
stealing Toral, Jesal's hand got caught in a nail in the stable.
This caused him great pain and his agonized cries brought
out the king to the stable. The king casually asked the person,
who seemed in dire pain, as to what he wanted from stable
at that time. To this Jesal cryptically replied, 'Toral'. At this
juncture, there was a twist in the story. Jesal was unaware
that just like the mare, Toral was the name of the queen as
well as the king's precious sword, surprising the king with his
earnest request.

---

[8] Shefalee Vasudev, 'Waiting for a Happy Ending', *India Today,* 15 December 2003, 13.

The king was a devout person, full of pious thoughts and religious abidance, as also a celebrated donor (daani or daanvir) who had taken a vow never to disappoint anyone seeking his charity. Having heard Jesal's request in good faith, he felt duty-bound to fulfill the same in the right spirit. The die was cast. The king's moral mind did not see any dilemma in Jesal's request and he dutifully handed over the three Torals, his loving wife, his coveted mare and his precious sword, all bearing the same name.[9]

On the boat journey back home, Jesal realized that Toral was not an ordinary woman. He was tormented by the guilt of having taken away someone from their house, who, out of loyalty and obedience, did not even question or remonstrate at her husband's decision. It is said that Toral *Rani* is remembered in Gujarati literature as a poet who composed and sang devotional songs. So, the enlightened company of the Queen completely transformed Jesal from his old ways of dacoity; he got indoctrinated into a reformed life. He joined the Queen's religious efforts and started spreading the message of god.

The inseparable companionship and platonic bonding of teacher and disciple is often discussed in literature, but scholars have assiduously avoided discussing the alliance between Jesal and Toral as it was a relationship between a man and a woman. Common people respect their unusual affinity and pious relationship, which even death could not change. The legend has it that when Jesal undertook *samadhi*, he called out to Toral from his grave to join him. Toral who was travelling then, intuitively heard his voice, came back to Anjar and immediately took *samadhi*. No wonder, the two souls have remained inseparable. Later toral, the mare, too was buried

---

[9] Ibid.

outside the temple dedicated to Jesal and Toral. A green and magenta *chaddar* (sheet), now covers the equestrian grave.[10]

The shrine of Jesal-Toral at Anjar has a great following and pilgrims recount endless tales of benignity, boons and miracles attributed to the couple's blessings. In the recent past, Kutch has endured two serious earthquakes, one in 1957 and another in 2001. Though these earthquakes caused widespread damage and devastation in the surrounding areas, the twin *samadhis* have survived intact and every time the people inside the shrine have escaped unhurt even as neighbourhood mourned the many faces of death. Even an old priestess recalls how she stood unmoving, with hands folded at the *samadhi*, during both the earthquakes; she said with utter devotion and sincere belief, 'Toral Rani saved me.' No wonder, the faith is implicit and unshakable. The number of pilgrims regularly visiting the shrine is witness to belief in this unconventional association and its supernatural powers to bless.

THE MYSTERY OF SORCERY

This is a tale from the times when Chhatrapati Shivaji's son ruled the Maratha kingdom. The legend goes that the *Maharaja* was informed of the great reputation of a certain woman in his dominion, for sorcery and fortune-telling. However, he did not believe in sorcery yet sent for her to be summoned to his court, with the intention to put her to death, but also to satisfy his curiosity. The woman duly appeared before the king. She was about forty years of age, very corpulent and not of an ill-presence.

As she appeared, he asked her sternly in an imperial tone, whether she knew why he had sent for her. She answered in the affirmative with utmost intrepidity and unconcern.

---

[10] Ibid.

She further elaborated saying, 'You have summoned me to take away my life. But before you proceed to that, I hope you will, for your own sake, permit me to give you a salutary warning.' Perhaps out of curiosity or interest or in consideration of the woman's last wish before death or else, even apprehension of possible witchcraft, the king assented to her cautionary request.

The woman demanded two fowls to be brought to the court; one of them being a cock and the other, a hen. The cock, full of life and spirit, was put down on the ground. Taking the hen in her hands, she desired and urged the *Maharaja* to watch the consequences of her action. With these words, she wrung the neck of the hen off. Almost immediately, the playful cock, though untouched by anyone, started undergoing all the convulsions and agonies of the hen and accompanied it in its death.

All persons in the court were amazed and dumb-struck at the act, while the woman determinedly called out to the king, 'This Sir, remember will be a type of your fate and mine.'[11] The *Maharaja* was over-awed by the events and took time to compose himself. He, then, not only desisted from executing his intention of killing the woman, but also entreated the woman to excuse him for his ignorance and mistaken belief. The woman was set free and the *Maharaja* was convinced of the acts of sorcery.[12]

SUFI DARGAH NEAR MOHALI HILLS

There was a time when sufi saints roamed the land of Punjab in search of spirituality and a peaceful place for meditation. One such sufi saint, Hazrat Hafiz Mohammad Moosa left

---

[11] *The Statesman*, 20 January 1992.
[12] Ibid.

home at the age of 15 years and started following a sufi saint in Ropar. He later left for the forests of lower Shivaliks and meditated, and returned to his 'master' after a few years. Happy with his disciple's progress, his master allowed him to start his own *khanqah*, a designated and accredited house of the *sufis*. With blessings of his master, Moosa first meditated in the nearby Majri village, but later shifted to Manakpur, where his *dargah* still exists, and out of respect, this place came to be called Manakpur Sharif.[13] Manakpur, back then, was predominantly a Muslim populated village, but its demography changed after partition of India in 1947. It is located just a few miles from Chandigarh; in fact, it is equidistant from the Chandigarh border and Sahibzada Ajit Singh (SAS) Nagar (Mohali) in Punjab.

This *dargah* has a history spanning nearly two centuries and the compound houses the graves of 25 followers of the 19th century sufi saint, Sharif Hazrat Hafiz Mohammad Moosa Chishti Saabri. The finely built 192-year-old, turquoise-coloured shrine looks majestic and imposing, like a fortress, even from a distance. The entrance itself is spell-bounding with an 85-foot dome-shaped structure with two minarets in the front and an 18-foot tall, green-coloured gate. The ceiling of the cross-arched dome is ornamentally covered with finely painted frescoes.[14]

Faqir Baba Mehdi Hasan, *gaddinashin* of the *khanqah*, proudly announces that the shrine has links to the famed Ajmer Sharif Dargah. He further explains, 'We are from the Chishti order of sufi saints, the one started by Moinuddin Chishti, in whose memory the Ajmer shrine has been built.' The Chishti order has its roots in the older Ahmadiya sect

---

[13] Siddarth Banerjee, 'Manakpur sharif: Sufi break near Mohali hills', *The Times of India* (Chandigarh Edition), 3 July 2019, 6.
[14] Ibid.

of Islam in India, whose seat is at the *dargah* of Hazrat Syed Mohammed Jeelani Shah Quadri Chishti Kaleemi in Hyderabad. The *dargah* at Manakpur Sharif is open to all, irrespective of their religion or caste. Anecdotes of miracles connected with the place are profusely narrated. Many may not believe in these miracles, but spirituality and religion are all about faith.

GURU LEADS TO DIVINITY

In popular perception, yoga is a set of physical postures or exercises for building bodily strength and flexibility. But this is not true yoga; the actual meaning of *yog* is to join or unite, and in Indian philosophy it means union with the Divine or the eternal God. But for most of us, Divine is unknown and mysterious and difficult to understand or grasp with our limited human faculties. This is where we need help and the *guru* comes to our succour; the concept of the *guru* stems from here. Thus, *guru* is a teacher who guides us onto the path of Divinity, which opens up before us and as we walk it, love, peace and grace begin to pour into our mind and seep into our consciousness.

The next stage is our introduction to the Divine and this can be bestowed upon us by a *satguru*. The word '*sat*' means truth and an alternative meaning of *guru* is knowledge or spiritual gravity. So, *satguru* brings to light or consciousness, the spiritual knowledge, inherent, yet latent, in a person. The *satguru* has the acumen to discern the deserving from the undeserving as well as the magnetism to attract the souls ripe and ready for revelation, so that he can simply guide them to tread the path of spiritual evolution.

The litmus test for a *satguru* is that he must bestow the three graces of *pranpat, shaktipat and shivapat. Pranpat* is the transmission of *pranic* life energy, where the teacher breathes through the breath of the disciple to diffuse negativity and evolve purity in consciousness. In the *shaktipat* stage, he transmits the *kundalini* healing energy, thereby awakening every chakra and connecting them to his own, to channelize goodness and benignity. Finally, through *shivapat* transmission, a teacher tends to share his enlightened consciousness of a stilled-mind. This is called the state of 'Living-in-the-Now' or 'Living-in-the-Present'. In this stage, distractions of a conflict-ridden world are discarded, and discords are shed. This provides an exclusive experience of essential healing at the individual level and the mind trains itself to tread towards stillness. In the process, human bondage is liberated, the Divine is realized and soul is enlightened.[15]

MYTHICAL POWERS THAT CURE AILMENTS

Rajasthan is, no doubt, a backward state battling with illiteracy, but its population harbours more than its share of myths and superstitions. One such belief is responsible for the ever-surging crowds at Mehndipur Balaji temple in Dausa district. It is believed that Hanuman *darshan* in this temple cures all kinds of mental ailments and also helps exorcise evil spirits. The powers may seem mythical, yet those who have benefitted vouch for the divine help.[16]

Again, in a somewhat prosperous district of Sri Ganganagar, a belief persists that snakes have mythical powers. In reverence of this belief, the festival of Gogaji (serpent deity) is held at Gogamedi. Legend says that before the *Gogaji* fair was started, every year hundreds of farmers used to die from snake-bites. This became too much for the community, so a *puja* (prayer) was offered to propitiate Gogaji deity. This annual celebratory *puja* ceremony, later, turned into a

---

[15] Yogiraj satguru Siddhanath, 'Pranpat, Shatipat and Shivapat', *Hindustan Times*, May 2008.

[16] 'Ten Myths and Miracles' in *Hindustan Times*.

full-fledged festival, in the belief that snakes do not bite a person who attends this *mela* (fair).[17]

STRANGE HAPPENINGS IN RAJASTHAN

In Rajasthan, in Pali district, there is a temple of Lord Mahavir of the Jainism religion. It has an idol of Lord Mahavir that is made completely of stone but, strangely enough, it has grown a natural moustache. This is a verifiable fact.[18]

At Bhilwara, in Jodhpur district, there is a temple of Aayee Mata (a mother deity), where an *akhand jyoti* (a light that is never extinguished nor extinguishes on its own) always burns (24x7), but strangely, instead of emitting black soot as a natural chemical process of burning, saffron stems drop from this light.

The hillock of Poorna Giri Devi is situated about 12 km to the west of Pali in Rajasthan. This hillock, on the auspicious night of Deepawali, starts glistening like gold. This does not happen on other nights.

Further, at Nadwal, in the Pali district, there is a temple with the idol of Asha Poorav Mata. This idol changes its physical appearance three times in a year. For four months, it assumes its childhood features; for the next four months, it assumes the characteristics of a young maiden; and for the remaining four months, it assumes the face of an old lady.[19]

AT DARGAH HAZRAT NIZAMUDDIN AULIA

Haji Syed Kashif Ali Nizami, *Sajjadah nashin* of Dargah Sharif, informs that the *dargah* (tomb) of Hazrat Nizamuddin Aulia

---

[17] Ibid.

[18] This and the following details relating to Rajasthan temples and its idols are from a report by Subhash Rawal in Urdu newspaper, *Hind Samachar* (Jalandhar), 21 November 1994.

[19] Ibid.

is one of the oldest and biggest *dargahs* in Delhi. It is more than 700 years old and a very popular destination for wish-making, with a high wish-fulfillment quotient. As per the custom, the wish-makers first visit and pay obeisance at Hazrat Amir Khusro's *dargah* located in the same premises and thereafter, go to Hazrat Nizamuddin Aulia's *dargah* to make their wish. The wish or *mannat* is marked by tying a red cotton thread around a hole in the latticed marble enclosure.

When the wish/*mannat* is fulfilled, the knot of thread tied earlier, has to be untied. But it may be difficult to recognize your own knot among the numerous other knots, so any knot can be untied and the ritual is considered to be complete. Apart from this, the blessed person has to offer a *chadar* (a sheet of flowers) to be laid on the *dargah* and comply with any other promises made at the time of wish-making. It is a secular shrine and open to people from all religious backgrounds.[20]

PARABLE OF THE HOMA BIRD

The Vedas speak of the Homa bird that is known to live very high in the sky, presumably flying all its life, never perching anywhere and certainly avoiding coming anywhere close to the ground. It is believed that they fly higher and higher to seek heaven right from birth. They are considered pious and auspicious and should, perchance, their fleeting shadow fall on a human being, he is deemed to be bestowed with greatness and may become a king or a saint or a celebrated soldier.

According to the Vedas, the Homa bird lives so very high in the sky that when the mother bird lays her egg, the fall takes many days for it to reach the ground. Meanwhile, in

---

[20] Namya Sinha and Jasjeet Plaha, 'May your wishes come true', *Hindustan Times City*, 30 December 2007.

the process of fall, the egg hatches and the chick continues falling. The fall of the chick too goes on for days and in the meantime, the chick develops its eyes and starts looking around. As it nears the ground, it becomes conscious of it closeness to the material world and instinctively realizes that it will meet certain death if it hits the ground. Frightened, it gives a shrill cry and shoots up towards its mother for shelter and safety and is not tempted to look anywhere else. The mother is believed to dwell high in the sky.

This story fits as a parable to a class of devotees called the *nitya siddhas* or those who have attained perfection. The members of this sect seek god from birth and do not enjoy any material offerings of the world. Their faith maintains that the outgoing nature of mind (pravritti) shows itself in the quest for external worldly pleasures and achievements. Its counterpart *nivritti*, represents the nature of the other part of the mind, which does not want to wander out and strives to seek the kingdom of heaven within oneself. The experience of this force of *nivritti* is the beginning of their religion.

A BENEFICENT TEMPLE AT ANANTPUR

There is a holy shrine at Anantpur in Andhra Pradesh that is famous by the name of Lepakshi Temple. The temple is made in the typical Vijayanagar architectural style. The structure of this temple is supported by 70 pillars made of granite stone. However, one pillar seems like it is hanging from the roof and does not touch the ground to support the proportionate weight of the building. Thus, there is a discernible gap between the pillar and the floor. Despite the fact that it does not touch or mesh with the floor, it is still deemed to be the main pillar of the building. There is the belief, embodying fear, that if it is taken off or removed, then the entire temple structure will collapse. Sensibly, nobody has attempted to prove this.

Lepakshi in Telugu means a beautiful bird, denoting Jatayu. The legend has it that Jatayu was lying injured here and was saved by Lord Rama during his sojourn in exile. The temple is now devoted to Veerabhadra. There is, of course, another belief that anyone who can pass his cloth in the gap between the hanging pillar and the floor, prospers in every way. Locals believe and testify that many have been bestowed with good luck by performing this ritual.

MIRACULOUS POOL OF GOOD HEALTH

Situated in Masuria locality of Jodhpur, Parcha Naadi is a place where even ghosts fear to go, yet this area hosts an annual fair of Baba Ramdev and has a shrine of his *guru*, Baba Balinath. But the main attraction is the pond in the shrine premises. A belief prevails that if a person takes a dip in its sacred water while chanting, '*yeh chamatkari paani hai*' (this water is miraculous), he or she will be freed of any evil spirit that might have possessed them. This miracle water is also believed to cure physical disorders and skin diseases.[21]

It is maintained that this pond is linked to the pool of Baba Ramdev, also called Chamatkari Bawdi (a well or pond with miraculous powers). This *bawdi* is located in Ramdeora temple near Pokhran in Jaisalmer district. Believably, Baba Ramdev had killed a devil at this place and the *bawdi* got sanctified. Faith ordains that a dip in this blessed *bawdi* will cure skin diseases including leprosy; people believe this from the heart and vouch for the miracles.

AUCTION OF HOLY WATER FOR THE CHILDLESS

Every year, on the festival of Ashokashtami, Mukteswar temple at Bhubaneswar witnesses an auction of a different

---

[21] 'Ten Myths and Miracles', *Hindustan Times*.

kind. Interestingly, the auction is for the holy water from the temple's sacred pond called Marichi Kunda. The anxious and eager bidders are childless couples from across the state as well as the country. A pot of the holy water used to get a final bid for around three thousand rupees, ten years ago. The auction rate would have escalated by now. The money realized is deposited in a fund for temple development.[22]

An ancient belief is that couples who fast and bathe in the waters of Marichi Kunda on Ashokashtami day will soon be blessed with a child. The temple authorities inform that childless devotees have been coming to this temple for a few centuries now, and though no statistics have been maintained, it is believed that hundreds of couples have been blessed with a child as indicated by the growing crowd every year. An Oriya scholar asserted, 'Science cannot explain it and rationale does not work here.' The belief has existed for too long to be doubted.

REVENGEFUL CROWS TARGET A MAN

Shiva Kewal, a daily wager of Sumela village of Shivpuri in Madhya Pradesh is scared of coming out of his house for fear of attack by crows. Every time he steps out of the house, he furtively looks heavenwards, to watch out for an aerial attack by crows that come cawing and clawing for him. Most of the times, a squadron of crows, heads for him with talons extended and beaks lunging, for a bite. Sometimes, it is a lone ranger that swoops down on him. Mostly, assaults are sudden and frightening. This happens every time he leaves his house. For locals, it is a matter of daily amusement.

It started three years ago, on the day when Kewal tried to rescue a chick that was stuck in iron netting. Unfortunately,

---

[22] Ibid.

it died in his hands and since then such attacks have become a regular occurring. They believe he killed the chick. How he wish, he could explain to them that he was only trying to save the chick to help it survive, and not kill it. The crows couldn't understand Kewal's intentions; scars on Kewal's head show how he had bled in this one-sided battle. He had been injured many times before he started carrying a stick to shoo the crows away, sometimes unsuccessfully.[23]

What surprises innocent and illiterate villagers is how crows apparently harbour grudges and remember human faces for taking their revenge. Incidentally, researchers in Seattle and University of Washington have revealed that crows have a sharp memory and can remember faces of humans who have offended them.

SNIPPETS

WISH-MAKING IN DELHI

Wish-making is one of the fascinating traditions popular among young Delhiites, who find different nooks scattered all over Delhi, which are famous for such wish-making. Only a select such places are described below, with their typically distinctive customs or rituals. No analysis of the wish-fulfillment quotient of these shrines has been attempted.

WISH-FULFILMENT AT CHHATTARPUR TEMPLE

Chhattarpur temple is one of the most popular wish-making places in Delhi and one of the few places where

---

[23] P. Naveen, 'Why this MP man is target of "revengeful" crows', *The Times of India*, 3 September 2019, 7.

wishes are made to a goddess, in this case, Goddess Durga. There are two holy trees, a peepul tree and a banyan tree, in the compound of the temple. Believers tie a red *chunri* on the branches of the trees while making a wish. The *chunri* has to be untied when the wish in fulfilled. One will be amazed at the number of *chunris* tied on the trees. The wish-makers need not identify their own *chunri*; untying the knot of any *chunri* is considered as due fulfillment of the ritual. However, there are people, who for identification, tie bangles, souvenirs, money or any other distinctive memento with their *chunri*.[24]

The other code of conduct is secrecy; one is not allowed to disclose the nature and content of the wish made until it comes true. Most people untie one knot to tie another. This means that human desires are insatiable and new ones keep cropping up; thus, the cycle of wishing before Goddess Durga continues.

AT DARGAH OF MATKA PEER

While driving from the Supreme Court of India in Delhi to Purana Quila, one will be surprised to see a huge tree on the left side of the road that grows *matkas* (earthen pitchers) rather than blossoms with flowers. Do not be surprised, it is the *dargah* of Matka Shah, where young couples come, even from far off places, to make a wish, believing it will come true. Once the wish is fulfilled, the wish-maker is required to offer a *matka* filled with jiggery, dried grams and other ingredients, to the caretaker. This custom dates back to a legend

---

[24] Namya Sinha and Jasjeet Plaha, 'May your wishes come true', *Hindustan Times City*, 30 December 2007.

of an ailing traveler, who was cured when Matka Shah offered him water in a *matka*. The emptied *matkas* are hung on the tree in the compound of the *dargah*. Many *matkas* fall and break during inclement weather or due to other natural causes, but nobody removes them on their own.[25]

AT DARGAH HAZRAT KHWAJA QUTUBUDDIN BAKHTIYAR KAKI

Located in Mehrauli, one reaches the *dargah* of Hazrat Khwaja Qutubuddin Bakhtiyar Kaki through narrow alleys. Like other places of wish-making, here also wishes are made by tying a symbolic red thread on the holy walls. Most people who come here are couples desirous of bearing children or wishing for other dire needs. As women are not allowed near the *mazar*, they only peep inside from the latticed window. Otherwise the place is open to people from all religious denominations. It is customary to offer token money once the wish is made. It is believed to bring luck and fruition of the wish.[26]

POORAM FESTIVAL OF KERALA

In the state of Kerala, Pooram festival is held at temples where elephants congregate in large numbers. Most of them are decoratively decked with local deities. It is believed that their loud and collective ritualistic trumpeting, pleases Lord Indra, the god of rain, and he sends dark clouds that bring rain for prosperity. It is also believed that dark coloured or black elephants are associated with rainfall while white elephants (or *prasadi*

---

[25] Ibid.
[26] Ibid.

hathi that does not do any labour and is decorously exhibited on ceremonial occasions with pride) are representative of snow.

A DIVINE PETITION

Chitai temple is situated around 8 km from the beautiful town of Almora in Uttarakhand. This temple is believed to be the abode of Golu Devta, known as the 'God of Justice' for his believers. For Kumaonis particularly, Golu Devta is justice personified. Externally, the temple comes across as a quaint place made in Kumaoni architecture. Golu Devta is considered to be possessing divine powers. The devotees approach the deity with applications of grievances seeking justice against perceived wrongs perpetrated on them. Once the prayer is heard and injustice is undone, the devotees are expected, in reverence, to offer a bell to Golu Devta. This is the reason why thousands of bells hang in the compound of the temple and letters are seen strewn around.[27]

There is another temple with bells hanging from a banyan tree in the same compound as the temple. This temple is located close to Digboi in Assam. People make a wish and tie a metal bell on the tree that is literally loaded with the hanging bells, thus presented. This is quite indicative of the wish-fulfilment quotient of the deity presiding there.

DEITY TURNS BANKER FOR LOANS

Taking loans from the local money lender or the institutional bankers is a common practice worldwide. But in

---

[27] 'Ten Myths and Miracles', *Hindustan Times*.

Andhra Pradesh, the temple of Goddess Vengamamba at Narrawada in Nellore district turns into a bank with the blessings of the Goddess. The temple loans are generally for ₹100, but in a few cases, people avail of loans of larger amount, which may go up to ₹10,000. The temple lends the money at a 12 per cent rate of interest, along with the blessings of the Goddess as a bonus. It is, however, informally expected that a loan of ₹100 will be returned as ₹150 after one year. The balance, if any, is treated as an offering to the deity. It should come as no surprise to anyone that the temple accounts have no long outstanding liabilities or non-performing assets.[28]

According to legend, anyone who takes a loan from the temple, with the Goddess's blessings, reaps good returns in whatever venture he or she invests the money. In fact, devotees treat the loan as token money and add to it their own capital while making investments in ventures. Owing to this belief, businessmen from different parts of the country and even abroad, flock to the temple to participate in the rituals and avail a loan from the Goddess during the Brahmotsavam ceremony performed in June every year. After the festivities are over, the devotees line up to clear their old dues and take fresh loans for new ventures.

---

[28] Ashok Das, 'Loan from God with blessings, 12% interest', *Hindustan Times*, 9 June 2004.

7

SADASUHAGS:
THE CROSS-DRESSERS

Veneration of the Oddities and
Peculiar Practices

In the evolution of human society and community living, religion, however primitive, elemental or minimalistic, has always had a place in some form or manner. Even aboriginal and tribal denominations had pseudo-religious totemic faiths, which many of them still carry with staunch fervour. Religion, for them, had a different meaning and purpose in life. It was more relevant to mundane things in life like warding off adversity, ill-luck, illness, etc. For some, religion was a shield against natural calamities like droughts and floods, earthquakes or volcanic eruptions. Religion, to this effect, treated everything incomprehensible as a god and worshipped it to propitiate for benevolence. Later, religion came to be sought and followed for higher virtues, spiritual values, after-life treatment and salvation from rebirth.

Religion has evolved with time as few spiritually enlightened beings were blessed with unique reverential experiences and divine revelations, which were interpreted differently by different groups of people, with shifting of emphasis on traditional tenets and prevalent rituals. As a result, small groups tended to branch off as separate religious sects with differential beliefs and varied pronouncements on attendant rituals. Gradually, these break-away branches developed their own tenets and conspicuous identities with separate prayer systems and anomalized ritualistic practices that came to be recognized as distinct from the main religion, acquiring a different name and calling.

The same happened for Sadasuhags. This sect, though originally part of mainstream Hinduism, leaned in a different direction, highlighting a prominent belief that all living persons are the brides of the Eternal God, irrespective of their gender. Thus, they remain brides forever and never get widowed because God is immortal and eternal. With this cognition and motivation, they dress as women, embellish themselves in feminine ways and mentally pray to please God, imagining him as the groom. With passage of time and growing disapprobation of cross-dressing by the prudish society, this sect went into hiding and has gradually disappeared. These days, few Sadasuhags are seen, either near temples or seeking alms.

Besides, social customs, at times, acquire oddities and unusual practices and turn into superstitions that defy common logic, where optical physicality tends to be illusory or remains unexplained in rational terms; for example, the Koovagam festival of transgenders, the weeping statue, prejudice against the number thirteen or the Spanish festival of Devil's Jump. While some oddities may be backed by reason like exaltation of pigs for economic necessity or the seasonal facts related to the Lenten Moon or Montanna for social justice. Thus, this chapter is a miscellany of narrations in diversity.

LORD RAMA'S BLESSINGS TO THE THEN UNBLESSED

India, particularly North India, has a custom of organizing a function of ladies' *sangeet* during weddings, mostly attended by ladies, though it is gradually becoming a common celebration for men and women, involving singing, dancing and merry-making. This is generally a private function of the household with select invitees. But visible signs of celebrations attract *Hijras* (eunuchs) to visit the household with such *sangeet* festivities. Apart from such celebrations, *Hijras* also visit the house celebrating other auspicious occasions and ceremonies like births and marriages, to bless the new-born or the newly-weds, and to solicit alms, which have, lately, escalated into hefty demands, bordering on extortion.

The origin of *Hijras* can be traced back to several myths during the times of Ramayana and Mahabharata. According to one legend, Rama while leaving for his 14-year-exile, found hordes of Ayodhian devotees following him. Rama disapproved of this and directed all men and women to return to Ayodhya and not to accompany him any further. Most of them, obeying his dictate, returned, but a few were still left and kept following. When Lord Rama enquired as to why they had not returned despite his strict instructions, they clarified that they were neither men nor women and, thus, his directive did not apply to them. Touched by their love, affection and fealty, Lord Rama bestowed on them a *vardaan* (boon) and gave them a benign power to confer blessings on people on auspicious occasions. The remaining followers, obeying Lord Rama's command and feeling highly blessed, came back to Ayodhya and started acting upon the boon conferred on them. Thus, started the tradition of '*Badhai*' by the *hijra* community.

Later on, the *hijras* were employed in the Mughal courts and *shahi* harems as guards and servants. This was because they could not sexually molest or exploit women, who were considered safe under their watch and ward. They could, with this immunity, enter intimate quarters of the kings and queens to fulfil any demands or meet any requests and were, thus, often, witness to many secret liaisons and private affairs. Their access to such vulnerable and damning information, including the clandestine activities of the royals, made them complicit and highly influential in royal affairs.

In India, transgender is an overarching term, yet loosely understood in meaning and equally loosely applied to a heterogeneous set of people and not to a homogeneous community. It, thus, covers and includes eunuchs, hermaphrodites and cross-dressers. Therefore, this connotation unfolds complex shades of their identity through some very subtle perceptions and some bold images. Eunuchs, as a community in India, is coming into its own and there are social and political stirrings among them to join the mainstream population as equals. Kaya, a non-governmental organization (NGO) has roughly estimated their number at about five lakhs, but it could be more.

KOOVAGAM FESTIVAL OF TRANSGENDERS IN TAMIL NADU

Koovagam is the time and place, when and where transgenders flaunt their uniqueness and sexuality in style without any fear of prejudice or stigma. Koovagam, a little-known village in Villupuram district of Tamil Nadu, hosts the biggest festival for the third gender or eunuchs, called *Aravanis* in Tamil. This festival lasts for one week and is celebrated with big rallies, beauty pageants, sports events, gala feasts and other festivities. People from the transgender community also tie nuptial knots with a deity at the local Koothandavar temple and freely consummate their marriage in the open fields under a full moon sky.[1] The final day of the week-long celebrations falls on a full moon night in April, every year.

Legend has it that Lord Krishna turned into Mohini, a beautiful woman, to marry a local boy, Aravan, for a night. This was because Aravan was to be sacrificed the next morning during the Kurukshetra war and no woman had come forward to tie the knot. Lord Krishna blessed him with this bliss of marital pleasure. The eunuchs, called Aravanis in Tamil Nadu, assume the role of Mohini every year and marry the legendary Aravan at the Koothandavar temple in a hallowed tradition.

The euphoric celebration has been accepted so far as an age-old practice, but has been condemned in the recent times, since the morning after the consummation of ritualistic marriage, the fields look like dump yard of condoms, which are often, in amusement, picked up by young children to the embarrassment of the parents and possibly constitute a bad influence on them. It has been seen lately that sex workers, homosexuals, bi-sexuals, bi-curious and even cross-dressers enter the fest and boldly mingle with their cognate peers. Besides, many seem in unusual hurry to have multiple sex escapades during this licentious time. This has vitiated the

---

[1] Avishek G. Dastidar, 'Celebrating their uniqueness', *Hindustan Times*, 23 April 2008.

solemn environment and local resistance to the festivities is growing. In any case, the present message being propagated is 'No sex around the temple'. This is how traditions are debased to attract a stigma.

SADASUHAGS: THE CROSS-DRESSERS

In a strange custom, Sadasuhags were men dressed up as women and sought alms from dancing girls and prostitutes. They would spend a lot of time dressing up gaudily and adorning themselves to look attractive and be liked by God as eternal spouses. They were, thus, also called cross-dressers. Sadasuhags are persons who always enjoys marital bliss with god and is never widowed. They are mystics in their own right and should not be confused with eunuchs or transgenders. However, they are rarely seen on the streets or elsewhere in public anymore.

The cult of Sadasuhags is an off-shoot of Sufism, in which the eternal beloved is the God Almighty, to whom all beings are attracted and attached or metaphorically married. They came to be known as Sadasuhags because the Almighty is immortal and can never die, so these persons never get widowed and remain forever wedded. They had a restless soul that yearned for oneness with God and perpetually strived for a spiritual union with that mystical lover.

Let it be clear that Sadasuhags are not *'dhongias'* who masqueraded in various disguises. They are *faqirs* (poor people) seeking alms from prostitutes who were looked down upon by the society as a depraved class. They did not mind accepting their charity in the name of the creator. Sadasuhags were followers of Islam but were greatly influenced by Indian ethos and culture.[2] Thus, they form a unique order about which the present generation is blissfully ignorant.

---

[2] RVS, 'The last Sadasuhag?' *The Statesman*, 22 February 1992.

There is a tale of a Sadasuhag who dwelt in a *'takia'* or piece of land, which also had the grave (dargah) of a Saiyyed *baba*. As is usual with the graves of saintly persons, there was a tamarind (imli) tree, a *neem* tree and a *gondini* tree for shade and fruit. The compound was small, but figuratively speaking was the resting place of this holy man. The Sadasuhag used to spend a lot of time dressing up and doing his makeup, much to the amusement of little boys peeping from the nearby windows. He would usually emerge in a green sari, jingling his green bangles that completely covered his arms and would go on his usual rounds for seeking alms.

The Sadasuhag died several decades ago and was buried under the *gondini* tree in the same *takia* compound along with the grave of the Saiyyed *baba*. It became a revered place of worship. Over the years, the *gondini* tree dried up, but the tamarind tree, though older than the *gondini* tree, survived and regularly blossoms and bears fruit for the devout and the urchins alike and continues to provide shade to the *baba's* grave. The blessings of the holy people buried there still pervaded the compound with benign influence.

One day a contractor hacked the trees down and leveled the place for a new construction project. However, destiny plays strange tricks. The contractor was murdered; his second son met the same fate and the third son went to jail. It could be a coincidence, of course, but the devout draw their own conclusions. They linked this *sarvanash* (devastation) with the destruction of the sacred trees; some deemed it as vengeance. Beliefs have their own logic and rationale. Now a new *neem* tree has been planted near the Saiyyed's grave, but the Sadasuhag's tomb vanished long ago.[3]

---

[3] Ibid.

HOMOSEXUALITY IS NO MODERN PRACTICE

Homosexuality has existed from times immemorial and cannot be proclaimed as a modern practice. An inscription on the pyramids of Egypt provides credible evidence of its existence over four millennia ago. In 1964, a newly discovered pyramid was being explored. The pyramid was located near the famous Step Pyramid in the necropolis of Saqarra that is a short drive from the Sphinx and the pyramids at Giza. As per the Egyptian practice, mortuary temples are the exclusive resting place of prominent men, their wives and children.

The new pyramid yielded no royal mummies or dazzling jewels. It presented a different sight in the form of wall art in the most sacred chamber. There, carved in stone, were the images of two men embracing each other with their names inscribed as Niankhkhnum and Khnumhotep. Though not belonging to the nobility, they were highly esteemed in the palace as the chief manicurists of the king, between 2380 BC and 2320 BC, during the time known as the reign of the fifth dynasty of the Old Kingdom. Grooming the king was then considered an honoured vocation.[4]

Archaeologists find it unusual for an elite tomb to be shared by two men of apparently equal standing and repute in the Egyptian custom. It is further intriguing to discover a couple of same sex to be depicted locked in an embrace, ostensibly in an intimate relationship. Other pictorial frames on the wall also show them holding hands and nose-kissing, which was an accepted and favoured form of kissing in ancient Egypt.

Analysis of the wall art by archaeology scholars and social scientists led to different interpretations and inspiring speculations. One such prosaic interpretation was that the two men

---

[4] Adapted from a NYT report, 'A mystery, locked in timeless embrace', published in India.

were brothers; another, equally unimaginative interpretation describes them as probable identical twins. Apart from these conjectures, a more credible analysis, which has gained much support from sociologists and LGTBQ (lesbian, gay, bisexual, transgender and queer) advocates, leads us to believe that the men were, in all probability, romantically involved. This seems to be the earliest depiction of homosexual relationship.

DURIG RITUAL OF SHAGAO

Shigao village in the Sahyadri hills of Goa is well-known for a tree-climbing ritual called 'Durig'. In local language, it means a high boundary wall. Durig is practised elsewhere in the state also, but not with such passion, dedication, cooperation and celebration.

The ritual begins each year with villagers going into the forest to identify and bring a suitable tree. This happens on a day before Durig and only the *suvari* tree is picked and used for this purpose. The selected tree is typically manually dragged to the village and no mechanized transport is used. On the night of *Panchami*, as per the Hindu calendar, the ritual begins around 11 pm. Accompanied with the playing of local folk music, the tree is shaved off its bark and its highly slippery trunk is uncovered. Then, the tree trunk is firmly set into the open courtyard of the Shanta Durga Temple for the competition next day.[5]

The ritual starts with the *mukhya gaonkar*, a respected and experienced person, chosen to climb the 20-feet-tall tree trunk. He climbs at a lightning speed. He is nimble, quick and leaves the crowd gasping in amazement at his dexterity, agility and skill. Once atop, he pulls up a *kalso* (pitcher) filled

---

[5] Gauree Malkarnekar, 'Here, a race to the top means climbing a tree', *The Times of India*, 17 March 2015.

with water and empties it slowly on the tree. The water licks the shaven trunk as it streams down, making it highly slippery for the human hands to grasp and hold onto the tree.

Eight boys in shorts gather below and size up the task of climbing the tree, while chanting prayers to the deity. These climbers are known as *gadde*, who on achieving the climb will win a *jhelo* (a garland of abolim flowers) and *valo*, a white cloth tied to the tree-trunk top. No doubt, it is a risky show of courage and grit achieved with the participants' cooperation and team coordination of a high order. But the risk to life and limb is worth a cure for their sufferings or for a blessing from the local deity. During the act of climbing, the heady native music energizes those who perform the ritualistic climb.

As the climbers struggle to cling onto the smooth and slippery trunk, lose grip, slide down or fall, the crowd roars in joy and cheers them to not to give up and keep climbing. They shout in exultation when one makes it to the top and earns the prizes of *jhelo* and *valo*. The next day villagers celebrate with *gulal* (red coloured powder) and that is why the local deity, Shanta Durga, is also called Ragaii or Mother of Colours. Legend has it that this village was located amidst dense forests and the ancestors had to survive tough weather conditions, animal threats and inhospitable environment.[6] Cooperation was the way to survival and Durig teaches them to honestly depend upon one another for common survival and collective safety.

MONTANNA: A TRADITION FROM YORE

The payment of *montanna* is a tribal practice that evolved as a social custom in Rajasthan and Gujarat; particularly in the districts of Banaswara, Dungarpur and Udaipur. *Montanna* is paid to a family, one of whose members has been murdered

---

6 Ibid.

in unusual circumstances. The payment of *montanna* is intended as a compensatory measure to help the victim's family. This shows tribal inclusiveness, kinship and altruism. Indeed, the members of the tribe lived for each other. The custom appears to be a mode of natural justice for unnatural deaths. Though not exactly same, it could fall into the genre of blood money sanctioned by Shariat among the Muslims for compounding crimes.

Perhaps, an account of such an incident will clarify the rationale behind this custom of compensatory justice. Deepa, a member of the Gamar community belonging to Semlia village in Gujarat was married to a Pargi community resident in Gau Pipla village of Udaipur district. Sometime after the marriage, Deepa's body was found hanging from a tree under suspicious circumstances, pointing towards suicide. The Semlia villagers maintained that since she died in the custody of her in-laws, the entire Pargi community residing in the Gau Pipla village should pay the bereaved Gamar family ₹700,000 as *montanna* (money for the dead).

The Pargi community dilly-dallied on the payment. Annoyed at the delay in *montanna*, the Gamar community comprising of about 2,000 men, women and children, staged an invasion (locally known as Charotra) of Gau Pipla village and there was burning and looting of 19 houses of Gau Pipla. Clashes with the police also occurred. After two days of stand-off, during which even the dead body remained hanging, negotiations were held in the presence of the police of Gujarat and Rajasthan, and *Pargis* were told to pay ₹400,000 to the *Gamars*, while Rajasthan government paid ₹100,000 to the family of the deceased woman. As per the customs, unless the *montanna* is paid, the offending community is not allowed to venture into the offended-community-dominated area.[7]

---

[7] Rohit Parihar, 'Death's Ransom', *India Today*, 8 November 2004, 68–69.

Lately, however, this benign custom of helping the needy victim family, has degenerated and become a means of extortion. Quite often now this practice is grossly misused for personal benefit or vested interests. Might and greed, and not justice, rule the people as evidenced by such recent incidents that keep occurring. Supporters of the *montanna* system and musclemen who lead invasions (*charotra*), act as judges, negotiators and protagonists of the aggrieved family, even without the family's express consent; and have succeeded in creating a demand for compensation for just about any unnatural death. These arbiters and goons pocket a major part of the realized compensation as fees for bringing it home.[8] One wonders, if this system could have prevailed without the complicity of the police and politicians. Nevertheless, the nobility of the medieval custom has suffered in reputation and literally lost its avowed purpose. State governments need to enforce the law and ensure justice is dispensed to all parties.

SNIPPETS

FORCING THE DEITY FOR A BLESSING

There is an ancient shrine of Nari-Semri near Mathura in Uttar Pradesh. A strange custom associated with this shrine is that, once a year, the devotees congregate here wielding bamboo sticks (lathis) instead of the usual reverential posture or prostration or offering of flowers or sweets. Ostensibly, it is a gesture to beat the deity and forcing her to bless them or to extort boons. This is the only goddess that is worshipped by the devotees with *lathis* in hand. Apparently, this seems sheer extortion, indeed!

---

[8] Ibid.

BLAME THE DEITY FOR LOSS

There used to be a tradition among Goan Christians, which provided that when they lost something precious, they would go to the church and bind the statue of St Anthony with a rope. The rope was untied and the saint was released only if the lost item was recovered. There are, however, no statistics as to how many times and how many statues were tied, released or tied again. The Church now frowns upon this practice and does not permit such tying of the statutes of St Anthony in churches.[9]

ALL ABOUT THE 'DEVIL'S DOZEN'

There is a belief or a superstition in the western world that the number 13 is unlucky. This fear of the number 13 is also called 'Triskaidekaphobia'. Therefore, in the hotels and high-rise buildings there is no 13th floor and hotels do have a room numbered 13 either. Of course, the 13th day in every month is unavoidable, but if the 13th falls on a Friday, the dread is compounded many times. In some Hollywood movies also, this fear surrounding the date and the human psyche when the date coincides with a Friday, has been emotionally depicted and exploited commercially.

In Scotland, the number 13 is referred to as the 'Devil's Dozen'. There is a further belief that if thirteen people dine together, one or more will die within a year. In France and Italy, the state lotteries never sell tickets with the number 13 because people declined to buy tickets so numbered.

---

[9] *The Tribune*, New Delhi, 7 May 1994.

The Turks dislike the number 13 so much that it was expunged from their vocabulary for sometime. Similarly, there is a superstition about names having thirteen letters of the alphabet because they bring devil's luck to the one so named. A few examples are Jack the Ripper, Charles Manson, Jeffery Dahmer, etc. Whether a coincidence or not, superstitions never dies easily. It really takes courage to break the taboos.

However, in India, there is no association of ill-fortune or bad luck with the number 13. In fact, this number is dedicated to Mahadev and is reserved for *Pradosh Vrat* (fasting). Most Hindus consider it lucky and many of the festivals and auspicious celebrations fall on the thirteenth day of a month, for example, Lohri and Baisakhi.

EXALTATION OF PIGS

The much-maligned pigs have also been exalted occasionally in some tribes. For example, certain Oceanic tribes used to measure family wealth and social status in terms of the number of pigs owned. Pigs were, no wonder, treated as a valuable asset and a precious possession. They were valued so much that in times of scarcity or drought, a mother suckled a pig in preference to her own child.[10] How ironic for the modern society to believe in this!

Further, in Perigord region of France, farmers grow truffles which are also called 'black diamonds of gastronomy'. The truffles generally grow from two to twelve inches below the ground and thus, it is difficult to find their location. In order to economize effort of labour for digging for the truffles, the farmers use pigs to sniff the ground

---

[10] Luis Fernandes and Pradeep Sathe, 'Kaleidoscope', *Hindustan Times*.

to reveal the presence of truffles and localize the digging effort with positive results.

The Cretans have revered and worshipped pigs in the past. Similarly, Vishnu, a venerated god of the Hindu pantheon, chose the form of a boar for his third incarnation as Varaha.

THE DIRTIEST QUEEN

Russia had a queen ruling it for ten years. History tells us that Queen Zarnina Anne ruled Russia from 1730 AD to 1740 AD and died at the age of 47 years. This title of Dirtiest Queen of the world stuck to her because during her reign of ten years she never took a bath, nor did she took the trouble to wash her face, hands or feet. However, it is known that sometimes she would smear hot butter on her hands and face.[11]

THE SPANISH FESTIVAL OF DEVIL'S JUMP

The village of Castrillo de Murcia in Spain celebrates the festival of 'El Salto del Colacho', meaning 'the devil's jump'.[12] It takes place on a Sunday after the Feast of Corpus Christi. As per the legend, the festival appears to be a blend of catholic and pagan rituals meant to represent the triumph of good over evil. During the celebrations 'the *colacho*' (devil) jumps over babies to protect them from evil and bring them good luck. Some historians believe that it may have started as a fertility ritual. The origin of this festival is unclear, but its celebration dates back to the 1620s.

---

[11] Extracted and translated from *Hind Samachar* (Urdu), New Delhi.
[12] *Times of India*, 25 June 2019, 13 (Times Global).

A STATUE THAT WEEPS

Displayed in the London Museum is a 16th century statue of Dr Edward Cook, which has been carved out of stone. The mystery is that this statue has been shedding tears for centuries. The secret of the tears was investigated by experts and scientists. It has been established that the stone material, of which the statue is made, is hygroscopic and has the characteristic of absorbing humidity from the ambient air. When the water content exceeds certain absorbency limit of the stone, it leaks from the eyes, giving the impression that the statue is shedding tears.[13] Thus, this phenomenon is no mystery and seems to have a scientific explanation.

THE NAKED TRUTH

The naked truth is an oft quoted refrain; it has certain truth behind the proverbial saying. The legend says that once Truth and Lie, perchance, went together to the river to take a bath. They jumped into the river together; while Truth was still busy praying, Lie came out quietly and mischievously donned the clothes of Truth and walked away unnoticed. No wonder, lies are often passed off as the truth in the first instance.

When Truth came out after the bath, he found his clothes missing and the clothes of Lie lying there. The predicament was embarrassing; Truth was enraged but had no choice. He, nevertheless, refused to wear the clothes of Lie and walked off naked; and has still not found his own clothes. Thus, the proverbial 'naked truth'.[14]

---

[13] Extracted and translated from *Hind Samachar* (Urdu) daily newspaper, New Delhi. Other details not available.
[14] Extracted and translated from *Hind Samachar* (Urdu) daily newspaper, New Delhi. Other details not available.

NIGHT BEFORE THE CROWNING

It is a British custom that the Monarch-to-be does not sleep the last night before the crowning at the Royal Palace or the usual residence. This last night is spent alone in a particularly appointed room in the building adjoining the Big Ben tower.[15] Records show that the coronation procession for Queen Elizabeth, as was usual, started from Buckingham Palace and came to Westminster Abbey.

It is not known when and why and how this custom originated, but seems to have been followed for ages. Believably, the last time this ritual was observed, was at the time of coronation of Queen Elizabeth in June 1953. The haloed room is still maintained in perfect order for such occasions in the future.

Incidentally, the coronation ceremony comprises of six parts, namely, the Recognition, the Oath, the Anointing, the Investiture including the Crowning, the Enthronement and the Homage, performed in this particular order.

QUEEN'S PROPERTY: CUSTOMARY LAW

All swans and all sturgeons to be found in the territory of England are customarily treated to be the property of the queen or the reigning ruler. Possibly, this law dates back to the 12th century. Messing with them or molesting them or torturing them, by any one, in any manner, is a serious offence and is punishable.

There is also a royal tradition of an annual census of these birds called Swan Upping. This is conducted on

---

[15] Mentioned by Amitabh Bachchan, anchor of infotainment programme on Sony TV, "Kaun Banega Crorepati," August 30, 2019. He claimed that he had seen this room.

the river Thames and involves 'measuring, weighing and checking swans on a stretch of the waterway between Surrey and Oxfordshire'. This exercise is usually held over five days during the month of July. The census has been cancelled for 2020 due to the outbreak of Novel Coronavirus (Covid-19) pandemic, though the report has not been confirmed by Buckingham Palace. The event was last cancelled in 2012 due to flooding in the country.[16]

---

16 *Times of India*, 'UK Royal Swan Census Cancelled Due to Pandemic', May 18, 2020, p. 9.

EPILOGUE

It may now be reiterated that faith, for the faithful, is not a binary predicament of black and white, but is lies somewhere on the spectrum of grey. It, thus, raises interesting possibilities of variations in belief that are possibly based on several factors like expectancy of spiritual bliss, ardency of fealty, familial grooming in certitude of cherished hope, adherence to a routine followed by an abider, compulsion of a societal norm or individual level of wisdom to reason out and evaluate the effort-benefit from ritual *vis-a-vis* its beneficial outcome or intended consequences. Nevertheless, faith is a baggage of inherited beliefs, rigid thoughts, accepted opinions, societal taboos or prejudices willingly participated in, for perpetuation; faith is believed to be for personal good, community betterment and collective prosperity.

Faith, customs and rituals, whether mediated or unmediated by religion, serve a host of interests of the person and the community assisting in sympathetic learning by the young ones, creating a social bond out of commonality of practices, forming a shared identity in solemn observance, a segregated cultural resonance and imbibing a cult mindset for achieving elevated divinity. Yet faith and customs are rarely tempered with rationality, tested on an intellectual template or selected by independent thought-process. Same way most personal rituals, like fasts, etc., have an aspect of religion and are believed to be for individual amelioration and spiritual purification.

Religion has been differently understood depending upon motivation and intensity of faith. It may, however, in our context, be defined as a social institution involving beliefs and practices based on cognition of the sacred whereas rituals are formal ceremonial activities. Thus, the pursuit and the observance of customs and rituals, though at times, promoted and motivated by religion, is mundane, instinctive and unquestioned. Despite this, customs and rituals are more meaningful in purpose and enjoyable in flavour by the followers who adore the practise of rites, appreciate their intended benefits, understand their intrinsic intent and instinctively comprehend subtle nuances.

It will become apparent to any reader that the stories of the myths and legends is global, and the narration so diverse that complete appreciation of the same would be nearly impossible without a deeper insight into these stories. This may be achieved through thorough research, extensive readings and dedicated interviews on the subject and personally surfing the websites to cull out information for confirming the veracity of these myths and legends. It may be honestly conceded that it is, therefore, difficult to unfold and truly express the ontology of these phenomena or grasp the group values or underlying motivations of society. This certainly points to multi-disciplinary implications that deserve to be researched and retold.

Thus, a deep-rooted psychological reality behind the societal manifestations craves to be unraveled and vindicated. Hence, the stories narrated in this book need more objective analysis and methodological research for truly understanding the different native milieu, cultures and mindset of the concerned tribal denominations and social groups. This is a big task, which has been left for the posterity due to old age of the author. This book is only a modest and elemental effort towards igniting the minds of interested scholars.

Certain customs and rituals, though widely observed, may not be agreeable to the prudish modern mentality or be congruent with millennial obsessions, yet the traditional heritage should not be traduced for sheer novelty or presumed repugnance. No one would like to barter the customary beliefs of yore for professed rationality of an outsider. Therefore, despite a level of discomfort with unusual observances, it would be unbecoming to condemn or castigate them for sheer uncomfortable novelty. It must be realized that every individual deserves space for personal inclinations and proclivities, which has to be rightfully conceded and willingly granted. Similarly, different social groupings and communities also deserve to have their own beliefs and faith.

However, the concept of personal space is not static; it is fluid, subjective and contextual. Its rules may have undergone dynamic transformation over the years, in relation to the extant milieu or due to the evolutionary processes, yet it essentially remains a balancing act of reciprocity or mutual adjustment between dissenting opinions or co-existing societies. Therefore, borders of personal space for individual needs, temporal demands, social occasions or celebratory purposes must be adjusted and accommodated with cordial understanding and convivial harmony, without undue intrusion or unreasonable protests or unnecessary fuss.

Customs as manifestations of society or celebratory occasions or personal observances are temporal human creations that tend to get perpetuated. Therefore, these are not divine impositions and cannot be frozen in time nor permitted to stand still. These are living institutions that have sustained over the years or eternalized themselves; they move forward with the passage of time, having adapted and transformed in response to the shifting values and changing mindsets of the new generations. Consequently, they become dynamic realities that are ever-transforming in response to technological developments, knowledge accumulation, newer thought processes, shift in social mores and broadening visions. Therefore, society can also not remain static, unaffected or impervious to the effects of social stimuli and by tools of societal change.

Let us, therefore, honourably accept that customs keep on evolving with metamorphic mutations in exterior complexion or endemic intent with the passage of time and birth of new values. Similarly, rituals of penance, self-mortification or motivated dare-devilry may appear, howsoever, misadventurous, unusual or unacceptable, yet for the devout, they are spiritual experiences of sublime bliss that transcend physical sensation by human faculties. Possibly, the thought process of reverdured divine deliverance has pain alleviating or agony obliterating effect. Nevertheless, these rituals keep undergoing sustained transformation with civilizational progression, societal maturation and governmental prodding. They ostensibly enrich with passage of time and dawn of new thinking; and tend to become less disagreeable as a result of the changed disposition of the community, temporal dynamics of societal action and reaction over a passage of time and societal tolerance in relaxation of disapproval or growing approval of customs and rituals.

Often observances may cause injury, like stone pelting in Himachal Pradesh; rituals may require painful penance and self-mortification like Thaipusam in Malaysia and *suttee* or *santhara;* some sacrifices may be gory like *bali*, whether relating to humans and animals. Such customs evoke compassion and consequent resistance and protests from humanists, rationalists and animal lovers. With sustained opposition movements and repeated demonstrations, world over, these rituals have often come under the gaze of vigorous democratic scrutiny and intensive media trial, which have led to stern legislative measures by the state administration and coercive action by the police against them.

However, in most cases, such legislative measures and deployment of forces, fail in their avowed purpose and official duty, respectively. This is because, in front of the determined devotees, either the police are ostensibly outnumbered or deliberately look the other side, so as not to trample over the sentiments of the ardent believers. Hence, our efforts to curb should not be tactically reactive but strategically educative and mentally reformative. Regardless of the social ramifications of the intense devotion, the ingrained religious element should not be politicized.

Age-old faith and public sentiment towards *gram devtas* and ethnic deities are a voice of collective conscience juxtaposed with individual reverence and solemn vibes. This, in essence, is the popular religion and its practice cannot be trampled in ruthless display of authority or wanton force by state instrumentalities. Notwithstanding the mandate of law, sensitivity in tackling emotional situations and determined human behaviour, is required. Patience and persuasion are other sensible responses against public susceptibilities.

I fervently hope you have enjoyed reading this book or parts of it!

ABOUT THE AUTHOR

Dr G. S. Sachdeva did his under-graduation in social psychology. He received his master's degree in economics from Delhi School of Economics, New Delhi. He culminated his education with a Doctorate in Law from the School of International Studies, Jawaharlal Nehru University, New Delhi. His varied interests, multiple subjects of study and diverse schooling have been his biggest assets. He always sustained an interest in sociology and allied studies of psychology, anthropology and theology. He, thus, remained a keen observer of society, its social processes and societal expressions. Religious customs, cultural festivals and social rituals fascinated him, and he delved into their origins, the legends behind them and the purpose of their ostensive observance.

He also had a chequered career spanning over five decades. He started as a Commissioned Officer in the Indian Air Force and took voluntary retirement in the rank of Wing Commander in 1986. This was his tryst with regimented life and its ramifications like strict discipline and hard duties yet with finesse in etiquette and social niceties. Thereafter, he worked for HCL Limited and loved the freedom of action in the competitive atmosphere of the corporate world. Next, he joined the German Embassy at New Delhi as a Legal Advisor and got elevated to Legal Counsellor, a designation rarely ever conferred on Indian staff. He enjoyed the suave atmosphere and the polite and cordial behaviour of his colleagues at the Embassy. This exposure and experience enriched his mind and gave him insight into different social orders and diverse cultures, which helped him understand the nuances of social expression.

He is, at present, Adjunct Professor, NALSAR University of Law, Hyderabad, and also works as an independent author and gets satisfaction from writing, which he deems as his return gift to the society. He has authored six books. He has published over 50 articles in professional journals in India and abroad, as well as contributed chapters in edited books.

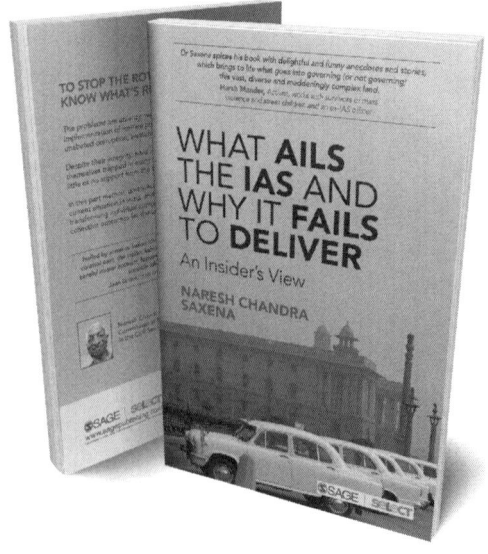

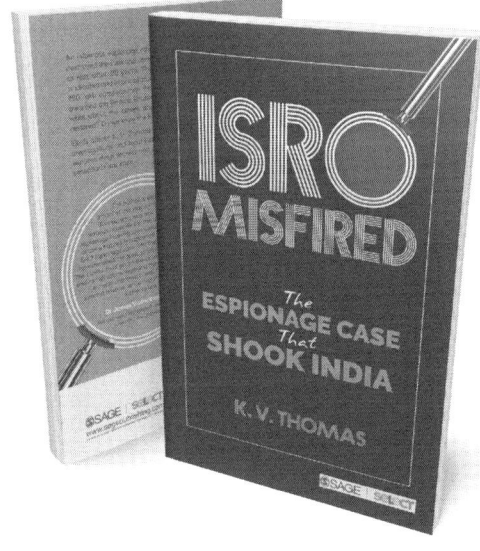